Lancashire & Cheshire Fauna Society

Registered Charity 50068

www.lacfs.org.u

Publication No. 12

ISBN: 978-1-9997312-

2020

Lancashire Bird Repo

The Birds of Lancashire and North Merseyside

S. J. White (Editor)

**I. Ball, D. A. Bickerton, B. Bracken, M. Breaks, P. Brennan, D. Broome,
S. Dunstan, S. Flynn, N. Godden, R. Harris, P. J. Marsh,
S.J. Martin, T. Vaughan, I. Walker, J. F. Wright.**

Contents

Cover images:
   Front: Eastern Black-eared Wheatear, Fluke Hall, Pilling (Steve Young)
   Back Top: Stilt Sandpiper, Lunt Meadows LWT (Steve Young)
   Back Lower: Pectoral Sandpiper, Mythop (Paul Ellis)

Introduction

Dave Bickerton

Once again it is my pleasure to introduce you to the latest Lancashire Bird Report in its new larger format that enables us to pack in more information and photographs about the birding year 2019. The price to non-members has increased slightly but membership remains the same at just £10. We hope you enjoy reading it and if you're not a member of the Lancashire & Cheshire Fauna Society, please consider joining (details at the back of the report).

As I write this, eight weeks into the coronavirus lockdown, I reflect on what it was like to simply go out onto my local patch or further afield meeting fellow birders with barely a second thought as to how circumstances might make a change to our activities. The first few weeks of lockdown certainly curtailed many plans but on the flip side, garden lists and local 'patch walks' became popular. The recording of nocturnal migration of Common Scoters over people's back gardens utilising social media applications connected birders from across the county and we birded vicariously through others images and messages.

As we did this, a few noted that they had been rather remiss in sending us their records in previous years. A few thought that Facebook was the place to find their records but this is virtually impossible to trawl without spending a lot of man-hours. Recording via Birdtrack is certainly something that many of you do already and it has excellent features such as breeding codes, comments, map-references and so on. The county recorder is sent a copy of the dataset at the end of the year which is disseminated to the report compilers. However, it rarely gives us a considered, perhaps anecdotal, local view of how species are faring. Local groups like East Lancashire Ornithologists Club and Chorley and District Natural History Society produce reports that are also supplied to us before we start writing. Fylde Bird Club, Rossendale Ornithologists Club and Lancaster and District Bird-watching Society send us their datasets and we get reports from main sites such as Heysham.

There are, of course, lots of areas that are not covered. This is where individual records and summaries are so useful in compiling the report, especially on the more common species; we are fortunate to get some terrific examples such as those from Paul Slater in south Liverpool, Chris Fyles in Southport and Bob Danson in Over Wyre. Some birders such as David Nuttall in Rossendale are meticulous in their recording of rookeries. All this helps in compiling this statement of record.

This year, as in recent years, the relatively novel technique of sound-recording speculatively to 'capture' bird calls and songs to be identified at a later time has been employed at Knott End by Chris Batty with some success. A benefit of this technique for bird recording is the potential length of exposure with, in 2019, Chris recording for over 2,000 hours from his coastal garden with resultant high totals of, in particular, Tree Pipits and Yellow Wagtails. I know a few more of you have dabbled in this so we look forward to receiving those records and the challenge of adjudicating the records of scarcer birds.

It was with great sadness that we learned of the passing of several long-standing contributors to the Society, three of which played an active role in the Society, for whom we've compiled obituaries later in the report. I had known Barry McCarthy from my earliest birding experiences as a fellow member of the Southport RSPB group in the mid 1970s when I used to trawl Ainsdale NNR and he, Formby and Marshside. I came across Malcolm Greenhalgh at KGV, Southport where he was a Biology teacher but only really got to know him in his later years. Andrew Cadman was pioneer ringer at Rossall and later took a prominant role in the Lancaster area. All were fine people, with the teaching profession, a passion for birds and the natural world in common and will be greatly missed.

Last and certainly not least, I'd like to thank those members who stepped into the breach at short-notice to help compile this year's report as well as the regular 'crew', many of whom spend days and weeks of their time to bring you this. Thanks to all those who've contributed their records and the photographers for the use of their images in this report.

Review of the Year 2019

John Wright

January

January started dry and settled but mostly cloudy, and it remained generally dry and often mild during the first half of the month but progressively less settled as the high pressure moved further away to the south-west. The second half was mostly cold and changeable with frequent north-westerly winds and some sleet and snow at times.

The year began with two male **American Wigeons** at Hesketh Out Marsh and on the Eric Morecambe Complex. Also, on the EMC was an astonishing gathering of 8200 **Black-Tailed Godwits**. At nearby Leighton Moss visitors were witnessing mesmerising murmerations of 130,000 **Starlings**.

Waxwings were once again present in the county, with a thin spread of records at both ends of the year, with the largest flock being 15 in Bootle from the 4th.

Fishmoor Reservoir was the place to be for larophiles with the regular presence of two first-winter **Caspian Gulls** in the roost along with an adult **Glaucous Gull**. **Iceland Gulls** were thin on the ground, but a juvenile was at Stocks Reservoir on the 20th. An impressive 1900 **Jackdaws** also roosted at Stocks Reservoir that evening.

The rise of the **Ring-Necked Parakeet** continues apace. Sefton Park in Liverpool is now the stronghold for this gregarious species with a peak count of 55 on the 27th. Another impressive count on the 27th was the 351 **Snipe** recorded on the Heysham Heliport.

At the end of the month the **Todd's Canada Goose** returned from Norfolk with **Pink-footed Geese** and was subsequently seen on both sides of the Ribble at Banks, Crossens, Hesketh Out Marsh, Marshside and Lytham Moss.

February

The month began cold with some snow in the east of the county, but from the 5th onwards it was generally mild. It was unsettled until the 10th and to a lesser extent between the 16th and 20th, but very mild and sunny weather developed widely between the 13th and 15th and again between the 21st and 27th, with record-breaking daytime temperatures in the latter spell. Overnight frost and fog developed quite widely during this period.

Goose-watching remained popular with the highlight being a **Taiga Bean Goose** which was faithful to the Eagland Hill area from the 9th to the 15th. Searching through the **Pink-footed Goose** flocks here also produced sightings of **Tundra Bean Goose** and **Greenland** and **European White-fronted Geese**.

A **Hooded Crow** was present at Todderstaffe Hall, Poulton-le-Fylde from the 13th and was the first of many sightings along the coast this year which probably related to a couple of wide-ranging individuals.

A magnificent immature **White-tailed Eagle** paid an unfortunately brief visit to the Eric Morecambe Complex on the 15th.

Twite flocks were regularly encountered at Banks Marsh, Knott End, Cockersand & Bolton-le-Sands with the largest count of 163 at Southport.

Following the major fire on Winter Hill in 2018 and its devasting impact on wildlife it was wonderful to hear the songs of over 50 **Skylarks** there on the 21st. Seventy-five pairs went on to breed here, an amazing testimony to the resilience of our wildlife.

March

The first half of March was dominated by an unsettled west to north-westerly type which brought frequent rain. It was generally mild, but occasionally cold enough for sleet and snow to fall to low levels. The second half was generally settled with high pressure close by. It was generally cloudy until the 23rd, but the last week was often very sunny.

For the second year in succession there was an influx of **Pale-Bellied Brent Geese** to Heysham with a high count of 43 on the 10th. Another notable sighting was the return of the **Grey-bellied Brent Goose** to the Ribble where it frequented Banks & Crossens Marsh from the 13th.

An out-of-season **Leach's Petrel** was a surprise find off Rossall Point on the 14th.

Common Redpolls are enigmatic visitors to the county and most confirmed records come from the ringing of flocks of **Lesser Redpolls.** This was particularly so this year with four birds all caught in a Rishton garden with one wintering and the others on spring passage on 4th, 23rd & 24th March.

A **Great Grey Shrike** wintered at Leighton Moss and continued to put in the occasional appearance up until the 5th, what may have been the same bird was seen on Warton Crag on the 29th.

A **Bewick's Swan** on Stocks Reservoir with a flock of 38 **Whooper Swans** on the 31st was an unusual record for the east of the county. A second-winter **Iceland Gull** that appeared at Otterspool on the 31st lingered in the area until the 6th May.

April

April started off with a cold and unsettled spell for the first five days. Easterly winds then persisted until mid-month, initially bringing warmer weather but it turned colder again from the 9th to 14th. The weather turned dry, sunny and very warm for most between the 17th and 22nd, coinciding with the Easter weekend. The last week was more unsettled.

A pair of **Black-necked Grebes** arrived at Lunt Meadows on the 3rd. They were seen displaying and mating in the first few days of their stay before disappearing into the reedbed. Unfortunately, there was no proof of breeding and they were last seen on the 24th May.

A **Great Grey Shrike** was found on the 9th on Wheelton Moor where it remained until the 17th.

A male **Green-winged Teal** which stopped off on the Eric Morecambe Complex on the 9th to 12th was closely followed by a male **American Wigeon** at the EMC from the 16th to 20th.

Hoopoe, Charnock Richard, 28 April (Tony Dunn)

The American theme continued with a delightful **Buff-breasted Sandpiper** at Marshside on the 20th. This was the county's 15th record in modern times and the first in spring.

A **Serin** was sound-recorded over Knott End on the 21st and was 5th record for the county. Another overshooting migrant was a **Hoopoe** which was found by a farmer at Charter House Farm, Charnock Richard on the 26th. Identified via social media this delightful bird was well watched by an appreciative audience until the 29th.

A trip of seven **Dotterel** that visited Pendle Hill on the 28th was a welcome return to form and a **Pectoral Sandpiper** appeared at MMWWT on the 29th.

Dotterel, Pendle Hill, 28 April (Craig Bell)

May

The month started off generally cool, with a cold northerly outbreak on the 3rd/4th, and often cloudy. The second week began wet but then high pressure slowly built and between the 12th and 24th the weather was often quite settled, dry and sunny. It turned more changeable from the 25th onwards, but the month ended very warm.

A **Lapland Bunting** seen on Newton Fells on the 6th was the only record in the county this year. The next day a male **Green-winged Teal** was present at Lunt Meadows.

Spring passage through Morecambe Bay was in full swing with a massive peak of 2910 exquisite **Arctic Terns** past Heysham on the 10th. These were joined by flocks of pristine summer-plumaged **Black Terns,** totalling 65 birds, and a record passage of 19 **Artic Skuas**.

Also, on the 10th a fine **Roseate Tern** was picked out amongst the **Arctic Terns** as they passed Morecambe. **Manx Shearwaters** were also on the move with a peak of 500 off Blackpool on the 11th

Another notable feature of the month was the passage of **Temminck's Stints**. Two appeared on the 11th, at Lunt Meadows and Aldcliffe Marsh, with one at MMWWT on the 14th and two on Newton Marsh on the 18th & 19th.

Migration continued apace with six **Pomarine Skuas** powering passed Rossall Point on the 18th and a fine adult **Honey-buzzard** north over Leighton Moss on the 22nd.

The highlight of the month (and the year) was a **Stilt Sandpiper** that graced Lunt Meadows from the 17th to the 20th. Since Lancashire's only other record was in 1967, this graceful American wader had been much anticipated and attracted admirers from far and wide.

More excitement came on the 18th with the discovery of a singing male **Iberian Chiffchaff** at Pilling Lane Ends. This was a text-book bird in both song and plumage and the third county record. It made an extended stay singing until the 23rd June.

June

June began fine and warm in the south-east but cloudier in the north. It was generally unsettled and cool from the 3rd to 20th, and particularly cool, cloudy and wet between the 10th and 13th. A ridge of high pressure brought dry sunny weather on the 21st and 22nd, then the rest of the month was mainly warm and humid, with a hot sunny spell from the 27th to 29th.

Summering **Knot** are regular along the coast but the flock of 109 at MMWWT on the 1st was a remarkable inland count. The breeding season was now in full swing and there were a number of success stories to report, most notably the gull colony at Belmont Reservoir. **Black-headed Gulls** saw a further increase there from 10,484 pairs in 2017 to 11,553 pairs in 2019. The colony is now considered to be the largest in the UK, estimated to be 8.3% of the UK breeding population and an astonishing 0.5% of the world population!

In amongst the Black-headed Gulls the colony of **Mediterranean Gulls** grew from 43 pairs to a minimum of 63 nests plus an additional nine adults on territory. This is the largest UK inland colony and the only substantial colony away from the south and south-east English coast.

Another species on the increase is the **Avocet** with thirty-two pairs on the Eric Morecambe complex 29 pairs at MMWWT, 32 pairs at Marshside, 27 pairs at Hesketh Out Marsh, seven pairs at Lunt Meadows, four pairs at Conder Green and two pairs on Newton Marsh. Whilst their productivity is highly variable the county breeding population is now well over 100 pairs.

Another species on the up is the **Gadwall**. An almost complete set of breeding records were received from likely sites giving a total of at least 106 pairs across the county. The RSPB Morecambe Bay properties held 40 pairs, a joint record for the site.

At Leighton Moss a full **Water Rail** breeding survey was completed this year. An impressive 112 pairs were recorded, with a further six pairs at Barrow Scout and three pairs at Silverdale Moss.

Also, at Leighton Moss it was exciting to have **Bitterns** breeding again with juveniles seen on the 10th & 24th June. With booming also heard at Lunt Meadows, MMWWT and Marton Mere earlier in the spring the hope remains that further breeding pairs may become established.

In the east of the county, **Nightjars** again returned and very excitingly were present at a second location in Bowland. Whilst there was no definitive proof of breeding the number of churring birds increased, suggesting this population is becoming established.

Another enigmatic summer species is the **Quail** and 2019 was the best year in the county since 2011. Fourteen calling birds were noted from eight sites, with five calling males in the Eagland Hill area on the 29th.

July

July started off rather cool with north-westerly winds. The first half was mostly dry and settled but with unremarkable temperatures. The second half was much wetter, due largely to numerous thundery outbreaks, but with an exceptionally hot spell from the 22nd to 25th which saw record-breaking temperatures and plenty of sunshine.

Little Terns are always a welcome sight in the county with inland records particularly noteworthy. A single at Foulridge Reservoir on the 17th June was followed by two at Brockholes on the 5th.

Exciting news from MMWWT where the first breeding record of **Bearded Tit** was confirmed. Two pairs nesting from a group of eight birds that turned up on the 21st February.

Spoonbills have yet to establish a breeding presence in the county but regular sightings in spring & summer continued this year with a peak of five at Leighton Moss between the 10th and 15th.

Glossy Ibises have also become regular visitors in recent years. One frequented Marshside from May to July and was sighted at Longton Brickcroft on the 13th. This bird was last seen at Marshside on the 14th and it or another was seen over Crawshawbooth and Waterfoot on the 25th.

An adult **Pectoral Sandpiper** was on the Eric Morecambe Complex from the 14th to 16th with a further sighting on the 25th.

The nocturnal overland passage of **Common Scoter** through the county is a well-known migration route. A rare day-time movement was observed late morning on the 27th when approximately 600 flew west between Brockholes and Alston Reservoirs.

Marsh Tits are infrequently seen away from Silverdale and one at feeders at Crawshawbooth from the 28th was only the sixth record in Rossendale and the first for 18 years.

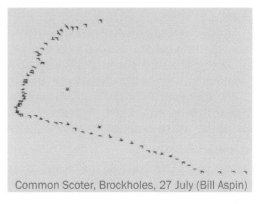

Common Scoter, Brockholes, 27 July (Bill Aspin)

August

The first three weeks of August were mostly dominated by bright showery weather, and after a relatively quiet start to the month, deep depressions brought wet and windy weather on the 9th/10th, 14th and 16th. A hot spell developed from the 21st to 27th, setting new record high temperatures for the Bank Holiday weekend. The weather turned cooler and more unsettled again from the 28th.

There was a very welcome increase to five successful **Hen Harrier** nests in Bowland, with all 22 chicks fledging. With the Bowland Special Protection Area being designated for thirteen pairs there is still much room for improvement.

In the spring four male and two female **Garganey** were present at Lunt Meadows and breeding was confirmed when a female was seen with a half-grown juvenile mid-month.

As summer turned to autumn a dispersing juvenile **Black-necked Grebe** arrived at Alston Wetland on the 11th and remained until the 24th.

The autumn passage of waders on the Ribble was well underway with a massive count of 39,639 **Dunlin** and 6363 **Sanderling** - the highest counts anywhere in the county since 2012 & 2014 respectively.

Two exciting finds rounded off the month with a dapper summer-plumaged **Long-billed Dowitcher** at MMWWT from the 20th to the 25th and a delightful male **Grey-headed Wagtail** amongst **Yellow Wagtails** at Hesketh Out Marsh on the 31st.

September

The first six days of September were dominated by changeable westerlies, then the weather turned more settled. There were numerous dry sunny days between the 13th and 20th, with warm days and cool nights. The weather turned very wet at times during the last third of September, which raised rainfall totals above the long-term average.

An adult female **Eastern Black-eared Wheatear** was a remarkable find at Fluke Hall on the 1st and another contender for bird of the tear. It remained there until the 17th and was well watched and photographed throughout. An extremely tricky identification process resulted in a consensus that this was this species rather than a Pied Wheatear, but this is currently with the British Birds Rarities Committee for consideration.

A **Red-Breasted Goose** was a surprise find with **Pink-footed Geese** at Marshside on the 8th. Another great find on the 8th was a juvenile **Montagu's Harrier** below Pendle Hill – the first in the county since 2014.

A juvenile **Caspian Gull** at Cocker's Dyke on the 13th proved to be another long-stayer and was last sighted on the 19th October.

More excitement followed with the discovery of a **White-rumped Sandpiper** at Hesketh Out Marsh on the 14th and the same day an adult **American Golden Plover** adult arrived at Lunt Meadows. Remarkably it was joined by another adult on the 15th and they both stayed until the 24th!

American waders remained centre stage with a pristine juvenile **Pectoral Sandpiper** at Mythop from the 18th quickly followed by two juveniles at Winmarleigh from the 24th.

During the same period a delightful juvenile **Red-necked Phalarope** was present at Marshside from the 20th to the 27th often to be seen alongside a flock of up to 15 **Cattle Egrets**.

At the month's end the first **Yellow-browed Warbler** of the autumn was ringed on Middleton Nature Reserve on the 30th. A localised arrival then took place between the 13th and 15th October producing a total of at least 14 individuals in the Heysham area.

October

The jet stream tracked over the county for most of the month, resulting in a wet and cloudy month. The weather briefly turned more settled on the 21st - 23rd, and colder quieter weather affected most parts from the 27th.

An obliging **Kentish Plover** was discovered with **Ringed Plovers** on the shore by Southport Pier on the 5th and remained until the 13th. This was the 25th county record and the first since 2011, so was well watched during its stay.

The only **Grey Phalarope** of the year was at Lytham on the 10th. Another adult **American Golden Plover** on Banks Marsh on the 18th moved between there and Crossens and Marshside until the 27th. With the two at Lunt Meadows these were the eleventh to thirteenth records for the county.

Banks Marsh continued a great run of form with a juvenile **White-rumped Sandpiper** and a male **American Wigeon** joining the **American Golden Plover** from the 26th and all found by the same diligent observer!

Also, on the 26th a female **Smew** arrived at Brockholes and remained faithful to the pools and adjacent River Ribble into 2020.

Two adult **Greenland White-Fronted Geese** then arrived at Banks Marsh on the 27th with a flock of **Whooper Swans**.

Bramblings were on the move and 244 over Belmont on the 27th coincided with a flock of 330 feeding in nearby beech-woods.

Nine **Cattle Egrets** were a notable sighting flying south-east over Knott End on the 28th and a record Lancashire count of 58 **Mandarin Ducks** was made in the Rivington and Anglezarke area on the 29th.

This busy and exciting month ended with a **Richard's Pipit** at Rossall School on the 30th.

November

The jet stream continued to track further south than usual, bringing further spells of cloudy and wet weather. The weather was more settled at times in the third week and on the last two days. Temperatures were mostly below normal, but it was mild early in the month and again around the 25th-27th.

An adult male **Long-tailed Duck** was a lovely find inland at Alston No 1 Reservoir from the 1st to the 8th. A small arrival of **Shags** brought three juveniles to Heysham on the 2nd and an adult on the 3rd, with five off Blackpool on the 15th.

A **Great Grey Shrike** was on Anglezarke Moor above Lead Mines Clough on the 8th & 9th, only a mile from the spring location on Wheelton Moor.

The great run of rarities continued with the discovery of a first-winter male **Ring-necked Duck** at Pine Lake on the 17th which remained into 2020

Three **Great Northern Divers** were seen this month passing Formby Point on the 11th and 18th and Knott End on the 26th. Formby Point also had a **Black-throated Diver** on the 18th and 156 **Red-throated Divers** passed Blackpool on the 22nd.

It was a good month for **Snow Buntings** with multiple reports from coastal and inland sites with peaks of eleven on Ainsdale Beach on the 17th and eight on Pendle Hill on the 20th.

December

December started with a spell of cold dry frosty weather with high pressure and plenty of sunshine, but it quickly turned mild and unsettled with westerly winds, and this regime persisted until Christmas. Temperatures fell close to the seasonal norm around mid-month. The last week was generally dry and mild and often cloudy.

A **Richard's Pipit** at Mythop was a great find on the 1st. A first-winter female **Long-tailed Duck** at Lunt Meadows on the 1st to the 17th was the first record for the site. It then relocated to Crosby Coastal Park where it remained into 2020 and was very confiding. A juvenile was also seen off Heysham on the 3rd & the 6th.

A juvenile **Purple Heron,** found and photographed at Eagland Hill on the 4th, was a truly remarkable record. It stayed until the 16th and the following day it was relocated at Marshside, over 16 miles to the south. It then disappeared until the 29th when it was relocated back at Eagland Hill! Here it stayed into 2020 catching voles and showing remarkably well at times. This was only the second record for both the Fylde and Marshside and was the sixteenth record for the county.

A notable influx of **Scaup** brought seven to Pine Lake, three to Marshside and two at

Purple Heron, Eagland Hill, 9 December (Mark Nightingale)

Yarrow Reservoir. The three at Marshside were with an impressive flock of 324 **Tufted Ducks**.

Fishmoor Reservoir produced a first-winter **Caspian Gull** on the 29th and two juvenile **Iceland Gulls** were also roosting there in the final week of the year.

Short-eared Owls were putting on a fantastic display at Lunt Meadows with a peak of seven on the 28th, while Champion Moor had a peak of six this month.

This marvellous birding year ended in spectacular fashion at Kemple End on Longridge Fell when completely unprecedented numbers of **Redwings** were discovered roosting. Numbers peaked at an astonishing 37,500 and attracted national media attention. Observers were also able to witness **Woodcocks** leaving the woods to feed with a peak of 25 seen on the 31st.

Systematic List

KEY TO STATUS (Based upon the results of the 2007-2011 atlas surveys & subsequent annual reports)

Breeding	Non-breeding
Rare: breeding in 1-6 tetrads or 1-10 pairs Scarce: breeding in 7-38 tetrads or 11- 50 pairs Uncommon: 51- 250 pairs Fairly common: 251- 1000 pairs Common: 1001-5000 pairs Abundant: more than 5000 pairs	Vagrant (or very rare passage migrant): 1-10 records in past 25 years Rare: 11-50 records in past 25 years Scarce: 51-250 records in past 25 years Uncommon: 11-20 annually Fairly common: 21-200 annually Common: 201-1000 annually Very common: 1001-5000 annually Abundant: more than 5000 annually

RED GROUSE *Lagopus lagopus*
Common breeding resident.

The annual systematic counts undertaken by the Game and Wildlife Conservation Trust on four shooting estates in Bowland showed a reduction in the spring density to 67.0 birds/100ha from 81.5 birds/100ha in spring 2018. Productivity was even worse than in 2018, with a ratio of just 1.2 young to one old (1.4 in 2018), albeit the July density rose slightly to 91.5 birds/100ha from 88 birds/100ha. In comparison, the figures from the excellent 2017 season were a ratio of 2.3 young to one old with a July density of 207 birds/100ha.

Following on from the poor 2018 breeding season that saw grouse numbers crash across Lancashire, it was estimated that a stock of 5000+ birds overwintered into 2019 on the Abbeystead Estate. This year's breeding season was initially looking favourable with good early broods noted across the county until a spell of heavy persistent rain arrived from the second week of June onwards, which resulted in high mortality of young. The ensuing shooting season was limited for the second consecutive year, with very few driven days undertaken on the Bowland Fells, albeit some moors on the Lancashire section of the South Pennines reported a good season and some shooting took place on the West Pennine Moors.

The almost continuous distribution across the higher ground of Bowland was amply illustrated by over 200 casual records received. The highest counts were 90 at Clougha on 7 Sept, 18 on Brennand Fell on 6 June, 18 in The Trough itself on New Year's Day and ten in Croasdale on 16 April. Confirmed breeding records included three broods totalling 15 young on Brennand Fell on 5 July and pairs with five and four young on the Trough road on 2 June. Records were also received from the Bowland outlying fells of Waddington, Newton and Grindleton with six pairs and four young seen at the latter site on 22 June and a single calling on the isolated Champion Moor on 9 Dec. The maximum count submitted from Pendle was ten on 30 April.

Away from Bowland, 14 were on White Moor above Salterforth on 3 May and three pairs in a sample area of Boulsworth Hill on 24 May; whilst reports from Lancashire and Walshaw Estate (that straddles the county boundary) in the South Pennines suggested the breeding and subsequent shooting season had been far more successful (with over 2000 birds shot during August) than elsewhere in the county.

Grouse are very scarce in central Rossendale, hence the two on Cribden Moor on 24 Feb was especially noteworthy particularly since the species was not recorded there (neither breeding or wintering) in either of the Lancashire Atlases.

In the West Pennine Moors, a survey of Darwen and Turton Moors realised 147 territories, up from the 130 territories in 2018. A strange sight was a male observed feeding amongst daffodils in the garden of Lords Hall on 30 March. The breeding bird survey for UU on Winter Hill, realised 17 territories on the Lancashire section affected by the major 2028 fire, with another 3+ territories on the unburnt section immediately adjacent. In the light of recent surveys and increasing management in the West Pennine Moors, it is estimated that the population of the SSSI is now in excess of 250 pairs. The first young were seen on Darwen Moor on 14 May with a very late half-grown brood of four seen on 4 Aug. Over 500 birds were reported present on Darwen Moor during grouse-driving in August with a poor 20 seen during a shoot on Belmont Moor on 17 Aug. The only other records received from the West Pennine Moors were seven on Anglezarke Moor on 26 June and three at Bull Hill on 29 Nov.

RED-LEGGED PARTRIDGE *Alectoris rufa*
Fairly common resident. Population maintained by regular releases in many areas.

The number of records received was down on last year with 388 reports (520 in 2018) from 119 sites (149 in 2018). Observer fatigue with this increasingly disregarded species is probably largely to blame as the scale of releases continues unabated.

The largest count received was 275 at Hareden in Bowland on 27 Nov with 30 nearby at Newton on 20 Dec, both at or near sites where large numbers are turned out with likewise the 50 at Fluke Hall, Pilling which is also a site of mass releases. The 14 birds/pairs in spring between Kirkby and Simonswood Moss were the result of 1000 being released in 2018 with the 20+ near the Knowsley Estate in May and on Plex Moss in October representing two other shooting estates on the outskirts of Merseyside.

The only reports of breeding concerned an adult with seven young near Bolton-by-Bowland on 21 June and adults with two young at Helks Bank on 5 July and seven young in Littledale on 29 July, both in north Bowland.

The annual contest for the most unusual location as to where this species can turn up was awarded jointly to singles at Seaforth in April, Oglet shore in May and in woodland at Brockholes in April.

GREY PARTRIDGE *Perdix perdix*
Common resident in the west, scarce resident in the east. Long term decline.

Year after year, Lancashire's Grey Partridges seem to be afflicted with poor weather at the most crucial time in their breeding cycle, which renders any resurgence in numbers unachievable particularly when linked with other factors such as increasing numbers of generalist predators and a farmed landscape largely unsympathetic to wild Partridges. 'Ascot week' in mid-June is traditionally when Grey Partridge young hatch, and it was precisely that week in 2019 when an extended period of heavy, persistent rain started with the inevitable dire consequences for broods. The number of records submitted was therefore not surprisingly down on last year, with 193 received in comparison to the 219 in 2018 and the number of locations also down from 103 to 81. However, a reasonable number of broods and coveys were recorded from summer through to the year-end which gives some hope.

The Lancashire 'strongholds' (such as they are) on the arable mosses of the south-west and the Fylde, again reported the majority of records. On the Fylde, records came from eleven sites with a maximum of 18 at Medlar on 9 Jan. Subsequently, some seven pairs were recorded between Lytham Moss, Peel and Cockerham Moss in the spring period, albeit the largest covey reported later was just five on Lytham Moss on 14 Sept. Further north, one at Middleton NR on 13 Aug was the first record there for many years.

Across the south-west mosses, records were submitted from over 30 sites with breeding likely at over 20 locations based on the presence of pairs in the April-June period. Highlights included three pairs at Lunt Meadows (three broods totalling 36 young seen), two pairs on Hesketh Out Marsh and a small population east of Birkdale. Coveys recorded included seven double-figure counts with 24 on Mawdesley Moss on 27 Dec, 21 near Mere Sands Wood on 6 Jan, 15 at Rufford on 1 Dec and counts of ten or more near Formby, Croston Moss, Hesketh Out Marsh and Tarlscough also notable.

Even more noteworthy is the population present on the farmland east of Liverpool; roughly in a triangle from Kirkby to Oglet and over to Rainford. Meticulous observations here suggest a population in excess of 30 breeding pairs in this area from the 43 multiple-records from 15 sites submitted. The Oglet area stands out with a covey of ten on New Year's Day, calling birds/pairs present at nine sites on 12 May and three coveys totalling 24 birds seen on 14 Nov.

In Lancashire's eastern pastoral and upland landscape, the species is now in a perilous state with just a handful of seemingly solitary, fragmented pairs present, mainly in moorland-edge habitats. In the central West Pennine Moors, a covey of 25 was near Belmont on 31 Jan and an estimated six pairs were in the area in spring, albeit only one brood (of two young) was seen later. However, all of the above are thought to originate from released stock and very few birds were present in the second winter period. Five records from five sites were received from Rossendale including a pair at The Hile for the first time in several years whilst in east Lancashire the decline continues with just eight reports from five sites (16 from eight sites in 2018) with a family covey of ten at Swinden Reservoir on 15 July and pairs at Cant Clough and Wycoller the only cause for optimism.

QUAIL *Coturnix coturnix*
Scarce summer visitor to west, often in influxes. Occasional evidence of localised escapees.

Whilst in no way a 'Quail year', 2019 was the best in Lancashire since 2011 with 14 calling birds noted from eight sites. The short stay of most indicated ongoing migrant birds that subsequently moved on, albeit mated birds exhibit much reduced vocalisations.

The first was recorded on Lytham Moss on 10 May with no further reports from that site until one again on 14 July. Elsewhere in the Fylde, the Bone Hill/Eagland Hill area hosted a remarkable five calling males on 29 June, three next day, two on 10 July with the last single on 20 July. Other Fylde records included two calling at Freckleton Naze on 3 June and one at Stalmine Moss on 30 June.

South of the Ribble, one male was singing at Longton on 5 Aug, one at Mawdesley Moss from 19-22 June, one at Lisieux Hall, Whittle-le-Woods on 23 June with up to two calling from Plex Moss from 6-13 Aug, the latter being the last record in the county in 2019.

PHEASANT *Phasianus colchicus*
Common resident. Population maintained at a high level in many areas by releases.

In excess of 4000 records were again received this year, despite the species being ignored by many birders. High casual counts from across the county included 180 in the January Lancaster Winter Survey, 88 on White Moss, Rainford on 16 Nov with fifty or more at Leighton Moss on 17 Sept, on the Old Coach Road on 11 Oct and in Longworth Clough on 19 Feb. Four 'white' leucistic birds and six 'black' melanistic birds were in with 500+ 'normal' birds at Belmont in November.

Elsewhere of note were 500 reports from east Lancashire that amply illustrated the species' widespread distribution, twelve pairs were at MMWWT, five territorial males at Lunt Meadows and 16 birds were at Marton Mere on 20 Feb whilst the Winter Hill Breeding Bird Survey for UU realised a moorland edge population of some 50 birds. The species is scarce in Rossendale, with a maximum of seven at Musbury on 19 May and only the odd birds are present in the Speke and Croxteth Park areas near Liverpool, albeit up to 16 were nearby at Oglet on 14 Nov.

Reports of successful breeding were, as usual, few and far between but included females with four young at Shireburn Park on 30 May, four juvs at Stocks on 5 Aug, nine near Chorley on 13 July and seven on Croston Moss on 19 Sept. The first young (three) were seen at Belmont on 5 May with a brood of eleven (some three weeks old) there on 24 May with eight further broods seen there later.

Ten on the island in Belmont Reservoir. on 30 Nov and one at Seaforth from January to October were two of the more unusual records received.

DARK-BELLIED BRENT GOOSE *Branta bernicla bernicla*
Scarce winter visitor.

All records in the first winter period were of singles with Pink-footed Goose flocks, and may even have related to just one individual. Following a bird at Hightown on 20 Jan there were February reports at Pilling Moss on the 7th, Pilling Lane Ends on the 10th and Marshside on the 16th.

Late year records were apparently all not with Pinkfeet. They comprised three at Cocker's Dyke on 26 Sept, six at Crosby on 12 Oct, a lone bird on the Ribble at Naze Point on 29 Nov and finally four again at Cocker's Dyke on 10 Dec.

PALE-BELLIED BRENT GOOSE *Branta bernicla hrota*
Scarce winter visitor.

'Grey-bellied Brant', Crossens, 4 April (Stuart Darbyshire)

For the second year in succession there was an influx of birds to Heysham in the late winter period from their normally-favoured haunts around Foulney and Walney in Cumbria. Following three on 8 Jan counts included nine on 19 Feb, 17 on 5 March, 21 on 9 March and 43 the following day before dwindling until the last record of five on 7 April. Variation in numbers was thought to reflect considerable turnover of individual birds, based partly on the presence or otherwise of ringed individuals. There was limited spillover to other nearby sites, although there were nine at Sunderland Point on 9 Feb, five there on 20 Feb and 17 on 27 March.

The ony record away from north Lancashire in the first half of the year was an adult at Crossens on 4-6 April. This bird, which had previously been in Norfolk, showed features suggestive of the Melville and Prince Patrick Islands form 'Grey-bellied Brant'. This taxon has not been formally described and eliminating a hybrid Black Brant x Pale-bellied Brent Goose may never be possible.

In the second winter period a first-winter was at Banks Marsh on 28 Sept, a family party of six at Knott End on 27 Oct and two adults also at the latter site on 15 Nov.

BRENT GOOSE *Branta bernicla*
Scarce winter visitor

Four not assigned to subspecies were reported from Southport on 21 April. One at Marshside on 18 Sept could conceivably be the Pale-bellied bird seen at Banks a few days later.

RED-BREASTED GOOSE *Branta ruficollis*
Vagrant and escapee

One was with Pinkfeet at Marshside on 8 Sept (M Nightingale, *et al*). This record has been accepted by the BBRC. It is surprising that it was not seen subsequently in Lancs or Norfolk, though any assessment of why that might be remains speculation.

Red-breasted Goose, Marshside, 8 September (Stuart Darbyshire)

CANADA GOOSE *Branta canadensis*
Common breeder, very common winter visitor.

Monthly peak counts at sites holding 275+ birds

	Jan	Feb	Mar	April	May	June	July	Aug	Sept	Oct	Nov	Dec
Aldcliffe										360		
Bretherton									300	400		
N Ribble	385							800		825		
Foulridge Res	289	264	133	88	24	179	177	193	237	198	263	226
Hesketh OM		1300							135			
Lunt Meadows								620	450	578	121	189
Marshside	250	100	40	100			550		400		225	300
MMWWT								470	330			
Mere Sands								131	1160			
Rishton Res	320			12	47	77	132		225	165	280	
Southport ML	30	44	70	38	45	293	223	28		128	42	
Wyre marshes									275	226	266	277
Seaforth	10	125	42	38	50	285	800	85	36	20	72	50
Stocks Res	150	60	68	44	61	350	130	116		120	81	
WeBS Counts												
MBS	161	8		7	12	11	72	4	178	109		11
Ribble	2013	440	316	161	352	937	765	1328	2147	3249	4276	1324

As can be seen from the tables the largest flocks are generally on the Ribble, though this year there were also over 1100 at Mere Sands Wood in September before numbers quickly dropped away.

A lot of breeding information was received this year. There were 50 pairs at Hesketh Out Marsh;. 39 pairs at Marshside fledged 143 young; there were 13 nests at Brockholes and nine pairs at Cuerden Valley Park, but only four young survived due to predation by Grey Herons. Leighton Moss had eight pairs and Silverdale Moss three; at least seven pairs nested at Lunt Meadows. Eleven nesting sites were reported in east Lancashire and at least seven in Rossendale. Birds nested successfully on six moorland sites six sites in the West Pennine Moors while there were just eight pairs at Belmont Reservoir, a 50% reduction, due to ongoing control measures by shooting and egg pricking.

While moult migration to Windermene clearly occurred, few obvious passage flocks were recorded, peak counts were 60 north at Starr Gate on 13 May, 45 there on 2 June and 59 north over Fleetwood Prom on 15 June.

Apparently wild individuals

A bird showing characters indicative of Todd's Canada Goose *B. c. interior* was seen with Pinkfeet at several sites on the south Ribble marshes between 30 Jan and 6 April including Banks Marsh, Hesketh Out Marsh, Crossens and Marshside (S Darbyshire, *et al*) and on 3 and 4 Feb it was on the Fylde at Lytham Moss. The record has been accepted by the BBRC.

Todd's Canada Goose with Pinkfeet, south Ribble marshes, 22 March (Stuart Darbyshire)

BARNACLE GOOSE *Branta leucopsis*
Uncommon wild winter visitor. Scarce feral breeder.

Apparently wild individuals
There were numerous records of birds with Pinkfeet flocks: in January and February up to were four at Marshside; the March peak was six at MMWWT and up to four were at Marshside again in late March and early April. Widespread ones and twos were noted wherever Pinkfeet frequented, including a number of locations on the Fylde as well as the south-west.

Potentially wild individuals began to reappear from early October; potential overshooting flocks included 26 at Warton slag tips on 2 Oct and 20 on the Eric Morecambe Pools on 14 Nov, although without ringing recoveries there is no certain way of ruling out wandering feral birds.

Numbers of birds with Pinks late in the year were generally lower than in the first winter period, peaks comprised two at Banks Marsh and Heysham Moss in December.

Feral populations
The flock in Knowsley Safari Park was estimated at 200 birds in the summer, and around half that in the first winter period.

A flock of 50 was at Stocks Reservoir. in January to 1 Feb but after that only single figures were reported until 19 June when 21 were present; single figures continued to be reported through the summer until 14 were present on 11 Aug. Later in the year a flock of between 40 and 60 was present either on the reservoir or on fields above it from 5 Oct to 24 Dec.

The flock which feeds in the grounds of Blackpool Zoo was only reported irregularly as the birds often leave the roost at Marton Mere early and return late; 64 were on Lawson Road field on 7 Aug, and 61 at the Mere on 3 Nov. Elsewhere on the Fylde five were with Canadas at Warton Bank in February and eight passed South Promenade on 3 June, and there were at least a couple of other wandering singletons.

Otherwise there was the usual scatterings of escapes or feral birds, generally with Canada Geese. Several records in east Lancashire included two together at Jackhouse Reservoir on 6-16 April. In the Chorley area one was at Bretherton Eyes on 30 Sept. Birds were noted at Brockholes in March and May and singles were at Lunt Meadows in May and June and Mere Sands Wood in September; there were also regular reports from Longton Brickcroft and three on Longton Marsh on 21 Aug. In north Lancashire one was at The Snab in the Lune Valley on 6-7 Feb and one on the Eric Morecambe pools on 1 Sept.

There was no concrete evidence of any nesting attempts this year.

LESSER SNOW GOOSE *Chen caerulescens*
Vagrant, escapee and wanderer from feral populations

The only confirmed record of the year was of 14 feral birds, eight white and six blue morphs, on 28 April. They were first seen circling Alston Wetland at 09.00 hours before leaving to the west, and were subsequently seen over Marton Mere later in the day.

GREYLAG GOOSE *Anser anser*
Feral: fairly common breeder and common winter visitor. Wild: scarce winter visitor.

Monthly peak counts at sites holding 250+ birds

	Jan	Feb	Mar	April	May	June	July	Aug	Sept	Oct	Nov	Dec
Lune Valley		521						350		620	360	800
Lune marshes	178						320			250		
Glasson	60									300		
Alston Wetland	400					127					280	140
Burscough Moss												660
EMC/LM	625	299	205	78	120	93	102	140	210	90	271	290
Wyre	171						75	155	641	235	336	299

	Jan	Feb	Mar	April	May	June	July	Aug	Sept	Oct	Nov	Dec
Marshside									550			
MMWWT	800					71	250	300	486	412	168	79
Preesall												
Silverdale Moss	164	16	31	107	55	24	3			154	506	
Stocks Res	122	118	96	37	180	426	70	30	2	15	60	41
WeBS Counts												
MBS	1162	100	26	43	123	93	129	677	372	187	302	392
Ribble	45	1	118	58	122	17	37	92	514	305	307	164

In areas not covered in the table above there was a site record 51 at Belmont Reservoir in July and up to 80 at Bretherton Eyes in October, whiet five over Whitworth Quarry on 5 May was apparently the peak count in Rossendale.

At Leighton Moss there were 26 pairs on the main reserve, 16 on Silverdale Moss and six on the saltmarsh; seven pairs fledged 26 young at Belmont Reervoirs where the species is filling the niche previously occupied by Canada Geese which are subject to ongoing control measures. Five pairs bred at Lunt Meadows and the same number of broods were noted at Stocks Reservoir.

The handful of records from coastal vantage points showed no particular pattern, though eight passed Knott End and three were also off Starr Gate on 2 June and these may have beenon moult migration.

With regard to birds of potentially wild origin in Pinkfoot flocks the situation remains confused by feral brds intermingling with the Pinks, for example on 13 Jan at Little Singleton no fewer than 55 were in a mixed flock. Singles, perhaps the same, at Eagland Hill on 2 Feb, Thurnham the next day and Eagland Hill were arguably the best evidence but in the absence of strong evidence such as ringing recoveries it may be best to regard these as likely to have been feral.

TAIGA BEAN GOOSE* *Anser fabalis*
Rare winter visitor

One was with Pinkfeet at Eagland Hill, Over Wyre on 9-15 Feb (SG Piner *et al*). This continues to be much the less frequent of the two Bean Goose species.

PINK-FOOTED GOOSE *Anser brachyrhynchus*
Abundant winter visitor to Fylde, Ribble Estuary and south-west mosslands.
International importance 5100; National importance 5100.

WeBS Counts

	Jan	Feb	Mar	April	May	June	July	Aug	Sept	Oct	Nov	Dec
Alt	4440	1300	2							11	860	450
MBS	4135	4395	1127	9	1		1	5	1508	1440	850	24
Ribble	4335	5419	15437	7956	8				3084	12411	11912	9091

In the co-ordinated roost counts, the totals of 46260 in Oct and 40231 compared with 54757 and 49598 respectively in the relevant months in 2018. At Simonswood it was reported that following acquisition of the shooting rights the roost there was now subject to wildfowling having not been previously.

Co-ordinated roost counts	Oct	Nov
Alt	16305	15300
Marshside	10770	2056
MMWWT	4350	7600
Pilling	7135	9450
Preesall	1200	1150
Simonswood Moss	1750	915
Wyre	4720	3760

In January an estimated 15000 were at Pilling Lane Ends, while counts of feeding flocks included 4000 at Lunt in January, and 9000 at Marshside, 7000 at Eagland Hill and Preesall and 6500 at Birkdale in early February. Issues with count accuracy were highligthed in the flock present for much of the time near the Heysham bypass, where 2000-2500 were regularly reported but other estimates of up to 6000 were reported. The last of 14 skeins over east Lancashire in the first winter period moved west on 17 Feb. There were 10000 at Crossens on 31 March.

Spring movements were often masked by local feeding flights but continued into May, including 52 past Starr Gate on 7 May with twelve late birds on the 23rd. At Heysham three late birds were noted on 13 May with one on the 15th possibly injured.

The usual scatter of feral of injured birds was reported, including singles with Greylags and Canadas inland as well as coastal birds. There were seven on Pilling Marsh on 18 Aug which were presumably summering, there may have been some overlap with up to five at Glasson in June and July. Four summered at MMWWT, and three apparently also summered on the saltmarsh at Leighton Moss.

Return from Iceland continues to get earlier. There were 21 over Bretherton Eyes on 2 Sept and 87 at MMWWT on the 3rd. A major early season movement at Heysham saw 1800 in many small skeins on 16 Sept, while the first autumn skein in east Lanashire was 60 south at Allsprings the 18th, with a total of 1885 on the 30th. There were no fewer than 10226 at MMWWT by the 22nd and an estimated 10000 at Pilling Marsh on the 30th. Other counts from MMWWT late in the year included 20000 on 3 Oct, 21000 on the 23rd and 20000 on 15 Nov. An estimated 15000 were in fields between Formby and Hightown on 2 Oct and 10000 flew over Birkdale to roost on 12 Oct with 8000 on Banks Marsh on 29 Oct. In the Chorley area up to 3000 were at Bretheron Eyes in November and December but the only records from Rossendale were c240 west on Christmas Day, presumably moving back from Norfolk.

TUNDRA BEAN GOOSE *Anser serrirostris*
Uncommon winter visitor.

All records were of singles until almost the year's end, and as usual all occurred with Pinkfeet. There was one at Marshside on 1-2 Jan, before widely scattered reports in February, including at Scronkey on the 1st, Eagland Hill on the 5th, 8th, 10th and 13th, Marshside again on the 16th, Aldcliffe Marsh on the 18th-21st, Crossens on the 19th, near the Eric Morecambe complex on the 23rd, Pilling Lane Ends on the 24th and the Eric Morecambe complex again on the 26th. There appear to have been at least a couple of individuals involved.

The second half of the year was quieter, again all records were with Pinkfeet. The first was at Downholland Moss on 20 Nov. There was one on Heysham Moss on 1 Dec and two were on Crossens Outer Marsh on the 29th.

GREENLAND WHITE-FRONTED GOOSE *Anser albifrons flavirostris*
Uncommon winter visitor.

in January singles were noted at various south Ribble sites early in the month, at several Over Wyre and central Fylde sites in mid- to late month and again on the Ribble at the month's end, with dates suggesting at least two adults were involved. In February all records appeared to be related to the Pilling Marsh Pinkfoot roost, with up to two at Over Wyre sites and Aldcliffe. All records in March were from Banks and Hundred End with up to two birds until the 17th. Following a gap presumably a new bird was seen in April at Crossens and perhaps the same at Burscough Bridge from the 10th until the 26th.

Autumn got underway with two at Banks Marsh on 27 Oct, remaining in the area until 2 Nov. There were few records after this, two again at Banks on 30 Nov and 15 Dec, perhaps the same pair at Crossens Outer Marsh on 21 Dec and finally a single in the Pilling Hall and Dam Side area in Wyre on the 29th.

EUROPEAN WHITE-FRONTED GOOSE *Anser albifrons albifrons*
Uncommon winter visitor.

There were several reports in January. South of the Ribble up to four were at Mere Brow, two at Banks and singles at Marshside and Crossens. Otherwise there was just one report at Elswick, Fylde on the 18th. February produced a wider spread of records with up to three in north Lancashire at Aldcliffe, four perhaps including some of the same birds at Over Wyre sites and also up to three at Crossens and Marshisde which were likely to have been different individuals. One in the Lune Valley at The Snab,

Gressingham on 6 Feb was presumably unrelated to other records with Pinkfeet. There were four on the north Ribble at Warton Bank on at least 8-11 March, up to three at Marshside and Crossens from the 22nd with records continuing at the latter sites until a single on 16 April.

There were significantly fewer reports in the second winter period. Two were at MMWWT on 28 Oct, with probably the same at Banks on the 27th-29th. There was again one in the Lune Valley, with Greylags at Arkholme on 27 Nov.

WHITE-FRONTED GOOSE *Anser albifrons*
Uncommon winter visitor.

Increasingly 'White-front' agg. records take two main forms, both related to electronic records submission quirks. Firstly, some observers are apparently inputting at species level not realising subspecies level input is possible. Secondly, other observers are presumably making errors in online checklists, reflected in counts of this species on strange dates or noted as 'present' without counts despite it being uncommon. Having stripped these out there were no records which were clearly different from those referred to in the subspecies accounts above.

MUTE SWAN *Cygnus olor*
Fairly common breeding resident.
International importance: 2400. National importance: 740

Monthly Peak Counts

	Jan	Feb	Mar	Apr	May	Jun	Jul	Aug	Sep	Oct	Nov	Dec
MBS WeBS	28	25	44	33	61	47	49	126	35	19	18	24
Ribble WEBS	49	32	24	45	24	54	34	11	24	48	70	45
Southport ML	103	109	104	84	113	137	127	153	162	110	145	97

The only breeding reports received from north Lancashire were of six pairs on the Eric Morecambe complex and two pairs at Middleton NR. The January survey of the Lancaster area located 131 birds. Site counts in included 52 at Thurnham and 35 at Melling in February, 20 on the Lune at Skerton Weir in July, 38 at Sunderland Point and 31 on the Dockacres complex in August, 40 at Leighton Moss in November and 16 on Middleton NR in December..

However, rather more were seen on the north Fylde coast, including more than 100 in January, February and March at Jeremy Lane/Moss Lane, peaking at 142 on 24 Jan and 10 Feb. Other Fylde peak counts included 50 at Cockersand on 29 Jan, 41 at Glasson and 30 at Braides in April and 64 at Stanley Park and 65 at Cockerham Quarry in December.

In Chorley two pairs bred at Yarrow Valley Park and adults were seen with young on the canal at Withnell Fold and the Douglas at Bretherton.

Limited records were received this year from Brockholes, which is usually a productive site: a peak of 58 on 7 July. Further east a pair raised three cygnets at Grimsargh Wetland and Alston Wetland where a pair failed at the egg stage. Elsewhere in east Lancashire six were at Rishton Reservoir on 1 May and five on 12 Nov, in the Calder catchment a pair on the Leeds/Liverpool Canal at Hapton raised six cygnets and one was on a nest also on the canal at Foulridge Wharf on 18 April. Later in the year twelve were in a field near Greenberfield Locks on 16 Oct, one was at Wood End Sewage Works from 20 September to the end of the year, a pair were at Slipper Hill Reservoir in September and six were at Salterforth on 6 Dec.

In the south-west, a male at Sefton Park, Liverpool, bred unsuccessfully with his third mate in twelve years of residency; numbers peaked at this site at eleven in early October. A pair bred again at Seaforth, successfully fledging four from eight young; a spring influx there peaked at 25 on 19-27 April. At Lunt Meadows three pairs were present early in the year but only two nested, one hatching five young. A pair that bred six young successfully at Mere Sands Wood was the first breeding record for the site.

BEWICK'S SWAN *Cygnus columbianus*
Uncommon and declining winter visitor.
International importance: 200. National importance: 70

Up to ten adults and one juvenile remained at Cockerham/Thurnham in the early winter period, until 4 March at Cockersand, where three were the first to return on 10 Nov; numbers increased up to a peak of eight at Thurnham on 31 December.

A juvenile briefly on Stocks Reservoir with Whooper Swans on 31 March was an unusual record for the east of the county.

On the southern shores of the Ribble Estuary, up to ten were seen at Banks/Hundred End/Marshside in January with u to four in February and the last in the area a single at Hesketh Out Marsh on 22 Feb. Four on 18 November at Banks were the first back and then just two were seen in the area until the end of the year. Two on 5 and 21 Dec were the only records all year at MMWWT. Turn the clock back two decades and a peak of 77 at MMWWT in December 1999 was the lowest there since winter 1978/79, such is the long-term decline of this species.

WHOOPER SWAN *Cygnus cygnus*
Common winter visitor.
International importance: 210. National importance: 110

Monthly Peak Counts

	Jan	Feb	Mar	Apr	Sept	Oct	Nov	Dec
Thurnham	490	450	400	70	4	12	160	212
Over Wyre	75	62	71		6	281	80	27
South Fylde	23	60	115	6	38	28	170	218
Ribble WEBS	202	175	144	2	0	20	561	279
MMWWT	1078		70					

Away from MMWWT, the largest counts at the start of the year included 528 at Thurnham on 14 Jan, 17 at Bretherton Eyes on the 19th and 218 at Banks on the 20th January; 610 were at Cockersand on 16 Feb and 120 at New Cut Lane, Southport on the 18th. The sight of 25 on 25 Feb at Hurstwood Reservoir, Burnley was notable, while 635 were counted at Cockersand on 3 March when 50 were in the north-east of the county at Crook o' Lune.

Spring migration along the coast was noted from 27 Feb to 11 April; their departure was highlighted by 72 still at Hesketh Out Marsh on 24 March, reducing to 46 by 6 April and nine by 8 April. Likewise, wintering numbers halved at Cockersand in the week 17-21 March. Inland numbers included two at Belmont Reservoir on 16 March, a peak of 25 on 20 March at Croston Finney, Chorley and 22 at Alston Wetland the same day. After counts of ten on 21 Jan and 16 on 27 Feb, Stocks Reservoir saw a peak of 38 on 31 March then 15 on 1 April and a late bird on 17 April. At Heysham, counts of passing birds included 44 on 24 March, 54 on 26 March and four on 7 April. A late flock of 48 migrants passed Knott End on 10 April. Two were at Thurnham on 3 May and a 1st-winter bird was at Freckleton Naze on 31 May.

Typically, MMWWT held a few through the summer, with up to five seen.

Up to 17 between Bank End and Winmarleigh on 25 Sept were the first of the autumn. Subsequent arrivals included three at Croston Finney, Chorley on the 5 October, two at Hesketh Bank and five at Marshside on 12 Oct, one at Alston Wetland and two flying west over Cant Clough Reservoir on the 14th and 252 at Pilling on the 18th; 15 flew east over Lower Foulridge Reservoir on 19 Oct when two were seen on Entwistle Reservoir, Blackburn, while 27 flying east at Ightenhill Bridge, Burnley on 20 Oct coincided with an arrival that day at MMWWT.

Birds were regular at Lunt Meadows from late October, peaking at 23 on the 24th. Two on Belmont Reservoir on 25 Oct had roosted overnight and 30 were on Alston Wetland that day; 34 headed south at Wesham Marsh, Fylde on 26 Oct and 80 in five parties flew west over Croston Moss, Chorley the following day, again coinciding with an increase at MMMWT. Numbers passing Heysham included ten on 29 Oct, twelve the next day and three on 7 Nov.

The joy of local patch birding was illustrated with eight at Rishton Reservoir, Blackburn on 8 Nov and six on the 12th being the first site records for the observer. Good numbers fed on Croston Finney with a peak count of 200 on 10 Nov; 28 in two parties flew over Jackhouse on 10 Nov, 56 moved southwest over Fleetwood on 15 Nov when 14 were at Foulridge Lower Reservoir. At Seaforth ten flew over on 16 Nov and 13 flew over Altham on the following day.

The biggest numbers late in the year on the Fylde were 240 at Cockersand on 15 Dec, while in Chorley 40 were on Croston Finney on 20 Dec, 83 on Bretherton Eyes on the 29th and eleven flew over Cuerden Valley Park on 18 Dec. In the south-west, 100 were on Halsall Moss on 21 Dec and 600 at Hundred End on the 27th.

At MMWWT, 20 on 2 Oct increased to 44 the next day and 127 on the 13th, 200 on the 20th and 350 on the 27th, while a count of 550 on 2 Nov increased to 800 on the 7th, 1000 on the 15th, 1088 on the 26th and a peak of 1322 on 4 Dec. Up to 921 were seen there to the end of December.

SHELDUCK *Tadorna tadorna*
Common winter visitor at coastal sites, common breeder. Scarce in east.
International importance 3000; National importance 610.

Monthly peak counts

	Jan	Feb	Mar	Apr	May	Jun	Jul	Aug	Sep	Oct	Nov	Dec
Alt WeBS	283	/	99	186	83	24	36	35	38	541	310	506
MMWWT	560	555	239	314	329	152	41	19	1	13	346	437
MBS WeBS	2796	1381	1218	972	705	613	488	145	1801	2063	2102	805
Ribble WeBS	1419	2860	1721	1808	1443	2698	1180	1037	2268	2117	3850	1494

For the third year in a row there was a small increase in Morecambe Bay while a small corresponding decrease occurred on the Ribble Estuary. In keeping with the regional trend, the wintering MMWWT population continues to decline following a peak around the turn of the century.

Inland records were fairly widespread but never numerous. The most notable records comprised moult migration flights of 125 over Brockholes on 5 July and 35 flying over Alston the following evening. Prior to this in mid-June there had been brief gatherings of over 300 birds on the Keer Estuary and at Banks Marsh.

On the Ribble Estuary 22 pairs bred at Marshside and 23 pairs reared 33 young at Hesketh Out Marsh.

MANDARIN DUCK *Aix galericulata*
Uncommon feral resident and escapee.

Double-figure counts in the first winter period included 13 at Croston and ten at Common Bank Lodge near Chorley in January. The Calder catchment produced regular sightings with maxima of c.18 at Barrowford and 14 at Foulridge Upper Reservoir. In the north of the county at least 17 were present throughout the year in a captive collection at High Tatham. A handful of records involving one or two male were received from the Fylde at Marton Mere, Lytham, Nateby and Myerscough Quarry but there were no reports from the former stronghold of Singleton.

Females were seen with young at Croston, Eccleston and Yarrow Valley Country Park. Two pairs with 16 young were observed at Foulridge Lower Reservoir. Other sightings of either one or two birds in east Lancashire came from Jackhouse, Slaidburn and Stocks Reservoir.

A Lancashire record count was made in private woodland in the Rivington and Anglezarke area on 29 Oct when an impressive 58 were seen. These large numbers remained through the winter with 38 seen on Anglezarke Reservoir on 25 Nov and 45 on 21 Dec.

GARGANEY *Anas querquedula*
Scarce spring and autumn migrant and rare, occasional breeder. Amber List (rare breeder).

The first record of the spring was a pair at Grove Lane Marsh near Padiham on 21 March. Another pair were at Marshside on 26 March, followed by single male at Brockholes from 5-17 April and Marton Mere between 7-20 April.

Spring sightings peaked in late April and early May when reports were received from Adlcliffe, Alston Wetland, Leighton Moss (up to three), Marshside, MMWWT (up to three), Newton Marsh (pair) and Wesham Marsh.

A male at Lunt Meadows on 24 April remained into May when it was joined by a female from the 3rd onwards; on 17-19 May an impressive four male and two females were present, one male remaining into June. Breeding was confirmed there when a female was seen with a half-grown juvenile in mid-August.

The first autumn record of one at Stanley Park, Blackpool on 11-23 Aug was quickly followed by another at Leighton Moss from 12 Aug to 4 Sept. Other short-staying August birds visited Alston Wetland, Brockholes, MMWWT and Seaforth. Brockholes hosted a further individual on 13 Sept and a juvenile was at Hesketh Out Marsh on 21st. A juvenile male was at Conder Green on 28 Sept until 6 Oct. The last record of the year was of one at Leighton Moss on 11 Oct that stayed until the extremely late date of 21 Nov. Remarkably, it was joined by a second bird from 12-21 Nov.

Male Garganey, Lunt Meadows, 21 May (Mike Jackson)

SHOVELER *Anas clypeata*
Common winter visitor to west and north. Scarce breeder.
International importance 400; National importance 180.

Monthly peak counts

	Jan	Feb	Mar	Apr	May	Jun	Jul	Aug	Sep	Oct	Nov	Dec
Leighton/EMC	168	118	136	54	22	12	3	14	80	82	145	161
Lunt Meadows	22	35	44	59	/	/	/	/	69	76	65	24
S Park/ M. Mere	30	24	22	13	1	4	2	12	45	30	15	28
Mere Sands Wood	26	13	41	2	2	0	0	0	13	20	37	51
MBS WeBS	74	106	125	45	7	0	0	0	13	21	8	157
MMWWT	19	10	22	24	23	10	6	18	48	37	3	11
Ribble WeBS	35	94	159	26	11	13	11	0	57	188	137	162

Declines compared to 2018 were observed at nearly all of the sites listed in the table. Numbers at Mere Sands Wood were down by almost two thirds compared to 2018. The largest site count of the year was 168 on the Eric Morecambe Complex in January. There were also notable flocks at other nearby wetlands including 42 at Holmere in February and 60 at Silverdale Moss in October. Counts of

34 at Myerscough Quarry on 6 April and 26 at Grimsargh Wetland on 18 Nov were notable for these sites. Seaforth held up to 36 in September.

Ten pairs bred at Marshside, an estimated seven pairs at Leighton Moss and a minimum of five pairs at Lunt Meadows, raising at least four broods and at least one pair was successful at Newton Marsh.

Shoveler brood, Newton Marsh, 9 June (Paul Ellis)

HYBRID SHOVELER *Anas clypeata*

A male Shoveler x Cinnamon Teal hybrid was found on the Eric Morecambe Complex on 15 Nov and remained there or at Leighton Moss into 2020. A male hybrid Gadwall x Shoveler was at Marton Mere on 17 Dec and remained there until the end of the year.

GADWALL *Anas strepera*

Fairly common in small flocks at western wetland sites. Scarce in east of county. Scarce breeder in southwest and north of county.

International importance 600; National importance 250.

Monthly peak counts

	Jan	Feb	Mar	Apr	May	Jun	Jul	Aug	Sep	Oct	Nov	Dec
Leighton/EMC	160	121	76	47	47	40	56	78	103	161	361	290
Lunt Meadows	22	15	25	75	/	/	/	/	/	26	20	14
Marton Mere	131	127	88	21	6	3	9	15	24	46	81	112
MMWWT	39	14	7	22	14	39	43	56	9	44	5	4
Ribble WeBS	2	50	41	82	49	14	5	9	31	89	78	53

A Lancashire site record count of 361 at Leighton Moss on 25 Nov came after a substantial long-term increase. The Stanley Park and Marton Mere population has also increased substantially in recent years and the 131 on 28 Jan at the former was another new site record.

The rapid development of Lunt Meadows is reflected by a peak count of 75 in April, more than double that of 2018 but the 60 at Brockholes in December was less than half the previous year's annual peak. The largest gatherings in east Lancashire were of 17 at Alston Reservoirs on 20 March and 34 at Grimsargh Wetland on 18 Nov.

It was also an excellent year for breeding both in terms of number of pairs and breeding success. An almost complete set of breeding records were received from likely sites giving a total of at least 106 pairs across the county. The RSPB Morecambe Bay properties held breeding 40 pairs, a joint record for the site; Marshside had 24 pairs. Productivity was high at several sites, notably eight pairs raised twelve young at Lunt Meadows and up to five pairs reared 21 young at Middleton NR.

WIGEON *Anas penelope*
Very common winter visitor to coastal sites. Smaller numbers at some eastern sites.
International importance 15000, National importance 4400.

Monthly peak counts

	Jan	Feb	Mar	Apr	May	Jun	Jul	Aug	Sep	Oct	Nov	Dec
L. Moss/EMC	569	496	440	10	2	5	2	10	60	290	440	710
MMWWT	740	833	7	3	1	0	1	0	15	123	297	449
MBS WeBS	3885	2963	130	25	2	3	2	0	197	1374	2954	4936
Ribble WeBS	51802	21788	1684	148	0	8	3	0	1234	30674	33684	25715

The gradual decline on the Ribble continued in line with the regional trend. Record numbers were found on the restored saltmarsh at Hesketh Out Marsh, peaking at 14315 in December. While falling short of the 2018 maximum, the five-year average in Morecambe Bay remains only just below the historical maximum reached in 2016. There were only relatively low numbers at MMWWT and the Eric Morecambe Complex. Elsewhere, 850 were at Myerscough Quarry in February and Alston Reservoirs held a peak of 396 on 19 Jan.

Several birds spent the spring at the Eric Morecambe Complex, MMWWT, Marshside and Newton Marsh but there was no indication of breeding. A lack of records has made it difficult to determine major autumn arrivals. The first flock reported was 60 at Hesketh Out Marsh on 30 Aug and this had increased to 455 by 15 Sept before the main arrival had taken place by the time of the October WeBS count.

AMERICAN WIGEON* *Anas americana*
Rare winter visitor.

The male on the Eric Morecambe complex during December 2018 was reported again on 1 Jan. The Hesketh Out Marsh male from 2018 also remained until 6 Jan and was seen again on 16 March. A male stopped off at the Eric Morecambe Complex on 16-20 April.

The only record from the second winter period was a male at Banks Marsh from 26 Oct to 3 Nov.

HYBRID WIGEON
A male Wigeon x American Wigeon was seen at The Snab on 6 Dec. The male Wigeon x Gadwall hybrid was seen occasionally at Hare Tarn from 17 Jan to 22 March.

MALLARD *Anas platyrhynchos*
Very common and widespread winter visitor and breeding resident.
International importance 20000; national importance 6800.

Monthly peak counts

	Jan	Feb	Mar	Apr	May	Jun	Jul	Aug	Sep	Oct	Nov	Dec
Alt WeBS	155	/	38	38	13	17	41	33	51	238	215	135
Leighton Moss	180	110	35	58	38	120	255	170	78	132	98	135
MMWWT	787	524	425	368	412	562	695	578	771	1075	335	607
MBS WeBS	310	290	99	86	78	183	205	500	589	176	290	332
Ribble WeBS	750	335	284	252	207	269	305	317	617	689	854	580
Stocks Res.	359	38	21	90	122	290	80	300	280	100	200	112

The decline of this species continues to be a cause for serious concern. There was no repeat of the counts of nearly 3000 at MMWWT in the previous two years and in fact October's peak of just 1075 was the lowest site annual maximum on record. The declines on the Ribble and Alt Estuaries both continued, the Ribble peak was the lowest since 1982. A slight increase on 2018 was seen in Morecambe Bay but the five-year average continues to decline.

Significant counts from east Lancashire included 359 at Stocks Reservoir in January and 390 at Alston Reservoirs and Wetland in December. Elsewhere, 277 were at Lunt Meadows in October, 200 at Bretherton Eyes on 11 Oct and 370 on a private pond at Belmont on the 26th.

Where comprehensive monitoring of breeding populations took place there were generally larger numbers of pairs present than in recent years although productivity was fairly low. Records were received from the RSPB Morecambe Bay properties (88 pairs), Marshside (56 pairs), Hesketh Out Marsh (31 pairs), Lunt Meadows (20-25 pairs) and Belmont Reservoir (15 broods) plus a nest was present at 420m above sea level on Winter Hill. Breeding was confirmed from 19 sites in east Lancashire.

PINTAIL *Anas acuta*
Common winter visitor to coast and western wetlands. Has bred.
International importance 600; National importance 290.

Monthly peak counts

	Jan	Feb	Mar	Apr	May	Jun	Jul	Aug	Sep	Oct	Nov	Dec
Leighton Moss / EMC	46	61	10	2	0	0	0	3	17	22	32	42
MMWWT	185	242	2	1	1	1	1	1	1	91	59	246
MBS WeBS	382	292	14	2	0	0	0	0	0	510	194	241
Ribble WeBS	216	418	6	5	0	0	0	0	5	71	512	1688
Stocks Res	8	13	2	0	0	0	0	0	1	0	26	8

The national and regional decline was reflected in the lowest peak count on record at MMWWT. However, there was a hint of a continued recovery on the Ribble and December's count was the highest since 2011. WeBS counts in Morecambe Bay were fairly stable but did miss what must have been a short-lived but significant autumn passage, as 1230 were at Cockersand on 20 Oct.

A female with a damaged wing spent the summer at MMWWT and another female was seen at Newton Marsh on 6 June only. There were no other records until 29 Aug when one arrived at the Eric Morecambe Complex. The autumn arrival was late and in fact the only double-figure counts in September were the 20 that passed Starr Gate on the 23rd and 66 on a flood at Winmarleigh on the 27th.

For the third year running there was no large influx to Stocks Reservoir; this year's maximum count was just 26 in November. A maximum of 40 were recorded at Bretherton Eyes on 12 Oct.

TEAL *Anas crecca*
Very common winter visitor to western wetlands, smaller flocks in east. Rare breeding species.
International importance 5000; National importance 2100.

Monthly peak counts

	Jan	Feb	Mar	Apr	May	Jun	Jul	Aug	Sep	Oct	Nov	Dec
Leighton Moss	460	310	280	112	5	2	2	4	40	304	205	408
Lunt Meadows	350	1200	450	/	/	/	/	/	200	700	456	258
MMWWT	1046	428	170	81	1	13	19	4	564	3188	509	1021
MBS WeBS	1475	725	281	101	0	0	11	39	587	1888	925	1399
Ribble WeBS	1285	2069	1163	256	0	18	20	248	850	3627	3023	5142
Seaforth	502	170	100	20	4	2	4	47	120	350	450	500

The year began with relatively low numbers across the key sites and clearly many birds had moved on since almost 9000 had been counted on the Ribble Estuary in December 2018. The five-year average remains relatively stable or slightly increasing on the Ribble Estuary and at MMWWT but declining slightly in Morecambe Bay.

There were few large counts from sites not included in the table but those included 200 at Marton Mere in January. Floods in low lying fields on the Fylde attracted 420 to Lathwaite and 575 at Winmarleigh on 15 Sept. The largest count from east Lancashire was 276 at Stocks Reservoir in October,

More breeding season records were received than usual, albeit breeding was only confirmed at one site. One or two pairs bred at Belmont Reservoir where a brood of five young was seen in late June and a further three females or pairs were recorded elsewhere in the West Pennine Moors. Teal in potential breeding habitat were reported from Nangreaves near Rossendale, Marton Mere, Silverdale Moss (three pairs), Marshside (two pairs) and Hesketh Out Marsh (four pairs).

GREEN-WINGED TEAL *Anas carolinensis*
Scarce winter visitor.

A male was present on the Eric Morecambe Complex on 9-12 April followed by another at Lunt Meadows on 7 May.

POCHARD *Aythya ferina*
Fairly common but declining winter visitor, scarce breeder.
International importance 3500; National importance 380.

Monthly peak counts

	Jan	Feb	Mar	Apr	May	Jun	Jul	Aug	Sep	Oct	Nov	Dec
Dockacres	18	18	3	0	0	0	0	1	0	5	32	28
Leighton Moss	6	13	45	25	16	9	7	4	1	5	2	1
MMWWT	51	60	7	6	2	3	5	1	/	8	12	37
Myerscough Quarry	21	22	8	0	0	0	0	0	4	/	5	4
Seaforth	12	12	7	1	0	2	2	1	2	5	7	8

A slight increase compared to 2018 was apparent at Dockacres and MMWWT. Stocks Reservoir saw up to 23 present in February and 15 in December. An unusual east Lancashire record of a mid-summer pair came from Alston Wetland on 18 July.

Twenty pairs bred across the RSPB Morecambe Bay properties, with at least six fledged young seen and six young were also raised at MMWWT.

RING-NECKED DUCK* *Aythya collaris*
Vagrant.

A first-winter male discovered at Pine Lake on 17 Nov (P Crooks) remained into 2020. The first record since 2014.

Ring-necked Duck, Pine Lake, 24 November (Paul Ellis)

TUFTED DUCK *Aythya fuligula*
Common winter visitor, scarce breeder.
International importance 1200; National importance 1100.

Monthly peak counts

	Jan	Feb	Mar	Apr	May	Jun	Jul	Aug	Sep	Oct	Nov	Dec
Brockholes	/	35	55	/	40	/	1	60	73	100	55	/
Dockacres	130	160	68	12	4	1	1	2	38	32	127	178
Glasson	56	65	7	21	15	8	5	8	40	66	48	33
Ribble WeBS	114	126	68	64	37	27	43	15	34	79	202	235
Seaforth	7	12	16	31	15	48	82	84	85	25	33	16
S Park, Blackpool	78	70	68	45	0	4	9	6	10	21	42	51
Stocks Res	47	36	4	16	3	4	24	14	9	18	22	65

Only Brockholes, Marshside and Pine Lake recorded three-figure counts this year as short-stopping continues to mean fewer birds reach Britain every winter. Marshside held an impressive 324 on 20 Dec but at MMWWT, which used to be one of the key sites in the county, numbers peaked at just 40 in January.

Wintering birds were widespread in low numbers in east Lancashire with peaks of 68 at Alston Reservoirs and Wetland in August and 65 at Stocks Reservoir in December. The largest count from the West Pennine Moors was 50 on Wayoh Reservoir in December.

The main breeding populations were found on the RSPB Morecambe Bay properties where 28 pairs bred. Elsewhere, MMWWT had 15 breeding pairs and eight pairs bred at Lunt Meadows. Successful breeding was also reported from Alston Wetland, Fairhaven Lake, Grimsargh Wetland, Marshside, Pilling Lane Ends and Stanley Park, Blackpool.

SCAUP *Aythya marila*
Uncommon and declining winter visitor, scarce inland.

The year began with several individuals remaining from 2018. A male at Glasson stayed until 28 Jan. A pair at Pine Lake was joined by another female on 9-15 Feb. A single female then remained in the area for a further two months before last being seen at Leighton Moss on 12 April. Other inland records came from Stocks Reservoir on 16 Jan and 2 April. The last sighting of the spring came from Starr Gate when a pair flew south on 26 April.

The first returning bird of the autumn was an early male passing Starr Gate on 9 Aug. There were then no further sightings until a female spent a day at Lee Green Reservoir on 16 Sept and one was at Lunt Meadows on the 18th. A mid-October arrival was apparent with sightings at Blackpool, Clowbridge Reservoir, Hesketh Out Marsh, Pilling Marsh, Aldcliffe, Leighton Moss (two), Eagland Hill and Conder Pool between 9th-20th. A pair made the briefest of appearances at Slipper Hill Reservoir on 30 Oct.

A notable congregation by recent standards saw six birds on a regular basis at Pine Lake during November and December, with a peak of seven on 20 Dec. Other wintering birds included up to three at Marshside throughout December and two males at Yarrow Reservoir on 5 Dec. For the first time there were no records from Seaforth.

EIDER *Somateria mollissima*
Common winter visitor to Fylde coast and Morecambe Bay, scarce elsewhere. Rare breeder.
International importance 12850; national importance 550.

Monthly peak counts

	Jan	Feb	Mar	Apr	May	Jun	Jul	Aug	Sep	Oct	Nov	Dec
Heysham/M'mbe	319	462	1083	455	100	29	11	32	4	20	23	27
MBS WeBS	516	599	1225	273	256	209	293	153	112	95	47	55
Ribble WeBS	5	15	14	289	113	164	99	10	42	26	2	0
Rossall Point	67	7	180	116	48	/	53	53	68	57	49	52

Following on from the exceptional numbers of Eiders seen in Morecambe Bay in 2018 there was a predictable drop in peak counts. In fact the annual peak in March was very short-lived and probably came from many birds moving across from the Furness coast. Up to 75% of the birds were males. The second half of the year saw numbers decrease rapidly after storms washed away mussel beds en masse. The smaller population on the Ribble Estuary reached its highest level on record.

It was a very poor year in terms of breeding records but surely a number of pairs went unrecorded amongst the larger number of non-breeding birds. Two pairs bred at Hesketh Out Marsh and just a single brood of four young was seen at Lytham. Breeding was not confirmed in Morecambe Bay but pairs were seen in suitable habitat on the Lune Estuary and in the Pilling-Cockerham area.

VELVET SCOTER *Melanitta fusca*
Uncommon winter visitor.

The first winter period saw just two records: one off Ainsdale on 17 Jan and a female flying out of Morecambe Bay past Heysham on 14 March.

Given the flocks of Common Scoters that remain offshore during the summer it was not too much of a surprise that a male was seen off Blackpool on 21 June; there were two further records there, a male on 30 Sept and a female on 3 Dec. Single birds were seen off Ainsdale on 17 Nov and the following day off Formby Point.

COMMON SCOTER *Melanitta nigra*
Abundant visitor to Liverpool Bay, especially in winter, although main flocks are hardly visible from land. Uncommon migrant to inland waters.
International importance 16000; National importance 1000.

Monthly peak counts

	Jan	Feb	Mar	Apr	May	Jun	Jul	Aug	Sep	Oct	Nov	Dec
Blackpool	1420	1700	545	445	1020	383	1300	1180	1125	830	620	1500
Formby/Alt WeBS	8000	2640	720	242	25	3	437	9500	11970	6800	5100	9100

Large flocks could be seen, usually distantly from the Sefton Coast but there were lower numbers than usual off the Fylde coast. Three sample counts of large flocks off Formby in August and October revealed that 95-97% of the birds were male.

Spring passage in Morecambe Bay began on 9 March with two off Morecambe Stone Jetty. A total of 1528 bird-days were recorded off Heysham and Morecambe by 28 May with peaks of 600 on the 18th and 450 on the 19th.

The first inland birds of the summer were seven on Anglezarke Reservoir on 24 June. Late in the morning of 27 July, several flocks totalling approximately 600 birds flew west along a flightpath between Alston Reservoirs and Brockholes NR before poor weather curtailed any further observation. The following day, 24 were at Stocks Reservoir and 14 at Carr Mill Dam. Very few records were received from other inland sites for the remainder of the autumn with sightings of ones or twos coming from Alston Reservoirs, Pine Lake, Stocks Reservoir and Yarrow Reservoir.

LONG-TAILED DUCK *Clangula hyemalis*
Scarce winter visitor.

It was a poor year for this species, which began with no records at all during the first winter period. The first sighting of the year was two females that flew north off Blackpool on 4 May.

The first record of the second winter period was an adult male at Alston No 1 Reservoir on 1-8 Nov. A first-winter female at Lunt Meadows on 1-17 Dec was the first record for the site. On 25 Dec it was relocated at Crosby Coastal Park where it remained long into 2020 aside from a brief visit to Seaforth on 26 Dec. A juvenile was seen off Heysham 3 & 6 Dec.

First-winter female Long-tailed Duck, Crosby Coastal Park, 31 December (Steve Young)

GOLDENEYE *Bucephala clangula*
Fairly common winter visitor.
International importance 4000; National importance 200.

Monthly peak counts

	Jan	Feb	Mar	Apr	May	Jun	Jul	Aug	Sep	Oct	Nov	Dec
Alston Res's	9	16	18	4	0	0	2	0	0	3	12	6
Brockholes	21	26	30	13	0	0	0	0	0	1	10	9
Dockacres	15	23	12	5	0	0	0	0	0	6	9	16
Lune Estuary	7	40	1	0	0	0	0	0	0	6	7	24
MBS WeBS	30	14	17	0	0	0	0	0	0	0	11	28
Seaforth	16	19	27	14	1	0	0	1	1	9	23	25
Stocks Reservoir	18	32	4	3	0	0	0	0	0	0	3	11

The wintering flocks at most of the regular sites saw numbers broadly similar to 2018 although in Morecambe Bay this means the population remains at just a fraction of the level of a decade ago. Research has identified short-stopping at sites further north and east in Europe as the main reason for the apparent decline in the UK.

Two very unseasonal birds were a surprise find at Alston Reservoirs on 12 July before the first of the autumn arrived at Seaforth on 9 Aug. One at Clowbridge Reservoir in September was an unusual Rossendale record.

SMEW *Mergus albellus*
Scarce winter visitor.

A female arrived at Brockholes 26 Oct and moved between the lakes and the River Ribble during its stay which extended into 2020.

GOOSANDER *Mergus merganser*
Fairly common and increasing winter visitor especially in the east. Scarce breeder.
International importance 2700; National importance 120.

Monthly peak counts

	Jan	Feb	Mar	Apr	May	Jun	Jul	Aug	Sep	Oct	Nov	Dec
Alston Res's	16	33	18	0	0	0	0	0	10	/	/	/
Delph Res	84	86	44	0	0	0	0	0	0	64	69	62
Dockacres	8	3	4	6	0	0	0	0	0	0	0	1
Mere Sands Wood	20	19	13	3	0	0	0	0	0	1	23	23
MBS WeBS	15	16	22	19	8	0	2	0	8	19	16	14
River Lune	50	80	82	44	33	19	19	44	18	31	35	29

For the fifth consecutive year the site record count was broken at Delph Reservoir, this time by just one bird on 15 Feb. Additionally, it was noted that larger numbers are arriving earlier in the winter than previously as shown by the October count when compared to no more than 18 in the preceding six years. Other sites recording notable counts, typically at roost gatherings, included 53 at Yarrow Reservoir and 26 at Barrowford Reservoir in January, also 16 at Foulridge Reservoirs in November. Up to 21 were regular at Cuerden Valley Park in December.

The first confirmation of breeding came from the River Hodder at Easington on 27 April where a female was seen with ten small ducklings. Other broods in east Lancashire were seen at Altham, Martholme, Feniscowles Old Hall, Barrowford and Stocks Reservoir. At least two pairs bred on the River Yarrow, two females with broods of six young were seen in the Croston and Eccleston area.

RED-BREASTED MERGANSER *Mergus serrator*
Fairly common but declining coastal winter visitor. Rare breeder inland.
International importance 1700; National importance 84.

Monthly peak counts

	Jan	Feb	Mar	Apr	May	Jun	Jul	Aug	Sep	Oct	Nov	Dec
MBS WeBS	26	40	29	35	7	0	4	2	11	28	38	53
Stocks Res.	1	1	5	10	7	5	1	1	0	0	0	2

The county's main population in Morecambe Bay remains relatively stable compared to recent years. The largest numbers were found in the vicinity of the Keer Estuary and Eric Morecambe Complex, peaking at 22 in October.

Inland, the first returning birds at Stocks Reservoir arrived on 16 Feb. Breeding was not confirmed in Bowland but considered possible given the presence of several birds at Stocks Reservoir during spring, along with other sightings from Whitendale and Bottoms Beck.

A handful of sightings of one to three birds off Heysham and Starr Gate in June indicated that a few non-breeding birds spent the summer at the coast.

NIGHTJAR* *Caprimulgus europaeus*
Rare passage migrant; has probably bred in recent years.

It is very pleasing that one of our most evocative nocturnal species continues the recent run of sightings in a potential breeding location. There were three records during June and July at the east Lancashire site where birds have been present in recent summers. All three sightings related to churring individuals, with the frog-like call also heard on one occasion.

Further optimistic news came with the sighting of two birds, including a churring male, on 15 June at a quite separate site in the south of the Bowland AONB more than ten miles away from the regular one (P Morris). Birds were also detected in this area in spring 2020 so it appears that this too has become an established breeding site.

SWIFT *Apus apus*
Common summer visitor and abundant passage migrant.

Swifts were a full three weeks later in 2019 than they were in 2018, although the 2018 record was close to our earliest ever. The first of 2019 were two sighted over Leighton Moss on 25 April. The first for the ELOC area arrived on 30 April in Slaidburn with other area firsts arriving around that date or creeping into early May; including Belmont on 28 April, MMWWT and Knott End on 30 April and Seaforth and Stanley Park, Blackpool on 1 May.

Subsequent higher passage numbers were recorded throughout May and June. On the Fylde, Fairhaven Lake had a group of 50+ on 9 May and Marton Mere recorded flocks in excess of 40 on several dates at the end of May and into early June. Leighton Moss recorded 100+ on 11 May, 120 on 31 May, and 56 on 17 June, with nearby Silverdale Moss logging 50 on 3 June. Lunt recorded its peak count of the spring with 180 on 19 May and also had a flock of 100+ on 31 May. In the Rossendale area, Ewood Bridge sewage works recorded 150+ on 26 May, and in the west, MMWWT held 50+ between 22 and 24 May. Brockholes had a 100-strong flock late in the afternoon on the 9 May. An exceptional 2126 were logged on Trektellen as moving southeast over Winter Hill on 18 June in just a three-hour watch.

Among the few breeding reports received, one nest site was noted at Conder Green on 12 July. Breeding was proven from Belmont village when adults were observed with juveniles on 10 July. Earlier in the year adults had been seen visiting nest sites in at least three locations in the village. In east Lancashire, possible breeding was reported at Clitheroe, Longridge, Padiham, Rimington and Downham. A pair frequented a known nesting-hole in Longridge in June, 40 adults were seen at a regular nest site at Burnley, and finally two probably bred at Weaver's Triangle Mills. In other areas, two family groups were recorded in Fulwood and one in Bispham during July. Ten probable breeding sites were identified in the Chorley recording area.

Summer feeding flocks and departure movements resulted in some reasonably high counts, the pick being 120+ at Pilling Lane Ends on 26 June. In the north, 60+ at Leighton Moss on 5 July, a peak count of 61 in Lancaster on 24 July, and 40 at Conder Pool on 22 Aug. In the south, Lunt Meadows recorded 100+ on 23 Aug, while on the Fylde 65 were at Wrea Green on 4 Aug.

A number of records in mid- to late September included ELOC's last at Clowbridge on 13 Sept, one at Seaforth and one at Shard Bridge on 15 Sept, one at Folly Clough in Rossendale on 16 Sept, and two at Crosby on 23 Sept. Two recorded by the Lune at Low Mill on 29 Sept were the final records of 2019.

CUCKOO *Cuculus canorus*
Uncommon breeding bird and double passage migrant, more numerous in spring.

One of our harbingers of spring, the first Cuckoo of the year at Marshside on 14 April was followed by one at White Coppice on the following day. Arrivals in various areas after that date included two on Longridge Fell on 18 April, Darwen Moor on the 20th and singles at Belmont, Marton Mere and at Langden Brook, Bowland on the 23rd, and at Birk Bank on the 24th. The first Cuckoo of the season at MMWWT was seen on 26 April, and the first two at Leighton Moss the day after.

In the ELOC region, 128 records were received from 33 different locations, the majority of these in the Bowland and Ribble Valley areas, but also from eleven other sites around the moorland fringes of the eastern towns. Bowland had a maximum count of five singing males on 16 June, one of which was the much-loved satellite-tagged bird, Larry. Sadly, Larry perished during his migratory flight back to Africa, his signal being lost around 29 July in Libya. He will be sorely missed by the birdwatchers of Lancashire.

Cuckoos were heard calling in at least ten locations in the Rossendale area, including Compston's Cross, Clowbridge Reservoir and Tong Lane, Bacup. On 15 May one at Calf Hey Reservoir with a distinct call was presumed to be a regular returning bird since at least 2017. It called until mid-June and was seen and heard all over Musbury and Grane reservoirs. Another was calling on the outskirts of Haslingden on 22 May.

In the west, MMWWT held up to three during May and June and a juvenile was seen there on 18-21 Aug. One was also seen at nearby Mere Sands Wood on 21 July.

Juvenile Cuckoo, Ridge Farm, Fylde, 27 August (Paul Ellis)

Surveys in the West Pennine Moors located one calling male at Clough House Farm, Turton, and two on Winter Hill with another immediately adjacent to the survey site. Calling males were recorded from ten sites in the West Pennine Moors and a female was observed for over an hour repeatedly looking for Meadow Pipit nests (and judging from unobserved periods in vegetation being successful) near Belmont on 28 May with a male nearby. Breeding was confirmed in that area of the county, when a recently-fledged juvenile was on moorland above Belmont on 1 Aug.

A juvenile was also seen on a daily basis on Croston Moss from 12-20 Aug.

In the north of the county, individuals were seen at Leighton Moss on 3 Aug, Yealand Conyers on 5 May, Aldcliffe on 6 May, and a juvenile at Sunderland Point on 5 Aug.

On the Fylde, there were spring records at six sites and autumn records at just four, although one west of the carpark at Fluke Hall on 3 Sept was our last Cuckoo of 2019.

FERAL PIGEON *Columba livia*
Abundant and widely-distributed resident.

Feral Pigeons were routinely reported throughout the period but as is seemingly the norm with this species, the larger counts were predominantly in the second half of the year.

Around the Preston area, the highest count was 40 in Moor Park on 7 Sept, but no counts were received from Preston city centre.

In the Rossendale area, a three-figure count of 120 was logged at Rawtenstall town centre on 27 Oct and 70 were recorded at Waterfoot on 10 Nov.

A number of larger counts were made in Liverpool and the surrounding area, with many of the city's parks holding high numbers, including 200+ at Taylor Park, St Helens on 11 Sept, 126 at Greenbank Park on 12 July, 78 at Newsham Park on 13 June, 70 at Sefton Park on 30 Aug and 58 at Stanley Park on 3 July.

In east Lancashire the number of records received continues to decline annually with only 20 records received this year, but these gave no information on population size, just indicating the presence of the species in various rural and urban locations, so it is impossible to say if anything is changing significantly.

On the Fylde, 150 were at Blackpool centre on 10 Nov, 100 at Little Singleton on 16 June, 80 around Stanley Park boating lake on 22 May and 40 at Fairhaven Lake on 3 & 27 Dec.

In the west, Southport held 180 on 4 Dec with 70 feeding around the Marine Lake on 2 Dec; 50 were at MMWWT on 6 Jan.

In the north, numbers were recorded in seven squares in the LDBWS winter survey, with the peak number being 43 in SD56.

No breeding data were received from any region but the multiple double- and treble-figure counts from July onwards indicate strong populations.

STOCK DOVE *Columba oenas*
Fairly common breeding resident; local flocks in winter.

Overall numbers and three-figure counts for this often overlooked species were slightly down on 2018, but several notable sightings were recorded during the year and records were still much higher than those logged in 2017.

Early year double- and treble-figure counts included a flock of up to 200 commuting between Croston Finney and Bretherton Eyes during January, with 250 being counted on Bretherton Eyes on 16 Feb; 100 were feeding at MMWWT on 24 Jan with 60 there on 9 Jan and there were 40 on farmland to the west of Croxteth Park on 16 Feb with 35 there on 19 Jan. Also recorded were 39 at Hesketh Out Marsh, 34 in the Cheesden Valley on 9 March, and 23 at Lunt Meadows on 25 Feb. More modest counts were 21 at Oglet on 1 Jan, 20+ at Warton Bank 19 Feb, and 17 at Lea Green Reservoir on 10 March. The LDBWS winter survey recorded small numbers in five squares with SD66 logging 14.

Breeding reports came in from nearly all regions. In the north of the county, two pairs were recorded at Challan Hall woodland near Silverdale as part of the RSPB breeding birds survey, while in the south-west three pairs bred at MMWWT and one at Seaforth. In the east breeding took place at New Laithe Farm where two pairs nested, with four juveniles present at the nest sites on 4 Aug, and three pairs probably bred at Foulridge singles at Altham and Burnley by the Leeds/Liverpool Canal. In the Chorley area two pairs bred in Cuerden Valley Park with eight young raised and one or two pairs were at the regular site at White Coppice. At least four pairs bred at Belmont Reservoir and two pairs at Withnell Quarry.

Post-breeding groups were observed in several areas including 49 in fields by Rainford on 5 June with 35 still there on 19 June, 28 at Peel on 3 May, and 14 at Condor Green Pool on 26 May.

Double-figure counts later in the year were seen across a number of locations with the Fylde hosting most of the higher numbers: 111 were at Todderstaffe Hall on 23 Dec, with 100 there 4 Oct and 70 on 9 Dec; Agglebys Pit held 60 on 17 Nov, and 30 were at Newton Marsh on 11 Dec. In other areas, 45 were at Hesketh Out Marsh on 27 Oct, 27 at Crosby on 26 Aug, 22 on Burscough Moss on 27 Dec, and 20+ at MMWWT on 29 Sept. Twelve birds were at Alston Reservoirs on 31 July and the 20 recorded there on 3 Aug provided ELOC's peak count of the year.

WOODPIGEON *Columba palumbus*
Abundant breeding resident; widespread winter flocks.

Big counts of Woodpigeons were made throughout the year, with the largest during the autumn passage as is typical.

Early in the year there were a number of larger counts, mostly concerning feeding flocks, but only one site with four-figure counts during this period, at Singleton, where 1000+ were recorded throughout February and early March. The next largest consisted of 450 near Crosby on 20 April with 289 there on 31 March. Other high counts included 300 at MMWWT on 2 Feb with 75 there on 26 April, 190 on a stubble field near Oglet on 1 Jan, and 180 near Croxteth Park on 22 Feb. Moss Lane, St Helens held 150 on 19 Jan, 75 were at Spring Mill Reservoir on 31 March , 60 at Marshside on 14 Jan and the same number at Brockholes on 1 April. The LDBWS winter survey had records submitted from 9 squares, the pick being 178 in SD66.

Breeding was recorded across the region from a variety of urban and rural habitats. In the south-west 15 pairs bred at Freshfield Dune Heath, eight pairs in the Aintree study area, eleven at Carr Mill Dam, and at least four pairs at Lunt Meadows. Surveys in two Liverpool parks produced some fascinating statistics: 41 nests were located and monitored at Sefton Park, where hatching success was 71.1% and fledging success 81.5%, giving overall breeding success of 57.9%; and 35 nests were monitored at Everton Park with overall breeding success of 59.7%.

In north Lancashire at least 18 pairs were on the various EDF properties at Heysham, and twelve pairs Challan Hall near Silverdale. In Chorley and the West Pennine Moors no pairs were found on the Winter Hill breeding birds survey but a number were noted in the plantations surrounding the site, and two pairs bred for the first time in the developing scrub at Belmont Reservoir. A total of 29 were recorded in two BBS squares in the Brindle area in late April, and there were at least eight breeding pairs in Cuerden Valley Park.

As usual there were numerous reports of post-breeding flocks and movements: 2500 at Lunt Meadows on 1 June was the reserve's highest count of the year, 325 were near Croxteth Park on 2 June, 300 at Singleton on 13 Aug and 100 in the Grane area on 21 July.

The subsequent autumn passage produced the highest numbers of the year. The highlight being from the Belmont area where some impressive hourly passage counts were logged in October and November. The birds per hour figures are summarised in the table below. Two flocks (of 450 and 300) on 20 Oct were at an exceptionally high altitude, undoubtedly involving a long-distance movement; 600 were feeding on Beech mast in the Belmont area on 6 Oct, with 400 at a nearby site on 20 Oct. Trektellen visible migration data from Winter Hill showed 36121 were observed during October and 22143 during November with a peak count of 9967 on 28 Oct.

10 Oct	14 Oct	15 Oct	17 Oct	20 Oct	23 Oct	25 Oct	27 Oct	29 Oct	9 Nov
110	49	98	854	3828	225	84	4653	2292	2442

In Merseyside 1020 were at Belle Vale on 25 Sept and 230 were at Rainford on 1 Nov and 394 were logged from the Rimrose Valley watchpoint on 8 Oct, while Rossendale recorded counts of 300 around Calf Hey Reservoir on 10 Nov with 200 there on 27 Oct, 200 were at Strongstry on 30 Oct, 250 from Lench on 6 Oct and 100 at Fern Island Wood on 6 Oct. In the north, Heysham recorded 159 on 4 Nov, and in east Lancashire 250 were observed making a westerly passage over Alston Reservoirs on 10 Aug with 200 there the following day, and 300 were at Wood End Sewage Works on 22 Aug.

Usually with this species, the high numbers tail off as the year ends, however 550 were at Staining on 19 Dec, 500 were near Belmont on 9 Dec, 400+ were over Waterfoot, Rossendale on 16 Dec, with a similar number near the ski slope on 30 Dec and 300 at Calf Hey Reservoir the day before. ELOC had a record of 800 on 14 Dec at Feniscowles Old Hall which also produced three other counts greater than 100. There were 387 at Jackhouse on 9 Nov and c250 at New Laithe Farm on 10 Nov. A group of 1000+ was on Croston Moss on 27 Dec, and at least 500 used a roost site in Cuerden Valley Park on a regular basis.

COLLARED DOVE *Streptopelia decaocto*
Common breeding resident, more local in the east; some coastal passage.

Early in the year there were a number of double-figure counts, including 32 at Bryning Hall near Lytham on 5 Jan, 20+ by Old Moss Lane near Formby on 28 April, 15 in a Belmont garden on 6 Jan and twelve were at Strongstry feeding station, Rossendale on 3 Jan. Seven double-figure counts were recorded during this period in east Lancashire compared to 14 last year, including the largest of the year of 23 on 24 Jan at Newton-in-Bowland, followed by 18 in an urban garden in Burnley on 3 Feb. In the Chorley district, birds were present in 18 of the 23 gardens surveyed during the Winter Garden Bird Survey. The LDBWS winter survey had birds in nine out of the eleven 10km squares with 40 in SD67 the highest. An interesting spring passage record was one seen to come "in-off" at Heysham on 15 April.

Breeding records received were rather sparse, but did come in from most areas. A number of pairs were noted in urban Heysham, while in east Lancashire ten pairs were confirmed breeding at Foulridge, a number at Jackhouse and a probable record at New Laithe Farm. From the Chorley area, just three individuals were recorded in two BBS squares in the Brindle area in late April, but at least four pairs bred in Cuerden Valley Park. A well-observed nest on Pilling Lane, Preesall fledged two young birds. The species continues to breed commonly throughout suburban Liverpool.

A number of double-figure counts were submitted from August to the year's end, predominantly from locations close to the coast. Pilling Lane, Preesall had the pick with 131 on 14 Oct, 97 on 11 Oct and 40 on 3 Sept. 40 were at Cockersand on 3 Nov, 33 on the Keer Estuary on 1 Sept, 29 at Glasson Marsh on 13 Oct, and 22 on Formby Moss on 19 Dec. Further inland, there were 15 in a Belmont garden on 25 Oct with 23 there on 1 Dec, and 14 in Speke on 21 Nov. Autumn movement on the coast at Heysham produced one on 21 Oct, and four (three + one) moving south on 25 Oct.

WATER RAIL *Rallus aquaticus*
Scarce breeder; fairly common winter visitor from central and eastern Europe.

This year 40 sites logged Water Rails compared to 75 in 2018. Perhaps the above-average wet weather that dominated the second winter period in 2019 restricted the availability of wintering sites.

The majority of sightings came during the winter periods and mainly involved single or occasionally two or three birds. Most records came from the west of the county, including six recorded at night over Knott End on five dates. There were no records from Rossendale this year, and few records in east Lancashire away from the regular wintering sites of Lee Green Reservoir, Lower Towneley Pool and Wood End Sewage Works.

Marton Mere and Lunt Meadows had a maximum of five birds in the first and second winter periods respectively. There was no confirmed breeding at either of these sites, although singles were reported from Marton Mere during the summer. A minimum of three were heard at Middleton NR during both winter periods, but call distribution suggested many more were present. Breeding was presumed here as a single bird was present on 26 July. MMWWT had a maximum of four during the second winter period, in addition to six breeding pairs in the summer. Similarly to last year, four were heard at Marshside during the breeding season.

At Leighton Moss a full breeding survey was completed this year when 112 pairs were recorded on the main reserve with a further six pairs at Barrow Scout and three at Silverdale Moss. This confirmed last year's prediction that the 2018 count was an underestimate. Winter maxima at Leighton Moss were 22 in the first period and eight in the second period.

Water Rail, Leighton Moss, 15 November (Craig Bell)

MOORHEN *Gallinula chloropus*
Common resident breeder.

Monthly peak counts

	Jan	Feb	Mar	Apr	May	Jun	Jul	Aug	Sep	Oct	Nov	Dec
MBS WeBS	24	10	20	12	6	2	11	27	30	24	23	14
MMWWT	52	34	19	36	15	93	40	29	30	175	91	100
Ribble WeBS	22	16	15	28	9	10	9	20	13	26	17	23

The Lancaster & District winter survey recorded 70, compared to the 119 in 2018 and 107 in 2017. Overall, recorded peak counts were lower than in 2018. Peak counts away from the main sites included 41 at Lunt Meadows in January and February, 28 in Stanley Park, Blackpool on 9 Sept, and 40+ in Sefton Park, Liverpool on 12 Oct.

Breeding records were widespread. In east Lancashire breeding was confirmed at twelve sites with others almost certainly going unreported. A record 16 pairs bred at Belmont Reservoir, including eight pairs amongst the Black-headed Gull colony, where it was noted that they coped well with brood-rearing in the tightly packed colony. Elsewhere in the CDNHS area, pairs bred at a minimum of ten sites with multiple pairs at the larger of these. MMWWT had 57 pairs, a significant increase on the ten pairs noted last year. No breeding numbers for Leighton Moss were received although 20 birds were present on 19 July and nine pairs were noted at Barrow Scout. Elsewhere, Lunt Meadows held at least ten pairs, while Marshside and Middleton NR both held seven pairs.

COOT *Fulica atra*
Common resident breeder; abundant winter visitor from continental Europe.
National importance: 1800.

The largest single count was 451 on Southport Marine Lake on 31 Oct. Additional high counts included 94 at Glasson Basin on 3 Feb, 50+ at Hesketh Out Marsh on 23 Feb, 108 in Sefton Park on 14 Aug, 252 on Eccleston Mere on 14 Sept, 111 at Newsham Park, Liverpool on 16 Oct, 150+ on the Knowsley Estate on 21 Oct, and 58 on Fleetwood Marsh NP on 27 Oct. The Lancaster & District winter survey recorded 202 at various sites.

Monthly peak counts at sites with maxima over 200

	Jan	Feb	Mar	Apr	May	Jun	Jul	Aug	Sep	Oct	Nov	Dec
Alt WeBS	34	10	12	9	7	12	38	82	125	19	46	22
Brockholes	200	200	56	16	15	50	115	33	/	/	100	/
Brookside	39	30	20	14	18	28	23	27	34	55	56	38
Leighton Moss	60	62	52	24	20	55	75	78	55	71	170	130
Lunt Meadows	43	113	105	93	87	119	50	31	28	18	29	30
Marshside	250	45	30	40	20	18	8	7	10	14	4	14
Marton Mere	164	175	45	25	6	/	61	/	83	40	45	110
MBS WeBS	88	54	55	43	29	9	21	98	102	99	99	80
MMWWT	50	80	16	24	20	53	60	40	38	206	40	269
Dockacres	164	190	16	1	2	4	6	25	22	67	105	126
Ribble WeBS	40	63	79	64	67	33	15	17	18	55	88	56
Seaforth	16	15	8	10	9	34	43	83	124	38	44	20
Southport ML	306	112	31	8	20	29	85	14	123	211	277	206
Stanley Park, Blackpool	48	32	17	8	6	17	69	51	25	/	/	42

Breeding birds and juveniles were reported across the county. These included 33 pairs at MMWWT, 26 at Marshside, 20 at Lunt Meadows, but with low fledging success noted, and 14 at Barrow Scout. Breeding was recorded at a minimum of eight sites in the CDNHS recording area, but with the usual high predation rate before fledging. There was a reduction in confirmed breeding reports from east Lancashire, with only six sites, compared to nine last year. Also, from a peak of eight pairs at Middleton NR, this year saw no breeding attempts.

LITTLE GREBE *Tachybaptus ruficollis*
Uncommon but increasing breeding resident.

Monthly peak counts

	Jan	Feb	Mar	Apr	May	Jun	Jul	Aug	Sep	Oct	Nov	Dec
MBS WeBS+	18	6	11	6	10	9	7	28	41	35	23	12
Silverdale Moss	/	2	10	8	6	8	2	10	/	/	/	46
Conder Green	10	7	3	/	/	1	10	15	21	22	10	15

+ includes counts from additional days where numbers exceed WeBS totals

The number of records received was the best in recent years; up to three individuals were reported from over 50 sites in at least one month of the year and a few sites reported their best figures in current times.

In addition to the table above both Glasson Dock and Fleetwood recorded more than nine in the first winter period. Subsequently around 20 sites returned counts of more than nine later in the year, some of which will almost certainly have been juveniles; these included: Aldcliffe, Bazil Point, Borwick Waters, Conder Pool, Conder Green, Crook O'Lune, Dockacres, Fell End NR, Folly Lane Pool Lancaster, Glasson, Holmere, Leighton Moss, Middleton NR, Pine Lake, Ream Hills and Thornton ICI Reservoir.

River sightings in east Lancashire included singles on the Hodder at Dunsop Bridge, on the Ribble at Brungerley and the Calder at Altham in January, and two at Altham in February. At the other end of the year singles were at Altham on 6 &17 Nov, with two on the Calder at Whalley in October and December and one on the Ribble at Brungerley on 29 Dec.

Breeding was attempted at the following sites, most being successful to a degree: Alston, Brookside (2 pairs), Common Bank Lodge, Fleetwood Marsh NP, Grimsargh Wetlands, Herons' Reach Golf Course, High Bullough Reservoir, Lee Green (2 pairs), Lunt Meadows (6 pairs), Marshside (3 pairs), Middleton, MMWWT (2 pairs), Myerscough Quarry, Pilling Lane Ends, Salterforth, Seaforth, Sefton Park Liverpool, Towneley Park, and Wood End Sewage Works.

GREAT CRESTED GREBE *Podiceps cristatus*
Uncommon but increasing breeding bird. Fairly common in winter.
International importance: 4800. National importance: 190.

Monthly peak counts

	Jan	Feb	Mar	Apr	May	Jun	Jul	Aug	Sep	Oct	Nov	Dec
MBS WeBS+	31	20	10	10	4	4	10	8	22	40	87	11
Alt WeBS	16	26	2	15	6	2	4	/	1	5	6	0
Foulridge Res	4	1	16	10	8	2	/	9	14	9	20	29
Brockholes	3	4	12	10	7	/	8	9	/	/	/	3
Carr Mill Dam	22	34	50	42	39	48	36	35	25	/	/	/

+ includes counts from additional days where numbers exceed WeBS totals

Birds were present offshore all year with increased counts compared to last year for both winter periods in Morecambe Bay, and in the first winter period on the Alt Estuary. Foulridge Reservoirs continues to be the east Lancashire stronghold but with falling numbers. Good numbers at Carr Mill Dam, St Helens appear not to have continued to the end of the year – were all these birds moving to the coast?

Successful breeding occurred at the following sites but how many juveniles survived to full fledging is mostly unknown: Blea Tarn, Brookside, Carr Mill Dam (9pairs, 19 juveniles), Clowbridge Reservoir, Croston Twin Lakes, Dean Clough Reservoir, Dilworth, Foulridge Reservoirs, Glasson Basin, Heapey Lodge, Kincraig Lake, Lunt Meadows (2 pairs), Mere Sands Wood, Marton Mere, Preesall Flashes, Stanley Park Blackpool and Yarrow Valley Park.

Unsuccessful breeding occurred at the following sites where most failures were due to fluctuating water levels: Belmont Reservoir, Holden Wood Reservoir, Hurstwood Reservoir, Leighton Moss, Lower Rivington Reservoir, MMWWT, Rishton Reservoir, Seaforth, Sefton Park, Springs Reservoir, Taylor Park St Helens, and Walton Hall Park, Liverpool.

Birds were also reported from a further 40+ sites.

BLACK-NECKED GREBE *Podiceps nigricollis*
Scarce visitor, mostly in spring and autumn.
International importance: 2800. National importance: 50.

There was the usual scattering of migrants but most significantly a pair at Lunt Meadows which went on to make the first ever nesting attempt in the county.

One appeared in Liverpool Prince's Dock on 11 Feb but no more were recorded until the pair arrived at Lunt Meadows on 3 April; They were repeatedly seen displaying and mating in the first few days of their stay but then became elusive, disappearing into the reedbed where it is assumed they nested, although no nest was seen and no young emerged. They were last seen on 24 May.

Elsewhere there were singles at Seaforth on 26 April, MMWWT on 5 May and Wards Reservoir, Belmont on 29 June, and juvenile remained on Alston Wetland from 11 to 24 Aug.

Black-necked Grebes, Lunt Meadows, 11 April (Phil Boardman)

OYSTERCATCHER *Haematopus ostralegus*
Abundant winter visitor. Common breeding bird.
International importance: 8200. National importance: 2900.

WeBS counts

	Jan	Feb	Mar	Apr	May	Jun	Jul	Aug	Sep	Oct	Nov	Dec
MBS	10180	18133	6952	5340	3248	2029	4973	12558	17351	19259	12650	17068
Ribble	8813	3604	3438	1919	942	962	1014	7742	7754	6286	6558	9382
Alt	1949	2909	2422	531	313	58	519	1661	1412	709	604	881

Numbers wintering in the county peaked in the early years of this century but have fallen by almost a third since (see below). This decline has been most significant in Morecambe Bay which has held the bulk of the county's population for many years but now appears to be in danger of losing this status to the Ribble, where (as on the Alt) numbers seem to be recovering a little.

Typically few wintered any distance inland but many began to move back during January and February; the largest pre-breeding gatherings reported were 137 at Dunsop Bridge on 25 Feb, 75 at Hodder Bank Farm on 1 April and 23 at Belmont Reservoir on 23 March.

Breeding was reported in all parts of the county but as usual the data were very incomplete. The RSPB Bowland wader survey of 34 farms (1459ha) located 77 pairs, the same as in 2018. Fifty pairs nested on the Eric Morecambe complex, 32 on Hesketh Out Marsh, 24 pairs at Marshside and ten pairs at MMWWT. Breeding pairs were on at least another ten sites in east Lancashire, eleven in the

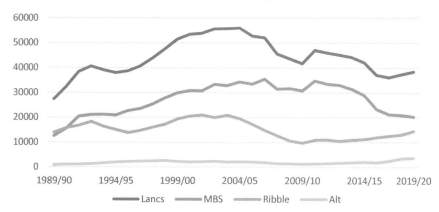

Peak winter counts (5-year rolling means) of Oystercatchers on the
main estuaries in Lancashire, 1989-2019

Lancs   MBS   Ribble   Alt

West Pennine Moors (including five pairs at Belmont Reservoir) and nine in Chorley, with low single figures on several sites in Merseyside, Rossendale and central and north Lancashire.

Post-breeding dispersal got underway in late June but there were few reports of any large gatherings inland – 65 at Stocks Reservoir on 5 July was the largest.

AVOCET *Recurvirostra avosetta*
Recently established uncommon breeding bird.
National Importance: 87

	Jan	Feb	Mar	Apr	May	Jun	Jul	Aug	Sep	Oct	Nov	Dec
Ribble WeBS	0	38	92	129	158	115	132	17	33	1	1	0
MBS WeBS	0	4	4	113	67	33	14	2	0	0	0	0

The first was on Warton Bank on 11 Feb but by the end of the month good numbers had also returned to MMWWT and the Eric Morecambe complex and Avocets were established at all breeding sites by mid-March.

Thirty-two pairs on the Eric Morecambe complex made 45 nesting attempts; many chicks were predated by Black-headed Gulls but 26 lasted until the heavy rains in June and only three fledged.

Avocet, Eric Morecambe complex,
21 April (Craig Bell)

Eight fledged from 29 pairs at MMWWT, 17 from 32 pairs at Marshside, four from 27 at Hesketh Out Marsh, one from two pairs on Newton Marsh and just one from seven pairs at Lunt Meadows. At least seven young were seen at Warton Bank and six at Conder Green, where four pairs nested. It seems clear that the county breeding population is now likely to be approaching 150 pairs.

A handful of migrants were seen at various coastal sites but more notable were singles in the east at Stocks Reservoir on 29 March, two at Alston Wetland on 19 & 28 April and 25 June, and Grimsargh Wetland on 19 & 26 April, possibly involving the same birds at these neighbouring sites, then a single at Alston on 25 June.

The last were at MMWWT on 23 Oct and Warton Marsh on 17 Nov.

LAPWING *Vanellus vanellus*
Abundant but decreasing winter visitor, common breeder.
International importance: 20000. National importance: 6200.

Monthly peak counts

	Jan	Feb	Mar	Apr	May	Jun	Jul	Aug	Sep	Oct	Nov	Dec
MBS WeBS	16006	3773	74	65	52	202	547	2369	3397	4721	8017	5798
Ribble WeBS	13144	6072	256	100	787	154	277	809	1261	3747	11278	15398

Inland counts during January included 2000 at Lunt Meadows and at MMWWT, while further inland numbers were as usual much smaller, including 323 at Alston Reservoirs, 200 at Bashall Town140 on Croston Moss and 120 at Ightenhill.

As demonstrated by the WeBS counts February saw the usual widespread move abroad and inland to Lancashire breeding sites. There were pre-breeding gatherings in excess of 100 birds at six sites in east Lancashire, 250 were at Brockholes on the 19th, 180 at Belmont Reservoir on 2 March, while the largest in Chorley was 300 at Brindle on 5 Feb.

The survey of in-bye on 34 farms in Bowland registered 306 pairs, 67 more than last year. The next largest site totals were 66 pairs at Marshside that fledged 32 young, 22 pairs at MMWWT fledging 17 and 25 pairs around Belmont Reservoir where at least ten broods were seen in one area of in-bye. Another 85 territories were recorded at a further 25 sites in the western and central West Pennine Moors, while smaller site totals included 13 territories at up to 430m asl in the fire-damaged Lancashire sector of Winter Hill, eleven pairs on the Eric Morecambe complex and at least ten pairs at Lunt Meadows. Breeding was confirmed on more than a dozen sites in east Lancashire, including eight pairs at Lamb Hill Farm but was reported more widely from farmland and wetland across the whole of the county. Overall, it would appear that the Lancashire breeding population may be holding up or at least is not showing any sign of dramatic reversal.

Post-breeding dispersal began in early June and a large influx came during July although numbers only began to build significantly on the coast in August. Post-breeding gatherings in Chorley included 80 on Mawdesley Moss on 10 July, 100 at Lower Rivington Reservoir on the 13th, 100 on Croston Moss on the 19th and 125 at Withnell Fold on 11 Aug. Similar records in east Lancashire included 142 at Stocks Reservoir on 29 June, 200 at Alston Reservoirs on 18 July, 150 at Grimsargh Wetland on the 23rd, 200 over Whitemoor Reservoir on the 29th and 200 at Upper Foulridge Reservoir on the 30th. However, no counts above 25 were received from Rossendale during this period.

Late summer counts away from the coast included 3500 at Lunt Meadows and surrounding farmland in August and 3200 in September but numbers fell to 400 or so thereafter; 1000 or so were also at MMWWT during September. Further inland the largest late counts included 300 at Rishton Reservoir on 1 Oct, 200 on Bretherton Eyes on 18 Dec and 564 at Whitemoor Reservoir on 14 Dec.

GOLDEN PLOVER *Pluvialis apricaria*
Abundant on passage and in winter near coasts. Scarce breeding bird.
International importance: 9300. National importance: 4000.

Monthly peak counts

	Jan	Feb	Mar	Apr	May	Jun	Jul	Aug	Sep	Oct	Nov	Dec
MBS WeBS	4382	739	36	/	180	/	16	39	613	2050	2042	2555
Ribble WeBS	1561	2454	1167	0	0	0	0	10	332	290	2605	2641

Notable Morecambe Bay counts missed by WeBS included 1500 at Cockersand on 3 March with 600 there on 9 April and 250 on 21 July, 1750 at Glasson on 10 Feb with 1500 there on 3 March; and on the Ribble 600 at Hesketh Out Marsh on 17 Feb.

Eight were on Pendle Hill on 8 Jan, six on Haslingden Moor on the 20th, 25 at Bretherton Eyes on 1 Feb, 46 on Winter Hill on 28 March and 200 at Thirteen Stone Hill on 19 March,, but there was no large-scale movement inland until April, when 800 were on farmland surrounding Lunt Meadows on the 6th, 250 on Croston Moss during the first week, 250 on Black Moss on the 7th and 823 in the Champion Moor area on the 4th.

In the east three pairs bred on Boulsworth Hill and two pairs on Pendle Hill, while in the West Pennines there were four territories on Winter Hill, three pairs being thought to have fledged young, and eight territories elsewhere in the western and central West Pennine Moors that included a pair with young chicks on the late date of 16 July.

Only a handful of inland records were received later in the year, among them 44 on Champion Moor on 10 Nov, eleven on Haslingden Moor on the 28th and four on Pendle Hill on the 29th.

AMERICAN GOLDEN PLOVER *Pluvialis dominica*
Vagrant from North America.

An adult arrived at Lunt Meadows on 14 Sept with a small number of Golden Plovers (P Boardman) and, remarkably was joined by a second adult on the 15th (S Young). Both birds remained until the 24th.

The third record of the year, another adult, was at Old Hollow Farm on Banks Marsh and Crossens Marsh on 18-27 Oct (S Darbyshire).

These were the eleventh to thirteenth records for Lancashire.

American Golden Plovers,
Lunt Meadows,
19 September
(Steve Young)

GREY PLOVER *Pluvialis squatarola*

Very common but declining, passage and winter visitor to coast.
International importance: 2000. National importance: 330.

WeBS counts

	Jan	Feb	Mar	Apr	May	Jun	Jul	Aug	Sep	Oct	Nov	Dec
MBS	291	382	545	125	0	11	0	0	117	235	237	351
Ribble	322	376	2360	1284	1319	13	28	98	570	361	726	172
Alt	439	358	977	1216	55	0	0	8	4	233	1	697

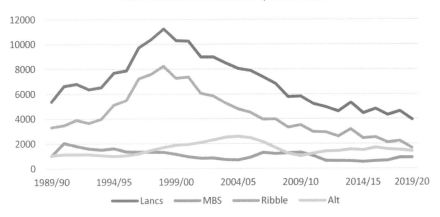

Peak winter counts (5-year rolling means) of Grey Plovers on the main estuaries in Lancashire, 1989-2019

Wintering Grey Plovers have undergone a massive 60% decline in Lancashire during the twenty-first century, accounted for almost entirely by falling numbers on the Ribble which has always held the lion's share of the three estuaries (see above). Numbers on the Alt have remained relatively unchanged and have now surpassed those on Morecambe Bay and are close to the Ribble's.

One-hundred and ninety-eight on 27 Aug at Ocean Edge, Heysham, and 242 at Pilling Lane on 26 Sept were missed by the WeBS counts on Morecambe Bay.

Grey Plovers are always very rare away from the coast, so one at Middleton NR on 13 Aug was most unusual. As were singles at Lunt Meadows on 6 April and Alston Wetland on 9 May.

Grey Plover, Preesall Sands, 19 October (Paul Ellis)

RINGED PLOVER *Charadrius hiaticula*

Common passage migrant in spring, declining as a winter visitor. Scarce breeding bird.
International importance: 540. National importance: 420

WeBS counts

	Jan	Feb	Mar	Apr	May	Jun	Jul	Aug	Sep	Oct	Nov	Dec
MBS	164	38	75	512	442	0	4	230	243	429	141	79
Ribble	296	34	91	1152	2314	2	41	1101	43	73	11	12
Alt	0	0	0	60	103	1	5	193	134	15	0	0

Ringed Plovers have always been primarily a passage species in Lancashire with roughly equal peak numbers seen during the spring and autumn movements, although usually more pass through in spring. Numbers have, however, been very variable over the years, reaching a peak of around 4000 in the late 1990s, followed by a decline before rising to a new peak of more than 5000 in the first decade of this century. Counts have fallen dramatically since then but appear to be flattening out; time will tell whether this boom and bust cycle is set to be repeated (see below).

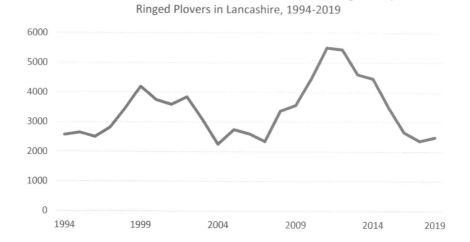

Peak passage (spring and autumn) counts (5-year rolling means) of Ringed Plovers in Lancashire, 1994-2019

Winter peaks have altered much less significantly during this period. The main change has been their loss on the Alt Estuary, accentuated by their complete absence from WeBS counts at either end of 2019 – although there was a single record of one at Seaforth in the early year.

The only inland winter records received were singles at Croston Finney on 24-25 Feb & 2 March, and MMWWT on 22-24 Feb.

However, a pair arrived at Brockholes on 18 Feb and went on to breed, joined by a second pair in mid-May, one of these pairs being seen with three fully-fledged young in early June. A pair nested at Marshside but failed. One in display flight at Long Lane Industrial Park in north Liverpool on 26 June was presumably breeding there. Worryingly, the only other breeding records received were of possibly three pairs nesting on the Lune gravels, three pairs at Lunt Meadows where three young fledged, and of a pair with two chicks at Cockersand in June. The county's breeding population has been in decline for some years but 2019 appears to have been particularly poor with, for example, definitely no pairs at either Heysham or MMWWT.

The first in east Lancashire flew over Alston Reservoirs on 30 March; it was followed by singles at Stocks Reservoir on 15 April and Alston on the 24th and 26th and a peak there of four on 9 May. The first of autumn were at Alston and Rishton Reservoir on 28 July with the last at Alston on 13 Sept. Inland passage counts elsewhere were sparse. They included five at Croston Finney on 23 May with one there on 9 Oct, two on Croston Moss on 19 Aug, six at MMWWT on 7 May with 26 there on the 26th and six on 15 Sept.

LITTLE RINGED PLOVER *Charadrius dubius*
Fairly common on passage. Uncommon breeder.

The first arrivals were at Newton Marsh on 22 March, Hapton on the 25th and MMWWT, Lunt Meadows on the 27th and Alston Wetland the next day. Birds were reported from more than 20 further sites by early May and it is likely that breeding was at least attempted at a good number of these.

However, reports of confirmed breeding received were very patchy across the county: a pair on Newton Marsh was the only one anywhere in the Fylde, and only the Lune gravels, where there were at least four pairs, reported breeding in north Lancashire.

Other definite breeding pairs included three at Lunt Meadows, where at least one brood of three fledged, three at MMWWT that fledged two, two on the reserve at Brockholes where at least one fledged with a third pair on the Ribble gravels there, and twos at Belmont Reservoir whose nests were flooded out, two at Hapton where all six chicks were predated and on Newton Marsh where one fledged. Single pairs were also at Springs Reservoir – also flooded out – and probably at Hurstwood Reservoir and Whitworth Quarry and the Grane reservoirs in Rossendale. A peak of five birds were at Rishton Reservoir on 2 May but territorial birds were continually disturbed by fishermen and did not settle.

The usual scattering of post-breeding birds was recorded throughout the county with the last of the year at MMWWT on 15 Sept, Croston Moss on the 16th and Winmarleigh on the 25th.

KENTISH PLOVER *Charadrius alexandrinus*
Very rare passage migrant.

What was probably a juvenile was on the shore at Southport from 5-13 Oct (J Wright). This was the 25th county record but eleven of these related to a returning bird at Rossall Point between 1992 and 1997; the last was at Cockersand on 3-5 May 2011.

Kentish Plover, Southport, 8 October
(Steve Young)

DOTTEREL *Charadrius morinellus*
Uncommon but regular spring migrant, scarce in autumn.

Spring passage on Pendle Hill produced more birds this year but was very brief with birds seen on just three days from 28-30 April: seven on the 28th, one the next day and finally four on the 30th.

Elsewhere, three were on Plex Moss on 8 May and one on Grit Fell in Bowland on 19 Sept, an unusual autumn record – our last autumn record being one flying over Knott End on 22 Aug 2016.

Dotterel, Pendle Hill, 28 April (Mike Jackson)
©2019 by Mike Jackson

WHIMBREL *Numenius phaeopus*
Common passage migrant, especially in spring.
International importance: 6700.

The first were at Alston Wetlands on 24 March, Banks Marsh on 3 April and Heysham on the 8th. Records then became more regular and numerous in most parts of the county, building as usual to a peak at the end of the month and in early May.

The evening roost counts recorded significantly more birds than in 2018, peaking at 1572 compared with 1210 last year (see table) – reinforcing the county's national importance for this species. Once again Barnacre Reservoir dominated the figures, accounting for more than half the numbers counted on 2 May. Only one other sizeable roost count was reported, 100 at Cockersand on 25 April but it is not clear of these were in addition to the evening's birds.

Our knowledge of where the birds feed has always been rather sketchy, although annual spring passage through the Chorley area farmland has been evident for many years. Flocks reported

Coordinated evening roost counts:	25-April	02-May
Glasson Marsh	100	111
Brockholes LWT	1	74
Alston Wetland	42	60
Grimsargh Wetlands	63	42
Barnacre Reservoirs	510	780
Longton Marsh	97	200
Clifton Marsh	106	144
Wenning Foot / The Snab	71	22
Chipping Moss	0	35
Burrow's Marsh / Barnaby's Sands	114	34
Little Singleton / Windy Harbour / Shard Bridge	131	28
Pilling Marsh	0	6
Barns Fold Reservoirs	85	30
Alt Estuary	33	6
TOTAL	**1353**	**1572**

from likely areas this year included 73 at Ulnes Walton on 19 April, 43 at Chisnall on 29 April, 41 on Jolly Tar Fields on 2 May (all in Chorley), 71 at Wenning Foot on the Lune on 26 April, 30 at North Moss Lane, Formby and 157 at Hothersall Hall in east Lancashire on 28 April, and 59 at Crossmoor, Fylde in a roadside field on 6 May.

Autumn passage was as usual a far more subdued affair with small numbers seen all over the county culminating with singles at MMWWT on 15 Sept, Fluke Hall on the 16th and over Knott End on 5 and 12 Oct. However, most unusually one first seen at Seaforth on 19 Oct continued to show up there irregularly well into 2020.

CURLEW *Numenius arquata*

Abundant winter and fairly common but declining breeding bird.
International importance: 7600. National importance: 1200.

Monthly WeBS counts

	Jan	Feb	Mar	Apr	May	Jun	Jul	Aug	Sep	Oct	Nov	Dec
MBS	1769	5990	2336	1386	130	289	2727	4480	3181	5603	1637	2959
Ribble	375	454	234	111	41	29	389	485	754	530	621	574
Alt	639	600	505	106	54	3	794	920	814	1022	1080	373

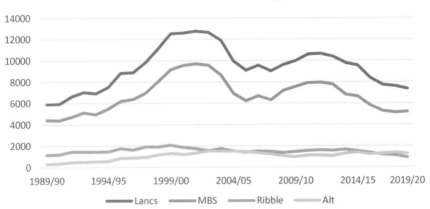

Peak counts (5-year rolling means) of wintering Curlews in the Lancashire sector of Morecambe Bay, 1989-2019

Morecambe Bay continues to support roughly three-quarters of the county's wintering Curlews but their numbers have been falling for the past ten years or so, having begun to recover from a very steep decline from the end of the last century (see above). Although both the Ribble and Alt Estuaries also appear to be declining this is not nearly as pronounced as in Morecambe Bay and the Ribble no longer supports nationally important numbers.

The only winter roost away from the coast was up to 135 on Aintree racecourse during January but a few birds had begun to move eastwards to the breeding grounds by the end of the month but, as usual, there were no sizeable pre-breeding gatherings until February. Counts in the east that month included 157 at Brockholes and 100 at Altham on the 19th, and 143 between Hodder Foot and Hurst Green on the 20th when 135 were near Raid Deep Wood, while in the West Pennines 177 were at Belmont Reservoir on the 27th.

Dispersal continued during March with notable counts including 100 at Brockholes on the 3rd, 150 at Grimsargh Wetland on the 7th, 172 at Belmont Reservoir on the 8th and 190 at Alston Wetland on the 29th.

The survey of 34 inbye farms in Bowland located 140 pairs, five pairs were on Boulsworth Hill, four pairs in the Foulridge area and there were others in the east at Procter's Farm, Lamb Hill Farm, Hareden, Hurstwood, Ightenhill Bridge and New Laithe Farm. In the West Pennines 24 displaying pairs were estimated in 10km^2 around Belmont in April with up to four pairs in 1km^2 near Belmont Reservoir where the first young were seen on 27 May. There were also seven pairs in 1.5km^2 of Darwen Moor in May, two territories in 1km^2 of Cranberry Moss in June, two pairs at Clough House Farm, Turton, four territories on Winter Hill and a further two territories immediately adjacent on unburnt sections of South Belmont Moor. Elsewhere, a pair fledged a single juvenile in a field next to Brockholes NR, 'a few pairs' were on the Anglezarke and Withnell Moors, while in Rossendale five pairs bred in the Cheesden Valley and four pairs in the Clough Bottom area and around the Grane reservoirs. Typically, post-breeding gatherings were more limited than in spring with the largest counts 60 at Belmont Reservoir on 20 June, 111 at Alston Reservoirs on 6 July, 50 at Slipper Hill Reservoir on the 26th.

BAR-TAILED GODWIT *Limosa lapponica*
Very common winter visitor.
International importance: 1500. National importance: 500.

Monthly WeBS counts

	Jan	Feb	Mar	Apr	May	Jun	Jul	Aug	Sep	Oct	Nov	Dec
MBS	1926	2622	132	40	160	42	4	56	403	247	1606	687
Ribble	3204	3861	279	21	162	25	42	4	188	888	2103	3070
Alt	2827	2010	910	233	97	130	171	1275	1173	89	582	1910

This year's WeBS counts merely confirmed the continuation of the decline which began in the late 1990s and which has been most marked on the Ribble. The Alt has been our most important estuary for this species for some years but this year's highest annual count there was the first ever below 3000. However, an estimated 2150 on the Fylde Coast were missed by the Morecambe Bay December count.

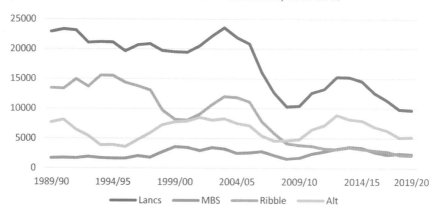

Peak counts (5-year rolling means) of wintering Bar-tailed Godwits on the main estuaries in Lancashire, 1989-2019

As with Knots an important change appears to be underway on the Alt Estuary with a significant shift in the numbers roosting at Seaforth and away from Formby Point, numbers at Seaforth reaching 250 in October and 700 in November.

First-summer birds began to build up at Seaforth in early June, reaching 148 on 6 June and 377 on 10 Aug.

The only inland records were one roosting with Whimbrels at Brockholes on 23-30 April, and one at Alston Wetland on 23 April which was joined by another until the 26th when both moved to Grimsargh Wetland.

BLACK-TAILED GODWIT *Limosa limosa*
Very common passage migrant and winter visitor. Rare breeder.
International importance: 1110. National importance: 390.

Monthly peak counts

	Jan	Feb	Mar	Apr	May	Jun	Jul	Aug	Sep	Oct	Nov	Dec
MBS WeBS	1290	1929	2386	5339	527	447	666	927	2164	1129	2340	280
EMC/L Moss	800	1150	2700	3050	470	460	800	970	2200	950	1700	550
Ribble WeBS	1230	2250	1504	295	156	53	1177	589	2667	4460	2557	386
Marshside	/	750	1200	/	/	/	1350	/	3000	3600	1500	/
MMWWT	20	23	60	/	214	500	2800	2500	600	100	100	10

2018 Correction: the wrong figure was published for the October peak at the Eric Morecambe complex – it was 2877 not 22902!

2019. Numbers continued to increase throughout the year on the two main estuaries but Seaforth remains the only Alt Estuary site for this species and numbers were unspectacular there this year with a peak of 390 in August.

Inland records have also proliferated in the past few years but it was only MMWWT that registered really significant numbers this year with site records in both July and August, while those at Lunt Meadows never exceeded 150.

Blackwits remain fairly scarce at any greater distance from the coast, however. They were seen on four dates at Brockholes, notably 30 on 12 May and 25 on 1 July. There were twelve on Croston Moss on 19 Aug, 14 at Bretherton Eyes on 3 Oct, up to four at Belmont Reservoir on 28 April to 12 May with one there on 29 June and three on 22 July.

In east Lancashire singles were at Alston Wetland on several dates in March and April with nine on 22 May. Early year peak counts elsewhere included eleven at Stocks Reservoir on 15 &19 April and eleven at Grimsargh Wetland on the 25th. During the rest of the year there were nine reports all of four or fewer except for eleven on 1 July at Alston Wetland, all from sites previously mentioned, the exception being three over Lee Green Reservoir on 4 Aug. The last was one at Alston Wetlands on 5 Sept.

Two pairs of nominate subspecies birds successfully hatched young on Newton Marsh this year; two young survived almost to fledging but all were ultimately predated.

A ringed nominate bird was on the Eric Morecambe complex from 10 July to 1 Sept.

TURNSTONE *Arenaria interpres*
Common passage migrant and winter visitor
International importance: 1400. National importance: 400

Monthly WeBS Counts

	Jan	Feb	Mar	Apr	May	June	July	Aug	Sept	Oct	Nov	Dec
MBS	299	73	391	197	8	0	0	435	352	718	443	619
Ribble	171	83	0	237	41	0	19	112	201	139	223	56
Fleetwood	120	/	100	50	/	/	50	10	191	176	280	
Alt	11	/	12	54	22	10	22	31	32	16	16	2

The October count on Morecambe Bay was the largest anywhere in the county since 1999 but in other respects it was an unremarkable year with numbers continuing to plateau at a very low level.

Turnstones are rare birds away from the coast so five at MMWWT on 26 Aug was noteworthy. Elsewhere two were at Stocks Reservoir on 16 May and singles at Lunt Meadows on 24 July and Alston Wetland on 20 Aug.

Turnstone, Crosby Coastal Park, 31 December (Steve Young)

KNOT *Calidris canutus*
Abundant winter visitor and passage migrant to coasts. Uncommon inland.
International importance: 5300. National importance: 2600.

Monthly peak counts

	Jan	Feb	Mar	Apr	May	Jun	Jul	Aug	Sep	Oct	Nov	Dec
MBS WeBS	12562	8771	7920	171		293	75	1	5117	7095	9664	10816
Ribble WeBS	1090	11940	30020	27975	4462	1397	577	152	10497	15585	17831	39802
Alt WeBS	19200	/	8131	13506	35	800	1032	7960	8000	7983	12808	16004
Seaforth	1050	2300	680	20	15	1500	3000	4500	8000	12000	10000	16000

Although the March count on the Ribble represented the highest annual total since 2009, average peak numbers there remain 50% lower than in the 1990s. The January count in Morecambe Bay was a little above the five-year average peak but numbers there have fallen by nearly 75% since the mid-1990s. Alt counts, however, have remained more or less stable during this period.

Until very recently roosting Knots were only usually present in large numbers at Seaforth during summer but that changed this year, especially during the second winter period when the reserve held the majority of the Alt's birds. The reason for this switch of roost site is far from clear: two possible explanations have been put forward, increased disturbance at Formby Point and/or Hightown, or a eastward shift of the main feeding grounds on North Wirral Shore encouraging use of the nearest undisturbed site. There is, however, no evidence to support either hypothesis.

Summering first-summer Knots began to arrive at Seaforth a little later than Bar-tailed Godwits but 500 were present on 13 June and numbers grew to 3000 in the third week of July – although some of these were presumably winter-plumaged adults.

There were some remarkable records inland in 2019, most strikingly 180 at MMWWT on 1 June with 30 there on the 9th. In autumn 18 flew west over Alston Wetland on 11 Aug, followed by eight at MMWWT on the next day and twelve there on the 13th, two on the 20th-23rd and one on 5 Sept.

RUFF *Calidris pugnax*
Fairly common passage migrant and winter visitor. Rare breeder.
International importance: 20000. National importance: 9.

Monthly peak counts

	Jan	Feb	Mar	Apr	May	Jun	Jul	Aug	Sep	Oct	Nov	Dec
MMWWT	70	60	50	0	0	1	24	60	50	50	30	66

Counts on the Ribble appear to have been much lower this year with 20 at Marshside in March and 30 there in April the only double figures received. The largest of an apparently poor year elsewhere – other than at MMWWT – included twenty at Lathwaite (Fylde) on 1 Sept, twelve at Lunt Meadows on 4 July and eleven on Newton Marsh on 9 March with 16 there on 12 Nov.

The only records further inland were singles at Alston Wetland on 6 and 17-18 May.

STILT SANDPIPER *Calidris acuminata*
Vagrant from North America.

A moulting adult or possibly first-summer at Lunt Meadows on 17-20 May (S Riley) has been accepted by the BBRC. This was the second Lancashire record and the first since 1967 – and needless to say enjoyed by considerably more birders.

Stilt Sandpiper, Lunt Meadows, 18 May (Steve Young)

CURLEW SANDPIPER *Calidris ferruginea*
Fairly common passage migrant.

The first of the year were at Cockersand on 25 April, Banks Marsh on the 28th and Marshside the next day. Birds were seen at another 12-15 sites during May, involving perhaps 25-30 birds but passage slowed considerably during June; no more than two were present on any site on a single day and few lingered longer than two or three days – an exception being a one-legged bird at Seaforth from 19 May to 10 June.

Virtually all were on the coast, exceptions being two at Alston Wetland on 9 May and one at Lunt Meadows on 6 June.

Autumn passage began on 22 July at the Eric Morecambe complex with records at Sunderland Point and Conder Green by the end of the month but the majority of birds passed through during August and September with peak counts of nine at Crossens Inner on 13-15 Sept, six at the Eric Morecambe complex on 13 Sept, and five on Hesketh Out Marsh on 28 Aug and at Lathwaite (Fylde) on 13 Sept.October records came from six sites and the last of the year were at Fluke Hall Lane on 3 Nov and Hesketh Out Marsh on the 16th.

All autumn birds were seen on the coast with the exception of five at MMWWT on 11 Sept and two at Lunt Meadows on the 15th with one there on 21-24 Oct.

TEMMINCK'S STINT* *Calidris temminckii*
Scarce passage migrant.

It was a productive year with records at four sites involving five birds, typically all in May: singles at Lunt Meadows on the 11th-12th (JE Taylor) and Aldcliffe Marsh (J Carter) and MMWWT on the 14th, and two on Newton Marsh on the 18th-19th (I Walker).

SANDERLING *Calidris alba*
Very common passage migrant and common winter visitor.
International importance: 2000. National importance: 200.

Monthly WeBS counts

	Jan	Feb	Mar	Apr	May	Jun	Jul	Aug	Sep	Oct	Nov	Dec
MBS	153	/	160	36	300	0	0	170	170	125	75	180
Ribble	690	1122	2335	1845	4867	11	209	6363	912	975	410	665
Alt	632	948	847	1142	48	0	46	2003	848	503	288	656

August on the Ribble produced the highest count anywhere in the county since August 2014. Otherwise it was an unexceptional year with peak winter and passage counts on all three main estuaries similar to 2018, indicating that the small revival noted in last year's report appears to be holding steady.

Inland, MMWWT had an unusually large flock of eight on 26 May with one or two remaining until 1 June, while in east Lancashire two were at Stocks Reservoir on 22 April with one there on 17 May, and two at Alston Wetlands on 31 May.

DUNLIN *Calidris alpina*
Abundant passage migrant and winter visitor. Scarce breeding bird.
International importance: 13300. National importance: 3400.

Monthly WeBS counts

	Jan	Feb	Mar	Apr	May	Jun	Jul	Aug	Sep	Oct	Nov	Dec
MBS	4123	7780	1052	1353	475	16	44	2182	519	1598	4178	3125
Ribble	9877	28398	8408	16186	9575	260	2828	39639	4678	7414	10154	12019
Alt	4327	/	510	2159	258	0	33	4619	429	251	403	684

Although the August count on the Ribble was the highest anywhere in the county since 2012, the five-year mean peak counts in both winter and on passage showed no real signs of recovery on any of the estuaries.

Dunlin are always very scarce inland in winter and the only records in the first couple of months were one at MMWWT in January, and one at Lunt Meadows and two at MMWWT in February. One at Croston Finney on 3 March and three at Brockholes on the 5th provided the first evidence of eastward movement but by the end of the month birds had also appeared at Alston Wetlands and Coldwell Reservoirs. Passage accelerated slightly in April but was at its highest in May when birds were seen regularly on wetlands in the south-west, including peaks of 36 at MMWWT but only five at Lunt Meadows, at five sites in east Lancashire, including twelve at Alston Wetlands.

The only reports of breeding came from the West Pennine Moors where three territories were thought likely on the moors around Belmont and one was confirmed on Winter Hill.

Autumn passage inland was an unspectacular affair with peaks at MMWWT of ten in August and eleven in October, and six at Croston Finney and seven over Alston Wetland in October.

PURPLE SANDPIPER *Calidris maritime*
Rare winter visitor.

Blackpool North Shore remained the most reliable county site but numbers were way down this year with just one seen during January and until 9 Feb, and up to two from 10 Nov until the end of year – in comparison to up to five seen during 2018,

Elsewhere there were singles at Heysham on 9 April and 26 Oct to 13 Nov, and at Fleetwood on 9 & 17 Feb, 9-11 March and from 30 Sept into December.

LITTLE STINT *Calidris minuta*
Fairly common passage migrant. Scarce winter visitor.

There were no winter records at either end of the year and only a handful were seen in spring: singles at Lunt Meadows on 5-6 May, Church Scar, Lytham and MMWWT on the 10th and Marshside on the 18th.

No more were seen until one at MMWWT on 11 Aug with two there on the 14th and three on the 20th, one on the Eric Morecambe complex from the 27th and one at Sunderland Point on the 30th. September continued in a similar vein with records of ones and occasionally twos from only five sites, notably the Eric Morecambe complex and the south Ribble Marshes, with one at MMWWT on the 14th the only autumn record inland. Finally there were singles at Banks Marsh and the Eric Morecambe complex on 3 Oct and Hesketh Out Marsh on the 26th.

WHITE-RUMPED SANDPIPER* *Calidris fuscicollis*
Vagrant from North America.

An adult was at Hesketh Out Marsh on 14 Sept (I Walker) and a juvenile on Banks Marsh on 26 Oct to 3 Nov (S Darbyshire).

These were the 17th and 18th county records.

BUFF-BREASTED SANDPIPER* *Calidris subruficollis*
Vagrant from North America.

The county's 15th modern record, at Marshside on 20 April (A Spencer), was our first ever in spring.

PECTORAL SANDPIPER* *Calidris melanotos*
Rare passage migrant.

Adults were at MMWWT on 29 April and on the Eric Morecambe complex on 14-16 July (SJ Dodgson) with possibly the same there on 25 July (PR Massey), followed by a juvenile at Ream Hills, Mythop on 18-23 Sept (P Ellis) and two juveniles at Winmarleigh on 24-26 Sept (C Piner).

A sound-recorded migrant over Knott End 24 Aug is still under consideration by the records committee.

Juvenile Pectoral Sandpiper, Ream Hills, Mythop, 18 September (Paul Ellis)

LONG-BILLED DOWITCHER *Limnodromus scolopaceus*
Vagrant from North America.

A moulting adult was at MMWWT on 20-25 Aug (A. Bunting). The record has been accepted by the BBRC and becomes the county's 16th record (after taking probable duplicates into account).

Long-billed Dowitcher, Martin Mere, 25 August (Tony Disley)

WOODCOCK *Scolopax rusticola*
Common winter visitor and fairly common breeder.

Woodcocks were reported from at least 50 sites in both winter periods; the latest seen on non-breeding sites were mostly at the end of March and the earliest returning migrants in mid- to late October.

Several of the largest counts were in the West Pennine Moors including at least 41 flushed by pheasant-beaters at Belmont on 23 March with 13 reported there on 30 Nov and 20 or more feeding in fields at Roddlesworth on 28 Nov; birds were also flushed from the moor plateaux at up to 430m asl, including five on 21 Dec. In east Lancashire Woodcocks were seen regularly at Kemple End, peaking at 25 on 31 Dec and ten were at New Laithe Farm on 20 Dec. Peaks elsewhere included seven at Whittle Bottoms, Charnock Richard on 4 Jan and five at Lunt Meadows during both winter periods and at Bartle Hall, Fylde on 23 Feb.

Woodcock, caught in car headlights, Todderstaffe Hall, 21 October (Paul Slade)

Very little information was received about breeding: three males were roding in the Belmont area, singles on Winter Hill and at Heatherlea Woods, Brinscall, and birds were present in breeding season at Stocks Reservoir and Collyholme Wood in east Lancashire.

JACK SNIPE *Lymnocryptes minimus*
Fairly common, though overlooked, passage migrant and winter visitor.

Reports were received from 40 or more sites during both winter periods with the latest in spring at Stocks Reservoir on 24 April and the first of autumn at Allsprings, Great Harwood on 13 Oct and Eccleston, Chorley the following day.

As usual, almost all records were of singles, occasionally two, but there were larger counts of nine on Croston Moss on 16 Oct, five at Cabin Hill on 13 Feb, four on the Heysham heliport in the first winter period and at Allsprings on 9 March, 29 Nov and 16 Dec, and three on Fairhaven beach on 27 Nov.

SNIPE *Gallinago gallinago*
Common but declining wintering and breeding bird.

Breeding information never achieves complete coverage but the county population appears to have been somewhat shaky this year. Thirty-four pairs were located during the RSPB's survey of inbye fields on 34 farms in Bowland in 2019, compared with 69 pairs on 39 farms last year.

Breeding numbers were, however, more or less unchanged in the West Pennine Moors with seven territories recorded around Belmont Reservoir and an additional 23 drumming birds on inbye and moorland elsewhere including three at Clough House Farm, Turton and five territories in small area of Winter Hill at 415-4545m asl.

Birds were present in the breeding season in east Lancashire at Allsprings, Alston Wetland, Barden Bridge, Black Moss Reservoirs, Calf Clough, Champion Moor, Upper Coldwell Reservoir, Collyholme Wood, Croasdale, Dean Clough, Gisburn Forest, Halsteads, Jackhouse, Lamb Hill Farm, Lower Towneley scrape, New Laithe Farm, Oswaldtwistle Moor, Stocks Reservoir, Twiston Moor and Wood End sewage works. Breeding almost certainly occurred on the Rossendale moorlands around the Grane reservoirs and several other sites.

For many years Grove Lane Marsh has been the county's most important wintering site but habitat loss has reduced its holding capacity more recently, although 54 there on 17 Oct was the highest count in east Lancashire.

This was overshadowed, however, by really large numbers on the Heysham heliport in the first winter period when 351 were recorded on 27 Jan and up to 240 until 24 Feb; numbers were much lower later, though, with a peak of 56 in late December.

There were also large numbers in the south-west: Lunt Meadows recorded several large counts with an early year peak of 150 on 20 March and an unprecedented August influx peaking in excess of 300 on 21-25 Sept with 120 there on 8 Oct, while MMWWT held 100 during January, 200+ in late August and up to 150 regular into November at least.

Large counts elsewhere included 103 at Glasson on 3 Nov, 100 at Bretherton Eyes on 25 Dec, 84 at Fleetwood Marsh on 17 Nov, 72 at Fairhaven on 27 Nov and 60 at Brockholes on 22 Sept and on Croston Moss on 16 Nov. The largest count in the West Pennine Moors was 40+ above Belmont on 27 Sept, and in Rossendale 34 at Edge Cote on 13 Oct.

RED-NECKED PHALAROPE* *Phalaropus lobatus*
Rare passage migrant.

A juvenile at Marshside on 20-27 Sept (D Owen) was the county's first since 2015.

Juvenile Red-necked Phalarope, Marshside, 21 September (Craig Bell)

GREY PHALAROPE *Phalaropus fulicarius*
Scarce passage migrant.

This year was something of a come-down after a reasonable crop of records in 2018 with just one seen – at Lytham on 10 Oct.

COMMON SANDPIPER *Actitis hypoleucos*
Common passage migrant, fairly common breeding bird. Scarce in winter.

One was at Myerscough Quarry into late March and one was in Avenham Park, Preston on 28 March. Elsewhere in the first winter period there were singles at Parsonage Reservoir during January (a bird from 2018 and possibly the same as one in 2017/18), at the Eric Morecambe complex on 19 Jan and Brockholes on 23 Feb, but there were only two records at the other end of the year, on Heaton Marsh on 1 Dec and at Parsonage Reservoir in November and December.

Singles at Fell End NR in north Lancashire on 26-28 March and Ightenhill Bridge in the east on 3 April had possibly wintered somewhere in the country but singles at Lunt Meadows on 6 April and the Eric Morecambe complex next day were presumably definite migrants. The expected wave of migrants then arrived throughout the whole of the country, both on the coast and on the breeding grounds, at its height in the second half of April and continuing well into May. The largest counts were eight at Stock Reservoir on 27 April, five at Brockholes on the 16th, Conder Green on the 17th, on the Lune at Halton on the 17th and Crook o' Lune on the 24th

Breeding was widespread in suitable habitat throughout east, central and north Lancashire, Rossendale and the West Pennine Moors but was, as usual, probably hugely under-reported and it is not possible to judge how well the breeding population is doing. The few site totals that were reported included seven pairs in the Langden Valley, five at Delph Reservoir and three at Belmont Reservoir.

Birds began to return to the coast in late June and early July but rather few large counts were reported this year; up to twelve on the Conder Pool and the Eric Morecambe complex in the first week of July were the only double-figure counts received. Only a handful remained beyond September.

GREEN SANDPIPER *Tringa ochropus*
Fairly common on passage, especially autumn. Scarce winter visitor.

Fifteen wintering birds were reported in January and February and into early March, mostly singles but with three at Brockholes on 23 Feb and two at Myerscough Quarry on 1 Jan. Typically most of these were in the Fylde but with single records in Chorley and Lancaster, and more unusually one in Liverpool on the Alt at Croxteth. Ten were reported at the other end of the year, although some November birds may have lingered undetected into December; all were singles at a similar range of sites to the first winter period but additionally at MMWWT, Alston Wetlands and Heysham Moss.

The first of spring away from wintering areas were at Cockersand on 6 March, Lunt Meadows on the 20th and Alston Wetlands on the 30th. Half a dozen arrived in April but the passage was over by the end of the month.

Autumn began with two at Freckleton Naze on 27 June-1 July with around 35 seen that month and similar numbers in both August and September. Movement slowed after that with probably only a dozen in October and five or so in November.

Autumn Green Sandpipers were seen throughout much of the county but there were only single records from the West Pennine Moors and Rossendale.

The largest counts included fours at , MMWWT on 29 July and 18 Aug, Freckleton Naze on 30 July and 11 Aug when there were also four on the Eric Morecambe complex, Myerscough Quarry on 21 Aug, Alston Wetlands on 7 Sept, Winmarleigh on 14-15 Sept and Todderstaffe Hall on 16 Oct.,

Green Sandpiper, Cuddy Hill, 7 May (Paul Ellis)

REDSHANK *Tringa totanus*

Very common passage and winter visitor. Fairly common breeding bird.
International importance: 2400. National importance: 940.

Monthly WeBS Counts

	Jan	Feb	Mar	Apr	May	June	July	Aug	Sept	Oct	Nov	Dec
MBS	2321	2143	2792	1395	12	28	606	2188	2979	3347	3564	1742
Ribble	532	1213	2819	234	76	69	135	1280	783	763	1230	278
Alt	362	850	365	190	0	0	121	392	685	315	671	510

The February total, all of which were at Seaforth, was the highest on the Alt since 2013 and the March Ribble count the best there since 2012. The year's peak on Morecambe Bay was a little lower than last year's but overall the county wintering population seems to be just about holding up.

As usual, very small numbers were seen inland during January and early February but some began to move back towards the breeding grounds at the end of the month and rather more during March and April. For example only one bird remained at Seaforth by 16 May.

After recording a significant slump in numbers on the RSPB survey of inbye land in Bowland to 14 pairs in 2018 the 23 pairs on 34 farms was a welcome return to previous levels. At least attempted breeding of one or two pairs was also confirmed in east Lancashire at Alston Wetlands, Lamb Hill Farm, New Laithe Farm, Swinden Reservoir, Stocks Reservoir, Dunsop Head and Foulridge Reservoirs, and possibly at Altham.

Twenty-three pairs bred on the Eric Morecambe complex, fledging 0.22 young per pair. Productivity on the south Ribble marshes was higher: 0.76 from 59 pairs at Marshside and 0.5 from 56 pairs at Hesketh Out Marsh.

Elsewhere, at least four pairs nested at Brockholes and two pairs at Belmont Reservoir.

WOOD SANDPIPER *Tringa glareola*

Uncommon passage migrant.

As usual virtually all records came from wetland sites in the west of the county; the only others came from Alston Wetland which had singles on 7-10 & 31 May, 3 June, 11 & 28-29 July and 8-11 Aug, Belmont Reservoir on 28 May, Croston Moss (two) on 27-28 Aug, Cuerden Valley Park on 1 Sept and Brockholes on 3 Sept.

The first of a spring passage that involved approximately 50 individuals began on the typical date of 24 April at MMWWT but with most records in May and a few until late June. Most were singles or occasionally two together but there were three at MMWWT on 2 May.

The return got underway in the last days of June with most seen in July and August and the last at Freckleton on 26 Sept; roughly the same numbers were involved as in spring with the largest counts four at MMWWT on 27 July and Carr House Green Common on the 31st.

SPOTTED REDSHANK *Tringa erythropus*

Fairly common passage migrant.

Monthly peak counts

	Jan	Feb	Mar	Apr	May	Jun	Jul	Aug	Sep	Oct	Nov	Dec
EMC/LM	/	3	3	1	1	/	/	1	3	1	/	/
Conder Est	/	/	/	1	1	/	2	/	1	1	/	/
Hesketh OM	3	3	4	/	/	2	2	1	9	3	2	3

Records received from the usual main sites were fairly scanty this year (see table), especially during both winter periods. The only other winter records were singles at Marshside and Banks Marsh in November and December, four sites in north Fylde in the early year and two sites in November and December, and a juvenile at Seaforth (where the species is scarce) from 26 Aug well into 2010.

Things were not quite so desperate during passage with birds arriving from mid-April through to early September at a dozen or so sites, all on the Fylde coast or in the south-west. Two were together at Barnaby's Sands on 4 Aug, Lytham Jetty on the 26th and Lathwaite on 1 Sept, but the outstanding record was the nine on Hesketh Out Marsh on 15-20 Sept.

GREENSHANK *Tringa nebularia*

Fairly common on passage, especially in autumn. Scarce in winter.

Monthly peak counts

	Jan	Feb	Mar	Apr	May	Jun	Jul	Aug	Sep	Oct	Nov	Dec
EMC/LM	4	3	5	4	2	4	20	23	18	12	6	2
Conder/Glasson	/	/	/	2	2	2	10	13	15	10	2	/

Away from the two main sites in the table there were winter records on five sites in the Fylde at both ends of the year, notably four at Wardley's Creek in January to March and again in November and December. Up to three were on Hesketh Out Marsh into early February and again in December. No other reports of wintering birds were received from anywhere in the county.

There were around six records of migrants in April including singles in the east at Stocks Reservoir on the 21st and Alston Wetlands on the 30th, but as usual the main spring passage took place during May, petering out during June and involving 40-50 birds. The highest counts were four on the Eric Morecambe complex in April and at MMWWT in May. Two at Holden Wood Reservoir on 30 June and one at Belmont Reservoir on 13 July were the only records in Rossendale and the West Pennine Moors respectively.

As ever it was difficult to differentiate the end of the spring movement at the end of June from the beginning of autumn's in early July. The passage extended into September and was as usual considerably larger than in spring, involving a minimum of 250 individuals. Large counts included those in the table at the Eric Morecambe complex and Conder Estuary with most of the rest in the Fylde, including 16 at Freckleton Naze on 22 July and ten at Wardley's Creek on 26 Aug; seven at MMWWT on 20 Aug and five on Croston Moss on 12 Aug to 9 Sept were the highest counts in the south-west and Chorley. A few continued to move through in October but by mid-November the passage was over.

Greenshank, Eric Morecambe complex, 18 August (Craig Bell)

KITTIWAKE *Rissa tridactyla*
Common passage migrant on coasts, fairly common in winter. Has bred.

Monthly peak counts

	Jan	Feb	Mar	Apr	May	June	July	Aug	Sept	Oct	Nov	Dec
Heysham	0	40	270	50	146	0	0	3	3	4	27	21

Coastal sightings started at Blackpool on 28 Jan with occasional records through February when onshore winds saw a total of 60 off Morecambe on the 8th, before the noticeable commencement of northward spring passage on 9 March at Southport (100), Morecambe (148) and Heysham (175). Counts remained most regular around Morecambe Bay off Heysham as shown by the table with notable numbers past on the 14th (270) and 17th (167).

Small numbers were encountered throughout April with 50 off Rossall Point on the 28th, and continued in May with the most significant numbers 146 off Morecambe on the 10th, 50 off Rossall Point on the 16th and 34 off Blackpool on the 27th. June saw five sightings, all from Blackpool with a peak of 14 on the 9th.

It was a disappointing year for inland observations despite starting with an unusual winter sighting of one in the gull roost at Lower Rivington Reservoir on 13 Jan; this was followed by one at Pine Lake on 12 Feb with an adult there on 27 March which sadly was found dead on 30th, and finally an unseasonal adult at Stocks Reservoir on 28 July roosting with local gulls during the afternoon.

The autumn passage saw small numbers concentrated in the south of the county, mainly from Blackpool with monthly peak counts of ten on 25 July, 23 on 31 Aug, a notable 153 on 26 Sept and 18 on 22 Oct. No winter onshore gale gatherings were noted. November records included 27 at Heysham on the 11th and two at Blackpool on the 12th. December followed a similar pattern with two records at Blackpool and three at Heysham with a peak of 21 on the 23rd.

BLACK-HEADED GULL *Chroicocephalus ridibundus*
Locally abundant breeding bird. Abundant winter visitor and passage migrant.
International importance: 20000. National importance: 20000.

WeBS

	Jan	Feb	Mar	Apr	May	Jun	Jul	Aug	Sept	Oct	Nov	Dec
Alt	2493	/	102	31	22	51	271	581	630	418	1308	904
Ribble	1183	1285	869	868	490	257	1100	3086	795	702	630	1434
MBS	1394	2953	1387	1393	1638	1479	4229	5211	2127	715	463	867

The year began with notable winter gatherings of 3000 at the Alt Estuary and 2000 at Pilling. Pre-breeding roosts started to build from late February with 5000 at Stocks Reservoir on the 24th through to the end of March.

The Belmont Reservoir breeding colony was subject to in-depth monitoring and a full aerial survey during 2019 as well as vegetation management carried out, making the island optimal for breeding Black-headed Gulls. Pre-breeding numbers rapidly increased from 3000 on 21 Feb to 24000 on 24 March and 25000 on 3 April. First incubation was recorded on 27 March with the first fledged juvenile on 28 May; the colony remained highly active through to early July. Results of the survey saw an increase from 10484 pairs in 2017 to 11553 pairs in 2019. The colony is now considered to be the largest in the UK, estimated to be 8.3% of the UK breeding population and an astonishing 0.5% of the world population.

Breeding numbers and success elsewhere were a somewhat mixed bag that included an increase to 932 nests at Leighton Moss from 820 in 2018, although productivity was poor with just 82 fledged young. Marshside experienced a significant fall from 838 pairs to 589 this year, and elsewhere in the south-west there were 313 pairs at MMWWT, and 35 at Lunt Meadows. Up to 70 pairs were present at Stocks Reservoir for a brief period late in the season during June and 40 nests were located but all failed as the colony demise continued – from 190 pairs in 2018. Unusual breeding records saw three nests at Conder Green and one at Alston Reservoirs, Longridge.

Notable post-breeding gatherings included 4000 at Thurnham on 11 Aug, 2714 at Leighton Moss on the 5th, while Skippool Creek saw monthly peaks of 1500 in August and 2000 in September. Early winter saw counts of 3000 at Formby on 2 Oct and 2000 at Thurnham on the 19th with 1500 there on 7 Dec. The winter roost off Morecambe saw a peak of 5200 during December, when 4000 were at Lower Rivington Reservoir and 2700 at Delph Reservoir in November was the largest site count there since 1999.

LITTLE GULL *Hydrocoloeus minutus*
Fairly common passage migrant and gale-blown winter visitor.

Monthly peak counts

	Jan	Feb	Mar	Apr	May	June	July	Aug	Sept	Oct	Nov	Dec
Blackpool	5	10	3	8	4	0	0	1	3	6	10	1
Rossall Point	2	0	51	2	5	0	0	0	0	0	2	0
Heysham	0	0	16	2	0	1	1	2	2	2	1	1

A species that in recent years has predominantly been seen off the coast, especially during onshore winter gales, with most regular sightings from Blackpool, Heysham and Rossall Point, as shown by the above maximum counts.

This year there were no notable winter period sightings as spring passage began in early March with one at Marshside on the 9th; small numbers were encountered from scattered coastal sites into April with one notable passage of 51 past Rossall Point on 14 Marc, while Seaforth saw a peak of 24 on 19 April. May brought sightings of singles from Leighton Moss, Morecambe, Hesketh Out Marsh, Marshside and Seaforth through until 18 June.

Inland one first-summer set up residence at Pine Lake from 15 April to 12 May, a significant arrival of ten stopped off at Foulridge Reservoirs on 16 April, up to 16 appeared at Lunt Meadows between the 17th and 21st, an adult was at Stocks Reservoir on the 18-19th, one was at MMWWT from the 29th with another there on the 18th, and a first-summer was at Rishton Reservoir on 1 May. During 2018 a first record for the Rossendale

Little Gull, Seaforth, 20 April (Steve Young)

recording area saw a second-winter bird at Spring Mill Reservoir between 19-25 Aug.

Late summer saw a gathering of up to seven adults at Formby Beach between 16 July and 1 Aug, one at Lunt Meadows on 16-17 Sept, a juvenile off the Stone Jetty, Morecambe on 11 Aug and one at Leighton Moss on 3 Sept. No notable winter gale-driven birds were encountered with just two at Cockerham on 11 Oct.

MEDITERRANEAN GULL *Larus melanocephalus*
Fairly common all year. Most numerous on the coast but increasing inland. Rare breeder.

Minimum number of individuals

	Jan	Feb	Mar	Apr	May	June	July	Aug	Sept	Oct	Nov	Dec
Heysham	2	2	0	2	0	10	60	76	60	18	3	3
Seaforth	1	0	1	2	0	6	16	15	10	2	2	2

Wintering birds were scattered throughout the coastal areas but with peak counts of two at Heysham and Heaton Marsh, Lancaster. Spring passage started in late February through March with peak day counts of four from Marshside, Brockholes, Lytham and MMWWT. Birds arrived at the Belmont

Reservoir colony in late February with numbers rapidly increasing to 63 on 28 March and to an estimated 110+ by 7 April. Leighton Moss saw a single notable report of ten on 31 May.

Belmont Reservoir was subject to in-depth monitoring and a full aerial survey during 2019 which resulted in yet another increase as the colony grew from 43 pairs to a minimum of 63 nests plus an additional nine adults on territory. Belmont Reservoir is the largest UK inland colony and the only substantial colony away from the south and south-east English coast. Sample counts in July of successful 'family groups' realised 89 juveniles with 58 distinct adults. Elsewhere in the county there were just two nests in the colony at Marshside.

Post-breeding gatherings at Heysham built from late June through to September with a peak day-count of 76 on 19 Aug setting a new record daily county count away from Belmont Reservoir. Numbers then dropped away before a surprising second peak of 60 on 11 Sept thought due to a sandworm-fest before numbers rapidly dropped again. Peak individual age-group counts included 38 adults/third-calendar year-birds on 19 Aug, 18 second-calendar-years on 17 Aug and 14 juveniles on 12 Aug.

Seaforth saw a decent gathering with up to 16 birds during July as shown in the table and elsewhere peak counts were predominately from coastal sites, including 16 at Skippool Creek and Glasson, 13 At Thurnham, six at Leighton Moss (6) and five at Lunt Meadows. Single wintering birds were recorded from scattered coastal sites as well as Pine Lake, Preston Dock, Cuerden Valley Park, Chorley, Hutch Bank Quarry, Rossendale and Alston Reservoirs,, with a peak count of three at Cocker's Dyke on 8 Dec.

The regular wintering Czech Republic veteran bird at Heysham (since 2003) was spotted back during October but there were no further sightings as a result of access being withdrawn to anglers and the public on the north wall.

COMMON GULL *Larus canus*
Very common winter visitor and passage migrant.
International importance: 16000. National importance: 7000.

Monthly Peak Counts

	Jan	Feb	Mar	Apr	May	June	July	Aug	Sept	Oct	Nov	Dec
Stocks Res	/	8000	/	1000	/	13	5	2	/	7000	6000	/
Alt WeBS	1196	/	190	45	10	24	51	82	102	152	340	248
Ribble WeBS	21	81	2	1	1	8	80	0	39	10	29	151
MBS WeBS	239	41	233	33	58	5	28	128	84	141	50	31

The Stocks Reservoir winter roost remains a prominent county feature despite several monthly counts being missed. Counts elsewhere in the county remain under-recorded with the WeBS data table providing the most regular information even though the survey methodology produces a poor measure of gull numbers. The year started with 800 at the Alt Estuary and 550 at Glasson during January; 24 Feb saw 465 at Skippool Creek and 450 at Glasson before numbers fell away during the summer months. The second winter period produced a low peak count of 1500 at Thurnham.

GREAT BLACK-BACKED GULL *Larus marinus*
Common winter visitor and passage migrant on coasts. Rare breeder.
International importance: 4800. National importance: 760.

WeBS

	Jan	Feb	Mar	Apr	May	June	July	Aug	Sept	Oct	Nov	Dec
Alt	210	/	50	35	19	34	9	27	72	134	95	43
Ribble	36	21	3	198	25	48	41	52	88	73	31	79
MBS	91	50	70	39	20	57	92	76	85	87	79	77

A largely coastal species with counts dominated by the WeBS survey results in the table. The most notable winter counts elsewhere were very significant numbers roosting at Fishmoor Reservoir, Blackburn where 200 were noted on 4 Jan with birds thought to feed at Whinney Hill Tip, Accrington.

Other notable counts were limited to a peak of 93 at Morecambe on 2 Sept and 70 later in the month at Cocker's Dyke on the 15th.

Heysham's breeding numbers halved to a single territory on harbour buildings and one on Heysham Business Park. Three pairs attempted to breed at Leighton Moss but all failed. Two pairs nested at Fleetwood Ferry and a pair at Layton. No survey counts were carried out for this species at the Bowland Fells or Ribble Estuary gull colonies where most recent figures showed 16 pairs at Tarnbrook Fell and nine pairs on Banks Marsh.

GLAUCOUS GULL *Larus hyperboreus*
Uncommon visitor, mostly winter. Usually more numerous and more coastal than Iceland Gull.

2018: There were two records in Rossendale, possibly of a single juvenile – at Holden Wood Reservoir on 9 March and Mitchells House Reservoir on 5 May.

2019: A disappointing year for the species from across the county with only a small number of first winter period records received. An adult roosted at Fishmoor Reservoir, Blackburn on 9 Jan and one was reported at the same site on the 11-12th. A juvenile was feeding on a seal carcass at Formby on the 30th, a second-winter at Fleetwood Marsh on 21 March and finally a juvenile flew south along the River Mersey at Otterspool on 8 April.

A late bird was at Whitworth Quarry, Rossendale on 5 May.

ICELAND GULL *Larus glaucoides*
Uncommon visitor, mostly winter.

It was a very poor year with no appearances by the two recently regular birds wintering at Marton Mere and Heysham. The first sighting involved a juvenile in the roost at Stocks Reservoir on 20 Jan before another juvenile was reported flying over Aigburth, south Liverpool on the 26th. There were no further sightings in the first winter period until a long-staying second-winter which frequented the Otterspool and Sefton Park, Liverpool area between 31 March and 6 May.

In the second winter period up to two juveniles were occasionally seen roosting at Fishmoor Reservoir between 27 and 30 Dec with additional sightings from Rishton Reservoir and Whinney Hill Tip, Accrington.

HERRING GULL *Larus argentatus*
Abundant winter visitor and passage migrant. Common breeding bird.
International importance: 13000. National importance: 7300.

WeBS data showed 4232 birds on the Alt Estuary in January with 2172 in March whereas the Ribble had a disappointingly low January count of 225. Small post-breeding WeBS counts on the Alt of 1453 in August and 1363 in September and 1026 on the Ribble held in August were outshone by 11500 on the Ribble in December although this count was significantly lower than the 25701 there in 2018. Elsewhere, 5000 at Fishmoor Reservoir was the largest count received; the few other counts reported included 3500 at Rishton Reservoir on 30 Dec and 2600 at Formby on 2 Oct.

See information for the Langden Head, Tarnbrook and Ribble Estuary colonies under Lesser Black-backed Gull for counts where Herring Gulls are estimated to represent a small percentage (around two to six percent) of the breeding totals. Around Heysham breeding numbers dropped with 32 nests on the buildings around the harbour and more from 44 to 13 nests at the Heysham Business Park with one nest at Ocean Edge. One pair successfully bred on the island at Stocks Reservoir. Urban rooftop nesters continue to be recorded throughout Liverpool, Southport, Fleetwood, Knott End, Lancaster, Morecambe, Cleveleys and 40 nests were recorded in central Blackpool.

Second-winter Iceland Gull, Sefton Park, Liverpool, 1 April (Steve Young)

LESSER BLACK-BACKED GULL *Larus fuscus*

Abundant breeder especially in Bowland and on the Ribble. Smaller winter population.

International importance: 4500. National importance: 1200.

The highest winter counts came from WeBS with 254 on the Alt during January and 333 on the Ribble in December, while the Ribble and Morecambe saw peak counts of 281 in September and 1049 in August respectively. Away from the breeding colonies the most noteworthy flocks during spring and summer were 840 at Stocks Reservoir on 24 Feb with 800 there on 28 July, 550 at Skippool Creek on 29 Aug, 500 at both Myerscough Quarry on 10 April and Alston Reservoirs on the 11th.

Regularly-returning adult Lesser Black-backed x Herring Gull hybrids were seen throughout the year in the area around Skippool Creek, MMWWT and Stocks Reservoir with additional sightings at Preston Dock and Fishmoor Reservoir.

No Bowland Fells census count was carried out but casual observations indicated a potential increase in some sections of the sub-colonies; 2018 had seen 4781 occupied nests at Langden Head and 6568 occupied nests at Tarnbrook. No separation from Herring Gulls was made but, contrary to previous estimates, a small sample this year suggested there may have been an increase in their contribution from two to six percent. No counts were received from the Ribble Estuary colony.

Breeding numbers around Heysham were up on last year with nests on non-operational land (nine nests), Heysham Business Park (an impressive increase from 55 to 103 nests), 38 on the buildings around the harbour and twelve at Ocean Edge. Urban rooftop nesters were recorded throughout Liverpool, Blackpool, Lancaster and Morecambe. A single pair bred in the Belmont Reservoir colony.

CASPIAN GULL* *Larus cachinnans*
Rare visitor mainly in winter.

The two previously-accepted first-winter individuals remained from 2018 at Fishmoor Reservoir until 19 Feb and were also seen occasionally at Whinny Hill Tip.

Three new records involved a long-staying juvenile at Cocker's Dyke from 13 Sept (C Batty) to 19 Oct. A first-winter appeared in the roost at Fishmoor Reservoir between 29-30 Dec (Mk Breaks) and potentially the same individual was at Altham on 31 Dec (WC Aspin).

YELLOW-LEGGED GULL *Larus michahelis*
Uncommon, most numerous in late summer and on southern coasts.

Seaforth had a quieter year with a second-calendar-year on 13 & 18-31 April, a second-summer on 29 June, a juvenile on 27 July with August producing a second-summer on the 4th, a juvenile on the 15th and two birds on the 24th.

A third-winter was at Lower Rivington Reservoir during January with two there on the 25th and a single bird on the 17 Feb. Elsewhere during February, a second-winter was in the roost at Fishmoor Reservoir on the 3rd and a first-winter frequented Cocker's Dyke between 14-24th. Early summer saw reports of an adult around Liverpool on 13-17 July, a juvenile at Southport Marine Lake on the 25th and an adult at Cocker's Dyke, Preesall on 14 Aug.

Late summer saw a first-winter at Lunt Meadows on 5-6 Sept followed by sporadic reports from coastal sites in the north of the county with an adult occasionally frequenting Cocker's Dyke between 22 Sept to 19 Oct while a first-winter was at Croston on 27 Sept and 1 Oct.

Second winter period records included adults at Stocks Reservoir on 10 Nov and Pilling Lane on the 27th, a third-winter at Fishmoor Reservoir on 7 Dec, and adults at Lower Rivington Reservoir on the 26th and 31st and Rishton Reservoir on 30th.

First-winter Yellow-legged Gull,
Cocker's Dyke, 14 February
(Chris Batty)

SANDWICH TERN *Thalasseus sandvicensis*
Common spring and autumn migrant on coasts, rare inland.

Morecambe Bay

A total of 562 bird-days was recorded at Heysham between 31 March and 28 May with peaks of 45 on 15 April, 91 on 26 April and 60 on 11 May. Sandwich Terns were seen at a handful of other sites but almost all in single figures, the largest exceptions being 50 at Morecambe on 30 April, 15 at Cockersand on 18 May and 32 at Knott End on 15 July. The last was on 6 Sept.

Liverpool Bay

Monthly peak counts

	Apr	May	June	July	Aug	Sept	Oct
Alt WeBS	33	104	25	186	632	495	0
Ribble WeBS	0	1	0	40	78	117	0
Sefton Coast	11	/	/	1000	700	110	0
S. Fylde coast	124	144	/	206	253	/	2

The first were one off Blackpool on 30 March and eight at Rossall Point the next day. Sightings became more regular during April and May but movement appears to have virtually stopped in June.

The year was, as usual, dominated by a steady post-breeding build-up of birds feeding close inshore and roosting on the beaches from early to mid-July. The largest gatherings were on the Sefton Coast between Formby Point and Ainsdale peaking at 1230 on 30 July with probably similar numbers there during August. The roosts thinned out during early September and the only October report was of two off Blackpool on the 22nd.

Inland

There were no records this year.

LITTLE TERN *Sternula albifrons*
Uncommon passage migrant on coasts, rare inland.

A fairly productive year began slightly earlier than average with one at Blackpool on 20 April, followed by additional spring singles in Liverpool Bay at Blackpool and Rossall Point on the 29th and Blackpool again on 6 May.

Similar numbers were seen in Morecambe Bay: off Heysham on 29 April (possibly the same as the Rossall and/or Blackpool records) and on 1, 10 & 13 May.

Several late (or perhaps early returning) birds turned up in June: singles on the EMC on the 3rd, off Blackpool on the 15th, at Foulridge Reservoirs on the 17th and at Cockersand on the 30th, and three at Seaforth on the 20th.

Two arrived at Brockholes on 5 July and one at Seaforth the same day. All other autumn records were in Liverpool Bay: four at Formby Point on 7 July, with one remaining the next day and three there on the 25th, followed by two on the 27th and singles on 30 July and 4 Aug. Seaforth had singles

Little Terns, Brockholes, 5 July (Bill Aspin)

on 5 July and 5 Aug, while further north three were off Rossall Point on 16 July, one off Blackpool on the 26th increasing to three the following day, and one there on 9 Aug.

ROSEATE TERN* *Sterna dougallii*
Scarce summer visitor.

In a fairly average year singles were at Seaforth on 7 May, 20 June and 27 July (AJ Conway, J Greep), and off Morecambe on 10 May (N Godden).

What was assumed to be the usual Common x Roseate hybrid was once again at Seaforth for a brief period in spring, seen on four dates between 9 and 23 May. Where it spends the summer remains a mystery.

COMMON TERN *Sterna hirundo*
Fairly common but localised breeder, very common passage migrant in Liverpool Bay.

Morecambe Bay
Migrant Common Terns were once again very scarce in the north of the county. In spring one was at Heysham on 19 April and twelve were with Arctic Terns on 10 May; later there was one there on 15 June, eight on 10 Aug and three on 6 Sept. The only other coastal records were singles at Cockersand on 5 May and 15 July with five there on 21 July, and finally one at Knott End on 4 Sept.

However, breeding was again successful at Conder Green where two pairs fledged five juveniles.

Liverpool Bay

Monthly Peak Counts

	Apr	May	June	July	Aug	Sept	Oct
Ribble WeBS	0	15	11	4	89	0	0
Alt WeBS	17	251	355	452	571	49	0
Seaforth	101	375	350	750	650	380	1

The first arrivals appeared on 15 April at Blackpool and Seaforth on the 18th. Birds continued to be seen off Blackpool fairly regularly throughout the breeding season with monthly peaks of 23 in May,

First-summer Common Tern, Seaforth, 29 June (Gavin Thomas).
One of only a handful of Common Terns proven to be this age that have been recorded in Britain.

21 in June, twelve in July and 31 in August and the last on 27 Sept. Only very small numbers were recorded to the north.

Numbers had increased rapidly by the end of April at Seaforth and 176 pairs went on to breed, hatching 203 young of which around 170 went on to fledge. Their numbers were swollen by migrants – probably primarily from Irish colonies – in July and August (see table) but there was a rapid clear-out by mid-September, after which only 20 or so remained with just one on 2 Oct before a very late bird on the 15th.

2018. The report of six pairs nesting on Hesketh Out Marsh was an error.

Inland

The colony at Preston Dock held 119 pairs but productivity was again very poor – only 19 fledged – due to gull predation. The smaller colonies fared rather better, though: two pairs attempted to breed at Brockholes, one successfully fledging three young, three pairs with six young at MMWWT and two pairs fledged two at Mere Sands Wood .

As usual there were a good number of inland records of migrant or wandering birds, including at Rishton, Stocks, Alston and Foulridge Reservoirs in the east, Belmont and Rivington Reservoirs in the West Pennines, Myerscough Quarry in east Fylde, Carr Mill Dam in St Helens, and Croston Twin Lakes, Bretherton Eyes and the canal at Sollom in Chorley.

ARCTIC TERN *Sterna paradisaea*
Very common on spring passage, especially in Morecambe Bay; less numerous in autumn. Rare breeder.

Morecambe Bay

After last year's unusual timing and relative low numbers on passage past Heysham and Morecambe Stone Jetty 2019 saw a return to normality, albeit peaking slightly later than usual, when 3783 moved north between 15 April and 19 May including a massive peak of 2910 on 10 May and counts of 83 to 200 on five other dates. The only other significant counts during spring passage were 54 at Cockersand on 18 May, 40 at Warton Slag Tips on the 11th and 30 at Jenny Brown's Point on the 10th.

Arctic Terns are always scarce at best in autumn and 2019 produced just a handful of ones and twos on seven dates between 7 July and 6 Sept; even fewer were seen anywhere else.

Liverpool Bay

The edges of the spring movement into Morecambe Bay are usually picked up on the Fylde coast but no really large numbers were seen this year south of the mouth of the bay. Peak counts were 275 off Blackpool on 10 May with 200 there on the 16th and 247 on the 17th.

Very few were seen further south: ones and twos were occasional at Seaforth and elsewhere on the Sefton Coast from 4 May and three were on the Mersey at Otterspool on 28 July.

Five pairs nested at each of the county's two breeding colonies, Preston Dock and Hesketh Out Marsh, but with quite different outcomes, five juveniles fledging at the latter but just one at the former.

Inland

One in Whitendale on 18 April, the first in east Lancashire, was followed by spring records at Stocks and Foulridge Reservoirs and Alston Wetlands, including five at Stocks on 8 May. There were only three records in the east in autumn, at Stocks and Alston and three at Rishton Reservoir on 29 July.

The very few records received from elsewhere in the county included singles at Brockholes on 8 May and 9 Oct, Belmont Reservoir on 28 July and MMWWT on 16 Aug.

BLACK TERN *Chlidonias niger*
Uncommon spring and autumn migrant. Usually more numerous and more coastal in autumn. Most northern records in spring.

This year's spring passage must be counted as a good one but it was almost entirely confined to Heysham, where flocks totalling 65 birds were caught up in the huge movement of Arctic Terns on 10 May, mainly a series of separate groups accompanying the Arctics. Subsequent records at Heysham were one on 11 May and two on 10 Aug.

Elsewhere the first were at Leighton Moss on 25 April and Seaforth and Blackpool on the 27th but they did not become more widespread until the period 7-11 May, when Black Terns appeared at several western sites and four in east Lancashire. The largest counts during this period were four at Seaforth on the 8-11th, three at Stocks Reservoir on the 8th, five at Lunt Meadows and three at MMWWT on the 9th, and 13 off Blackpool, six at Alston Wetland, five at Leighton Moss and three at Marton Mere on the 10th, but single-figures were also at Brockholes, Cockersand, Preston Dock and Leighton Moss.

Spring concluded with one at Seaforth on 14-18th May and no more were seen until three at Formby on 25 July and one at Belmont Reservoir on the 27th, followed by one at Heysham on 10 Aug, one at Marshside on the 31st and two juveniles at Seaforth the same day – the last of the year.

GREAT SKUA (BONXIE) *Stercorarius skua*
Fairly common passage migrant

Morecambe Bay

There were just two singletons in spring past Heysham/Stone Jetty on 28 April and 2 May. Autumn passage was also poor with singles off Heysham/Stone Jetty on 17 Aug, 5 Sept and 8 Oct and others off Cocker's Dyke on 29 Aug and Knott End on 4 Sept.

Liverpool Bay

There was a northbound flurry off the Fylde coast with singles off Blackpool on 25 & 27 April and three off Rossall on 28 April. More difficult to work out what they were doing date-wise were two off Blackpool on 26 May, one there on 20 June and two on 9 June.

Presumably on early autumn passage were singletons south off Blackpool on 11, 18 and 24 July. More typical autumn passage timing saw singles off Blackpool on 17 Aug and 6, 13 and 26 Sept and three there on 10 Oct. Other unduplicated Fylde autumn sightings were two off Fleetwood Promenade on 4 Sept and one off Norbreck on 13 Oct.

There was a complete absence of any submitted records south of the Ribble.

POMARINE SKUA *Stercorarius pomarinus*
Uncommon passage migrant

Morecambe Bay

Pomarine Skuas were more regular than Great Skuas in spring, usually during either easterlies or south-westerlies. The following records off Heysham and/or Stone Jetty undoubtedly included some of the Rossall birds: single north-east-bound pale morphs on 19 April, 20 April and 6 May, two together on 10 and 17 May and three together on 26 May.

Liverpool Bay

Singles flew north-east off Rossall Point on 20 April and 6 and 10 May, while six were seen from there on 18 May with an additional dark morph seen the same day off Fleetwood promenade.

The only autumn records were an adult pale morph off Fleetwood Promenade on 15 Aug and another pale adult off Crosby on 4 Sept.

ARCTIC SKUA *Stercorarius parasiticus*
Fairly common passage migrant with rapid transit in spring and a prolonged autumn passage with several lingering birds

Morecambe Bay
Forty-seven recorded at Heysham and/or Stone Jetty on spring passage between 9 April and 30 May were bolstered by a record count of 19 during the major seawatching day of 10 May. Elsewhere, there were singles from Cockersand on 10 and 18 May heading up the Lune flight-line, and one was off Knott End on 11 May. Yet again they were absent from the inner bay.

Autumn records were limited to singles off Knott End on 16 July and 1 Sept, four there on 4 Sept (all adults), Heysham on 22 Aug, Pilling Lane on 26 Sept and three at Cocker's Dyke on 27 Aug

Liverpool Bay
Spring passage sightings between Blackpool and Rossall saw two early birds off Blackpool on 30 March and thereafter 32 between 6 April and 23 May. Summer sightings from the same area saw singles on 22 and 29 June, 10 and 16 July with two on 12 July.

Autumn passage along the same stretch of the Fylde coast produced 13 between 28 Aug and 26 Sept, while the only Sefton records received saw off-passage sightings at Formby between 25 July and 2 Aug, peaking at eight on 1 Aug and four on migration on 19 Sept.

The only unidentified skua submitted was an Arctic or Pomarine off Rossall on 11 Sept.

GUILLEMOT *Uria aalge*
Common passage migrant; uncommon winter visitor

The first report of the year was on 7 Feb when ten were seen at Heysham with a single there the next day. Four were off Blackpool on 31 March and birds were seen regularly there between 1 April and 28 May and other Fylde coast sites, the highest count being 139 on 11 May.

South of the Ribble four were off Formby Point on 6 May and 87 on 21 May. Finally in the first half of the year seven were off Blackpool on 9 June, two on the 20th, singles on the 21st and 27th and four on the 30th.

On 4 Aug birds were present at Glasson Dock and during the month singles were seen off Blackpool on four dates, one at Preston Dock and five at Formby Point on the 27th.

Autumn passage produced two at Knott End on 2 Sept and one on the 6th with regular sightings off Blackpool between the 6th-30th with 14 on the 25th the highest number. Three were found dead on the strandline at Formby Point on 15 Sept.

Sighting continued throughout October and November off Blackpool with a peak of 33 23 Nov, while Formby Point had five on 2 Nov and four on the 14th.

The last sightings were four on 3 Dec and one on the 31st, both off Blackpool.

RAZORBILL *Alca torda*
Common passage migrant; uncommon winter visitor.

The first sighting was one off Blackpool on 28 March and there were regular records throughout April, May and June to 1 July from various Fylde coast sites; large counts included 68 on 11 May, 49 on the 13th and 51 a day later.

Autumn passage was limited: two were at Knott End on 4 Sept (one dead) and one on the 6th, while in November Blackpool recorded sightings on six occasions, the highest count being nine on the 6th.

None were seen anywhere in December.

UNIDENTIFIED LARGE AUKS
The largest counts off Blackpool were 256 on 15 May, 218 on the 24th, 191 on the 14th and 170 on 13 May. Other large counts included 231 off Rossall Point on 27 May and 169 off Formby Point on 21 May.

BLACK GUILLEMOT *Cepphus grille*
Scarce passage migrant; rare winter visitor

There were three records, all in spring: singles off Blackpool on 4 April and 16 May, and off Heysham on 18 May.

PUFFIN *Fratercula arctica*
Increasingly regular spring migrant, especially Rossall; rare at other times

Four were off Blackpool on 14 May with two there the following day, two on both 15 and 16 May at Rossall Point and finally one at Formby on 21 May. Possibly the same birds as seen at Rossall were observed floating into the Bay from Heysham on 16 May before flying off towards Walney.

RED-THROATED DIVER *Gavia stellata*
Fairly common winter visitor and spring passage migrant. Scarce inland.
International importance: 10000. National importance: 170.

Monthly peak counts

	Jan	Feb	Mar	Apr	May	Jun	Jul	Aug	Sep	Oct	Nov	Dec
Heysham	/	2	31	15	13	/	/	/	/	1	1	4
Blackpool	26	26	51	46	20	1	1	1	51	11	156	30
Formby Point	34	47	2	13	2	/	/	/	18	31	51	2

Seasonal movements were fairly typical with moderate numbers seen from the main seawatching sites in the table during both winter periods and more substantial passage movements in spring and autumn.

Numbers off Formby Point were almost certainly underestimated this year as virtually the only records received came from the once-monthly WeBS counts with very few of the usual focussed seawatching data.

Recording off Blackpool was, however, far more complete with peak counts of 51 on 26 Sept, 87 on 21 Nov, 156 on the following day and 67 on the 25th, all flying south, and double-figures remaining fairly regular into December, notably 30 on the 22nd.

The only record away from the main sites was one off Knott End on 31 Oct.

BLACK-THROATED DIVER *Gavia arctica*
Uncommon annual winter visitor, mostly on coast.

In the early year there were singles off Formby Point on 24 Feb and 24 March, Blackpool on 1 March and 27 April, and Rossall Point on 26 April.

Two off Heysham on 27 May was the last of spring. The only later records were singles off Formby on 18 Nov and Blackpool on 27 Dec.

GREAT NORTHERN DIVER *Gavia immer*
Scarce, less than annual, mostly on coast.

Great Northern records were quite similar to those of Black-throated Divers this year.

There were singles off Heysham on 16 Jan and Rossall Point on 2 March (possible only) and 29 May, followed by a long gap until the final singles of the year off Blackpool on 23 Sept, Formby Point on 11 and 18 Nov, and Knott End on 26 Nov.

LEACH'S PETREL *Oceanodroma leucorhoa*
Fairly common offshore in variable numbers during September and October gales.

There was only one early year record, a single off Rossall Point on 14 March, all other records were mainly in September.

The first were reported on 2 Sept when there three at Heysham and two off the Blackpool coast, followed by one at Rossall Point the next day; six off Formby Point, four at Heysham, two off Knott End and one off Blackpool on the 4th were followed by eleven at Blackpool on the 6th with singles at Knott End and Rossall Point. Three remained at Heysham on the 7th with four there on the 9th, which marked the high point of the passage with twelve at Blackpool and nine at Formby.

There was a final September record at Blackpool on 11 Sept and then the last of the year there on 10 Oct.

FULMAR *Fulmarus glacialis*
Fairly common on coasts in late summer and early autumn during onshore winds.

The first was a single inshore at Heysham on 9 Feb. March produced further singles on two dates at Heysham, on three dates off Blackpool and three at Heysham with two there on the 15th.

Spring continued with very occasional ones and two at Heysham/Morecambe or off the Fylde coast during April and May but no more were seen in Morecambe Bay until singles at Knott End on 1-2 & 6 Sept with there on the 4th when was also at Morecambe.

Birds were a little more frequent in Liverpool Bay, mainly off Blackpool with twelve bird-days in April and 18 in May, peaking at six on the 26th. There were records there on three days in June and later three on 17 July and three on 29 Aug, with last off the south Fylde coast four off Rossall Point and Blackpool on 11 Sept.

MANX SHEARWATER *Puffinus puffinus*
Common offshore in late summer-autumn, especially during onshore winds.

The first appeared ten days later than last year off Blackpool on 25 April, with two off Rossall Point on the 29th. May then produced a flurry of records with three-figure counts at Blackpool as follows:

Daily peak counts in May off Blackpool

11th	13th	14th	15th	23rd	26th	27th
500	340	210	145	116	621	401

Passage was poorly recorded at Formby Point as almost the only records came from the monthly WeBS counts and the only sizeable count there this year was 31 on 5 June. Heysham was a little more productive with single figures seen during both passage periods and peaks of 70 on 27 May and 32 on the 30th.

However, Blackpool dominated throughout the whole year with further notable counts including 110 on 22 June, 220 on 1 July and 300 on 11 Aug. Numbers declined everywhere during September and the last of the year was at Blackpool on 10Oct.

GANNET *Morus bassanus*
Common summer and autumn visitor offshore in variable numbers. Scarce in winter.

Most records came during the period March to September from Blackpool with a few stragglers into October and November; the first were on 2 March and the last on 26 Nov.

Monthly peak counts off Blackpool

	Mar	Apr	May	Jun	Jul	Aug	Sep	Oct	Nov
Days recorded	11	29	31	16	19	10	18	5	3
Peak count	26	65	74	67	52	18	24	3	2
Peak date	10th	27th	11th	30th	14th	2nd	26th	10th	26th

Additional significant Blackpool counts included 61 on 25 April, 66 on 27 May, 58 on 23 June and 34 on 11 July.

Gannets were only reported from Formby Point on WeBS count days between 21 April and 13 Aug with peaks of 59 on 17 June and 30 on 13 Aug. Peaks at Heysham included 71 in April and 42 in May.

Smaller numbers were logged at a few other coastal watchpoints and five were seen inland: singles at Pine lake on 4-7 Sept, Marton Mere on the 6th, Yarrow Valley Park on the 7th, where it died after an hour, over the canal between Higher Wheeton and Withnell Fold on 13 Oct and on Belmont Reservoir on the 15th.

SHAG *Phalacrocorax aristotelis*
Uncommon but probably increasing on coasts. Most records are of immatures.

Records were confined to Heysham and Blackpool.

At Heysham a sub-adult (3CY) was present on 15 Jan before appearing again between 15-16 March and then again on intermittent days between 2 and 14 April, and an adult or near-adult was there on 14 July. In the second half of the year one was seen on 2, 4, 6, 9 & 11 Sept, three juveniles on 2 Nov and an adult and juvenile on the 3rd, and finally an adult on nine dates between 10 Nov and 31 Dec.

Blackpool's waters were less productive but at least one was reported for at least one day in all months except July, August and October. Two were present on 10 May, four on 13 Nov and five on 15 Nov.

CORMORANT *Phalacrocorax carbo*
Common and increasing on coasts and estuaries. Local but increasing inland.
International importance: 1200. National importance: 350.

Monthly peak counts

	Jan	Feb	Mar	Apr	May	Jun	Jul	Aug	Sep	Oct	Nov	Dec
MBS WeBS+	350	355	192	97	220	38	81	257	234	224	178	153
Ribble WeBS	166	440	39	110	254	321	91	174	428	398	1006	643
Alt WeBS	380	/	138	73	91	75	228	219	451	1224	333	147
Seaforth	200	52	208	106	30	17	20	200	222	464	187	45
Stocks Res	22	38	46	11	12	11	47	52	45	49	43	15
Rivington Res	64	/	85	8	/	/	/	/	/	35	44	51

+ includes counts from additional days where numbers exceed WeBS totals

Brockholes, Foulridge Reservoirs and Mere Sands Wood that have regularly been included in the table in the past failed to record sufficiently large number throughout the year in 2019. At Mere Sands Wood there was an inexplicable decline from previous four-figure counts to an annual high of just 253 on 15th Sept.

Away from the coast elsewhere double-figure counts were recorded throughout the year from almost 100 sites; were of less than 50 birds but with continued increases some sites will break into three-figures for at least a couple of months of the year within a short time frame.

Brockholes reported a yearly peak of 27 in March, Lunt Meadows 33 the same month, 25 at Leighton Moss in September and 29 at MMWWT in December. Other maxima included 17 at Alston Wetland, 22 at Barrow Lodge, 23 at Clowbridge Reservoir, 50 at Slipper Hill Reservoir and 48 at Whitemoor Reservoir 48 in November; there were routinely 7-8 in south Liverpool at Sefton Park.

Apparent *sinensis* race birds were reported from five locations throughout the year involving a maximum of four individuals: two at Glasson Basin/Conder Green on 3 and 7 March, four at Preston Dock on 30 June) and singles at Leighton Moss on 12 Oct and Stanley Park, Blackpool on 23 Nov.

GLOSSY IBIS *Plegadis falcinellus*
Scarce visitor.

The first report coincided with exactly the same date and location of the previous year on 3 May at Marshside. The presumed same bird was seen again on 24 May at Marshside where it was present throughout June until it was last seen on 14 July.

It is possibly safe to presume that the same bird was seen at Longton Brickcroft (G Moran) on 13 July and then further east on the 25 July at Crawshawbooth and Waterfoot in Rossendale (C Bell *et al*).

SPOONBILL *Platalea leucorodia*
Scarce visitor, has bred.

Spoonbills appeared at the two regular sites, namely the Ribble Marshes and Leighton Moss/ Eric Morecambe complex. The first was on 28 Feb at Marshside and a second bird on 7 March with the first at Leighton Moss on 6 April.

On Merseyside there were flyovers at Seaforth on 6 and 8 May and presumably the same bird at Lunt Meadows on 3 June. A single bird was photographed in flight over Fairhaven Lake on 15 April.

Twos were present throughout May and June at both Leighton Moss and Marshside, while a notable five birds frequented Leighton Moss between 10-15 July.

The last record was two at Leighton Moss between 31 Oct and 10 Nov.

BITTERN *Botaurus stellaris*
Rare breeding bird, uncommon winter visitor there and elsewhere.

It is pleasing to report that Bitterns bred successfully in the county this year.

The first winter period produced records of ones and twos well distributed across the county: at Leighton Moss, Marton Mere, Brockholes, MMWWT, Lunt Meadows and Belmont from 01-03 Feb.

At Lunt Meadows the two from the previous year were present until at least 9 March with one half-heartedly booming from 22 February. Booming was also heard at MMWWT from February through to May and although breeding was not confirmed this is very encouraging. Similarly a single Bittern at Marton Mere on the 30 July provides some optimism for future breeding attempts.

Breeding was confirmed at Leighton Moss on 10 June when one fledgling was seen and then again on 24 June when three fledglings were seen.

Bitterns started to return to their wintering areas in September and singles and doubles were seen throughout the second winter period at Leighton Moss, Brockholes, Marton Mere, Lunt Meadows and MMWWT.

Bittern, Leighton Moss, May (Gary Waddington)

CATTLE EGRET* *Bubulcus ibis*
Scarce visitor but in increasing numbers.

According to WeBS the peak British population increased roughly fourfold between 2017/18 and 2018/19. The county trend is the same as the national statistics with increasing accounts year on year.

The year began with seven by the RSPB Offices at Banks on 1 Jan, possibly the same six birds that flew from the roost at Southport Marine Lake on 3 Jan. Bryning in Warton hosted the first on the Fylde on 5 Jan and two at Bolton-le-Sands on 25 Feb were the first in north Lancashire.

In line with recent years numbers started to increase in early autumn and continued through to October. East Lancashire recorded a single at Coldwell Upper Reservoir on 19 Aug while nine birds flew south-east over Knott End on 28 Oct and five were seen during November at Cockersand.

Double-figure counts were noticeable this year with 16 reported at Marshside on 28 Sept and 12 Oct and the October Ribble WeBS count recorded 20 birds.

The species' increase in the county provided 'first for reserve' records for both Lunt Meadows where two birds flew over on the 7 March, and Seaforth where two birds flew north on 16 Nov.

GREY HERON *Ardea cinerea*
Scarce breeding resident.

Monthly peak counts

	Jan	Feb	Mar	Apr	May	Jun	Jul	Aug	Sept	Oct	Nov	Dec
MBS WeBS	34	8	19	16	20	16	36	32	26	25	4	9
Ribble WeBS	29	10	4	9	19	16	19	13	30	23	22	5
Silverdale Moss	1	4	0	3	1	7	2	6	4	3	3	34
Alt WeBS	7	2	0	3	4	5	0	3	12	4	2	2

In the West Pennine Moors the heronry in Delph Plantations continued to decline from the eleven active nests in 2016 down to just three in 2019 and the Entwistle Plantations heronry declined sharply from 30 nests in 2018 to 20 in 2019, the lowest total for 20 years. The Rivington heronry was more-or-less stable with 30 active nests (31 nests in 2018). The decline in the three heronries from 69 nests in 2015 to the 53 nests in 2019 cannot be explained, albeit the loss of nesting trees at Entwistle and Delph is in part no doubt responsible, although seemingly suitable trees in abundance exist adjacent to these heronries.

The breeding situation elsewhere is unclear as not all heronries are reported but the county trend probably reflect the picture shown by the BTO Heronries Census of a slow decline in numbers.

Number of Active Nests at Monitored Herenories

North Lancashire	
Ashton Hall	6
Skerton Weir	9
Centre Farm Forton	5
Rough Hey Wood Claughton	12
Tunstall	25
Silverdale Moss	4
East Lancashire	
Winckley Hall	39
Stocks Reservoir	2
Jackhouse	2

Fylde	
Hackensall Wood	5
Stanley Park	34 (individuals)
Chorley	
Cuerden VP	3
West Pennine Moors	
Rivington	30
Delph Plantations	3
Entwistle Plantations	20
Rossendale	
Warth, Waterfoot	10

PURPLE HERON* *Ardea purpurea*
Vagrant

The county's sixteenth record was photographed in the Eagland Hill area on 4 Dec and identified as a juvenile from the photographs (G Pinder). It was relocated the following day along Bradshaw Lane, just north of Eagland Hill village, where it stayed until 16 Dec. The day after on 17 Dec, it moved to the saltmarsh at Marshside, over 16 miles to the south. This proved to be just a one-day visit with no more sightings until 29 Dec when it returned to Eagland Hill until the end of the year.

This was our first wintering record, all others have been in spring with the exception two in early autumn.

Interestingly for this species, which is normally a reedbed specialist, it spent its time feeding on flooded farmland where it was seen frequently to prey on Field Voles.

Purple Heron with Field Vole, Eagland Hill, 31 December (Paul Ellis)

GREAT WHITE EGRET *Ardea alba*
Scarce but increasing , mostly in winter.

Monthly Peak Counts

	Jan	Feb	Mar	Apr	May	Jun	Jul	Aug	Sept	Oct	Nov	Dec
MBS WeBS	4	1	3	1	0	0	0	0	3	3	0	1
Silverdale Moss	1	2	0	0	0	0	0	0	1	0	0	4
Ribble WeBS	2	1	0	0	0	1	0	3	6	6	4	0

Good numbers were present in the county's two main wintering areas at both ends of the year with up to five in the Leighton Moss area and possibly six birds on the Ribble Marshes – four south of the river and two on Warton Marsh.

Away from these two populations good numbers of sightings were made across the county, illustrating how this species can wander: in the east one was at Salterforth between 25-27 Jan, while A one day visitor at Eccleston on 5 March marked the species' presence in the Chorley area, and Brockholes had its first multiple record when two flew east on 29 Oct.

Away from Warton Marsh birds were seen on the Fylde at Little Singleton, Cocker's Dyke, Myerscough Quarry, Herons' Reach Golf Course, Marton Mere and Carr House Green Common. A mobile bird was also seen regularly in the second winter period between Warton and Newton Marsh which was a different bird from the two on the Marsh.

At Heysham early year sightings were on the eastern boundary on 17 and 23 Feb and flying east just south of Ocean Edge on 31 March. Elsewhere in north Lancashire one was at Gressingham by the River Lune in February. One was seen in flight over Middleton on 16 and 20 Sept, then fairly regularly from 4 Nov to the end of the year. What may have been an additional bird flew north over the wooden jetty on 5 Nov and there were two birds together flying south-east over Middleton NR on 18 Nov that and were probably the two roosting at Ashton Hall in the latter part of winter.

One flying east over Mount Park, Fleetwood on 7 April was the only new spring bird, but on 24 Aug two were seen from Fairhaven Dunes coming down the Ribble, where they briefly landed at Church Scar, Lytham before heading south. On Merseyside two seen at Seaforth on 26 Aug may possibly have been the same two birds moving through.

LITTLE EGRET *Egretta garzetta*
Common and increasing visitor, mainly to coastal marshes. Rare breeder, first in 2014.
National importance: 50

Monthly Peak Counts

	Jan	Feb	Mar	Apr	May	Jun	Jul	Aug	Sept	Oct	Nov	Dec
MBS WeBS	45	39	74	22	37	39	79	130	162	146	60	27
Eric Morecambe C.	1	6	12	7	9	3	1	36	19	103	56	9
Ribble WeBS	49	55	52	78	34	61	46	105	155	111	82	26

The table illustrates the recent county trend in which the population peaks in early autumn. This is highlighted by the numbers recorded roosting at Ashton Hall in Lancaster, where counts peaked at 184 in July, 160 in September and 175 in October, and at Fairhaven Lake where monthly peaks were 124 in August and 143 in September. It is clear from these figures that the county's autumn population is now likely to be substantially bigger than 300.

While still regarded as primarily a coastal species the number of inland records continues to grow. Multiple sightings during January, February and March in the Chorley area mainly came from Bretherton Eyes, Croston Moss and the Eccleston area. Further east singles were at Heapey and at Hoghton Bottoms on 11 April, while in Rossendale one was feeding on the River Irwell in March with another at Clowbridge Reservoir on 13 May.

As in the Chorley area, multiple sighting were received in the first part of the winter period from east Lancashire, notably at Hodderfoot and the Hurst Green area and on the river Calder, Altham. Roosting birds were recorded in the east of the county towards the end of the year at Sawley in November and December. Several records were received in December, possibly relating to three separate individuals in the Chorley area. One could be found in the White Coppice and Heapey Lodges area for much of December, another along Syd Brook, Eccleston and a third on Croston Moss.

Breeding was confirmed at Ashton Hall with 16 nests present and six nests were evident at Tunstall and two at Skerton Weir, but no report was received from Southport Marine Lake this year.

OSPREY *Pandion haliaetus*
Fairly common passage migrant, mainly in spring.

An early record was well inland at Stocks Reservoir on 19 March. A minimum of 43 were recorded on spring passage through the county during March to May. In addition multiple records of one or two occurred at or around Leighton Moss, with three there on 15 May.

Two spring records at Marton Mere involved birds hunting over the mere, but otherwise none were reported as lingering anywhere.

There were two June records and another single in July in east Lancashire, which presumably involved wandering non-breeders. One was at Brockholes from 13-16 June and June and July also saw many records from the Leighton Moss-Morecambe Bay area. The latter area also saw many August records, masking the start of any autumn migration, which involved widely scattered birds. The last of the year was Leighton Moss on 24 Sept.

HONEY-BUZZARD* *Pernis apivorus*
Rare passage migrant.

Only one accepted record, at Leighton Moss on 22 May, which was probably an adult male (G Thomas). It was our first record since 2013.

SPARROWHAWK *Accipiter nisus*
Fairly common breeding resident, uncommon passage migrant.

Nests from which juveniles fledged were reported in the Chorley recording area (Shaw Hill and two pairs at Cuerden Valley Park), in Fylde (Lytham St Annes, Pilling and Preesall), at Heysham and Ormskirk. Productivity was reported as high, with nine eggs in two nests at Pilling and Preesall resulting in eight fledged juveniles and four fledged juveniles at Lytham St Annes.

Spring migrants were recorded moving north at Heysham on 25 March (2), 6 April (2), 18 April (1) and 23 April (2).

Autumn migrants were also noted moving south over Heysham on 21 Sept (1), 18 Oct (3) and 23 Oct (1). Other autumn migrants were noted at Winter Hill in September, four on the 14th and two on the 23rd, all moving south-east from Lancashire into Greater Manchester.

The highest reported site counts were of six at Gisburn Forest on 29 March and seven at MMWWT on 18 Sept.

An interesting observation was made on 31 Jan at Alt Meadows, Croxteth, where one was seen to emerge at speed from the River Alt culvert running beneath the East Lancashire Road, at such a speed that it was deduced to have passed through the full length of the culvert. The observer had been present for some time without seeing it enter from the side where it exited. A female was seen to take and kill an incubating Lapwing at Belmont Reservoir on 11 Apr.

Sparrowhawk in rain shower, Roby, January (Steve Young)

GOSHAWK *Accipiter gentilis*
Rare breeding resident and escapee.

A female was over Longridge on 22 Feb before flying north. An adult was photographed at Jackhouse, Accrington on 24 Feb.

Display was recorded in Bowland in early spring, but no evidence of breeding could be found. However, a pair was seen at another east Lancashire site in March-April and probable breeding was confirmed with a juvenile male in the area from 26-28 June.

There were two June records in the Chorley area but for the remainder of the year the sole record was a juvenile in Rossendale on 21 Oct.

MARSH HARRIER *Circus aeroginosus*
Fairly common passage migrant, scarce in east. Rare breeder.

First winter period peak counts were six at Leighton Moss on 30 Jan and 31 March, four at Warton Bank on 14 Feb, and three at Lytham Quays on 4 Jan and at Martin Mere on 15 Feb.

Returning migrants were recorded in April at Marton Mere, Crosby and Brockholes and one at Warton Bank 22-23 May. Other May records were restricted to MMWWT on four dates from the 7th to 15th, Lunt on the 17th-19th and the Leighton Moss-Morecambe Bay area. June records on three dates in Fylde included one seen moving north at Arm Hill on the 16th. Non-breeding birds were noted as being regular visitors to the Bowland Fells During spring.

Four nests involving four females and a male were recorded at Leighton Moss, two of them each fledging three young while the others appeared to fail late in the chick stage. A pair possibly nested again at the now traditional site on the south-west mosses but was not proven.

July records were restricted to the Ribble, south-west mosses and Morecambe Bay-Leighton Moss areas but dispersing birds began to appear elsewhere during August, including one in Chorley at Croston Moss and Bretherton Eyes from the 26th, where it was joined by another in early September. Other scattered September records included singles at Champion Moor on the 7th and Anglezarke Moor on the 17th.

Peak post-breeding counts were seven at MMWWT on 23 Sept, with the same number on the November Ribble WeBS count and at Leighton Moss on 8 Dec, and five at Lunt Meadows during October. The final record away from established wintering areas was at Seaforth on 10 Nov.

HEN HARRIER *Circus cyaneus*
Fairly common visitor to coasts and hills outside breeding season. Rare breeder.

The south Ribble marshes held up to three birds in January, while on the Fylde side of the river, two ringtails and a male were at Warton Bank in February. The last of spring on the Ribble was on 6 April, while singles were at MMWWT on 2 and 13-15 April.

There was a very welcome increase to five successful nests in Bowland, with all 22 chicks fledging. However, this is still well below the breeding numbers in the first decade of this century. With the Bowland Special Protection Area being designated for thirteen pairs there is much room for improvement.

An early isolated record back on the coast was at Banks on 3 July. The next were at Marshside on 6 Sept, Leighton Moss on the 7th and St Michael's on Wyre the 10th. An exceptional autumn to year's end period saw at least seven birds passing through the West Pennine Moors, with several lingering. The only records of the year at Lunt Meadows were of two on 28 Sept and a single on 30-31 Dec.

MONTAGU'S HARRIER* *Circus pygargus*
Vagrant.

A juvenile was photographed at Pendleside Farm, Barley, Pendle on 8 Sept (S Grimshaw), following two unconfirmed reports there in the preceding days – the first in the county since 2014.

Juvenile Montagu's Harrier, Barley 8 September (S Grimshaw)

RED KITE *Milvus milvus*
Scarce passage migrant and rare winter visitor from successful reintroduction schemes.

The first record of the year at Leighton Moss on 9 Feb was followed by singles at Warton Crag on the 12th and Skippool the next day, before another single at Leighton Moss on 24 Feb. March produced singles at Lunt Meadows, Mere Sands Wood, Martin Mere and Bowland.

Elsewhere in the county, 19 bird-days were recorded in east Lancashire from 23rd March to 23rd July, singles were seen at Leighton Moss on 10-12 April, MMWWT on the 14th and over Rivington Service Station on the 24th. Finally, fleeting singles were on the West Pennine Moors in June, Brockholes on 7 July, Lunt Meadows on 8 Sept and in the Chorley area at Great Knowley on 2 & 5 Oct.

WHITE-TAILED EAGLE *Haliaeetus albicilla*
Vagrant.

One, an immature, flew over the Eric Morecambe Complex on 15th Feb (A Physick).

BUZZARD *Buteo buteo*
Fairly common breeding resident.

Records were widespread all year, as expected. High counts in the first winter and early spring period included six in Little Bowland on 10 Feb, eleven at Brockholes on 23 Feb, five at Salterforth, Pendle the same day and at The Kilns, Burnley on the 25th, twelve at MMWWT on 27 Feb, eight at Lunt Meadows on 19 March, 18 MMWWT 20 March, five at Dunsop Bridge on 21 March and twelve at New Laithe Farm, Newton on the 23rd.

Visible migration in spring was reported from Heysham, with singles north on 25 & 28 March and Winter Hill, where eight went north-west on 6 April. Migrants were also noted at Seaforth in April and May.

Seven pairs were monitored in the Pilling-Preesall area, which laid thirteen eggs, hatching ten young which all fledged. Other reports of successful breeding came from Eccleston, Belmont (at least three successful pairs from five territories), Lunt Meadows and Aintree.

Post-breeding and autumn migration was noted at Seaforth between August and October, while at Heysham single migrants flew south on 16 & 17 Sept. Significant numbers of migrants were recorded moving south-east at Winter Hill in September, this direction being influenced by the topography of the site, which birds navigate around when moving in a general southerly route; September counts of birds moving out of Lancashire into Greater Manchester airspace were of fifty on the 7th, 15 on the 8th, 32 on the 13th, eleven on the 20th, , 42 on the 23rd and eleven on the 26th.

Other significant autumn counts in included eight at Woodhouse Lane, Slaidburn 20 Sept, eleven at Brockholes on 23 Sept, nine at Bank Hall, Bretherton 1 Oct and ten on the November Ribble WeBS count.

A leucistic individual was noted as still being resident at Belmont.

Buzzard, Thurnham,
8 December (Paul Ellis)

BARN OWL *Tyto alba*
Uncommon breeding resident, most numerous in the south-west and in the Fylde.

The status of Barn Owls in Lancashire is rather uncertain at the moment, particularly since there is little systematic monitoring and we receive rather few breeding records. In spite of this, there is little evidence that their situation has changed significantly in recent years beyond an expansion into eastern parts from their stronghold in the south-west, and they remain widespread throughout the county.

Reports of breeding success in 2019 were inconclusive, except in east Lancashire where it appears to have been a poor year.

The Fylde Bird Club website received 185 records during 2019 from all parts of the region. As in previous years, Eagland Hill had the highest counts with twos and threes on numerous occasions and four on 7 Feb. Two were at nearby Bradshaw Lane on 20 Jan and two adults were also seen at Pilling, Cockersand, Lytham Moss, Freckleton and Marton Mere. Breeding was proved at Nateby, Medlar, Marton Mere and Freckleton Naze. Four young were ringed at Brockholes.

Individuals were recorded from eleven locations in the south-west – almost certainly a gross underestimate; these included young heard calling at two sites near Rainford, while MMWWT held three breeding pairs, resulting in an excellent eight fledged chicks.

In the Rossendale area, one dedicated recorder logged breeding at five sites including two pairs at Cheesden Bridge.

In the north, singles were reported at twelve sites, but there were no breeding records submitted. The LDBWS winter survey recorded Barn Owls in SD65, 66 & 67.

East Lancashire reports were down 27% on 2018 with many daylight hunting records indicating a struggle to find food and only 14 breeding records were received compared to 27 in 2018.

In Bowland as a whole, only ten pairs were found to be breeding, compared to 31 in 2018. Only 30 chicks fledged in 2019, showing a fairly dramatic fall from 82 in 2018 and 124 in 2017.

There were a number of sightings across the year in Chorley. Birds were noted at 5 sites in the early winter period, and a pair was observed at a site at Mawdesley on 31 March. There were no confirmed breeding records, but records from seven sites were received in autumn and winter. However, in the West Pennine Moors at least seven were out hunting in mid-afternoon in the Belmont area in January

Barn Owl, East Lancashire
(Gary Waddington)

including some (atypically) on moorland at up to 380m above sea level. Two pairs bred at Belmont fledging five and three young, a pair bred at Roddlesworth fledging one young, and several other territories were occupied in the West Pennine Moors with breeding proven at two of those.

TAWNY OWL *Strix aluco*
Common and widespread breeding resident.

Our most vocal owl, the Tawny Owl's distinctive pair of calls was heard across the county throughout the year. However, as usual it was under-reported and its true status in the county is poorly represented by what follows.

In the north of the county, Tawny Owls bred on four RSPB sites: Leighton Moss, Barrow Scout, Warton Crag and Challan Hall woodland. Three were at Crook O' Lune on 1 Jan, and singles were recorded at Stodday, Tower Lodge and Heysham.

MMWWT held two breeding pairs and both fledged two chicks, adding to the already healthy population of fledged owls at that site in 2019.

ELOC received 120 records in 2019 from every month of the year, mainly in ones and twos but Wilpshire had four on 11 Feb and Stocks Reservoir three on 5 May. Breeding was confirmed at a site south-east of Nelson and an adult was seen carrying prey at Ribchester on 21 July, and two pairs were also logged at Foulridge but breeding was surely much more widespread than this.

The Chorley area reported adults from three sites in March and breeding was confirmed on Anglezarke Moor, at Eccleston and at White Coppice. In the autumn/winter period mostly singles were noted at eight locations including Bretherton, Eccleston and Euxton.

On the Fylde, records were received from ten sites in the early part of the year and breeding was confirmed with the presence of juveniles by three nest sites in Fulwood, Mowbreck Hall and Salisbury Woodland.

Birds were reported from 15 sites in Merseyside but breeding was only confirmed at a handful, including a well-established territory in Kirkdale Cemetery in inner-city Liverpool.

Finally, in the Rossendale area three breeding records were received from a total of six monitored nestboxes. These three pairs fledged at least six young between them. Juveniles were also seen or heard at Mill End, Waterfoot and Deeply Vale. Waterfoot had at least seven birds calling on 2 Jan around the village, and adults were also heard at ten other sites in the area.

LITTLE OWL *Athene noctua*
Uncommon and widespread breeding resident.

Our smallest owl, but one that is seen quite regularly due to its use of historic sites and favoured perches.

The Fylde database received records from ten sites, with sightings throughout the year at a number of those. The most popular were the pairs at Marton Mere, Eagland Hill, Newton-with-Scales and Green Dick's Lane. The only records of juveniles came from a site near Medlar, where three were seen on 13 Aug.

In and around Rossendale, records came from eleven different sites. A pair was at Lee Quarry, the site which provided the most individual records, and a presumed juvenile was seen at The Hile on 16 July.

In the south-west, a pair was seen regularly at Lunt Meadows and was presumed to have bred. Two were at Coach Road Farm, Rainford on 28 Jun, one was calling at Walkden House Farm, Bicker-staffe on 11 Oct and one was seen along Cut Lane, Kirkby Moss on 30 Nov. Singles were at Red Cat Lane, Burscough on 29 July and at nearby Windmill Farm on 2 Nov, and the regular site in Banks produced a scattering of records throughout the year.

Carnforth Slag Tips provided the only confirmed breeding In the north, with two juveniles noted as part of the RSPB breeding bird survey. Sightings were also made at three other sites, Quernmore, Dockacres and Borwick.

Further inland, a pair was recorded at Belmont Reservoir, and ELOC received 104 records which was similar to 2018; 74% of these came from just five well-watched sites, four in east Lancashire and one on the western edge of the Ribble Valley, which produced three juveniles. Only one record came from Bowland, a single on 18 Sept.

In the Chorley area, one was at Withnell on 21 Feb, with another at Croston Finney on 20 March, and singles were in Runshaw Lane, Euxton on 24 May, and at. Bretherton Moss and a farm near Eccleston in July. One was recorded on Croston Moss in August, and then further records from the sites already noted were received later in the year.

LONG-EARED OWL *Asio otus*
Uncommon breeding resident.

It was a poor year in terms of records for the first of our stunning *Asio* owls, and the second year running that no records were received from the traditional winter roost at Marton Mere.

One pair in Rossendale was seen on a number of occasions and they raised three young. A pair nested in an old crow's nest at a confidential site in West Lancashire, where four eggs were laid, and two young hatched, but unfortunately the nest failed. Also in the west, one was seen near Skelmersdale on 3 April.

Near Belmont, at least one was seen regularly in suitable habitat during the first half of the year. Another separate individual was seen at an additional site close to Belmont on 14 Feb. ELOC received no records this year partly due to the sad passing of a long-term watcher who regularly submitted records for this species.

No autumn migrants were noted, and no winter roost records were received either.

SHORT-EARED OWL *Asio flammeus*
Scarce upland breeding bird; fairly common winter visitor.

A tale of two seasons for the second of our Asios with an impressive series of wintering records at both ends of the year but breeding records much reduced.

Nearly all records from the early part of the year were coastal, and most originated in the southwest and on the Fylde. However, the north fared better than in recent years with up to three seen regularly at Sunderland Point until 22 March, and three were recorded at Middleton Nature Reserve.

Short-eared Owls, East Lancashire, 24 June
(Craig Bell - taken under licence)

There was also at least one in the Leighton Moss area, with six records logged between 1 Jan and 16 April.

As in recent years, Lunt Meadows had the highest counts, with up to four there during the period until the last report on 9 March. Fourteen records came from Marshside, four from Hightown, and three from Ainsdale and Birkdale. Fylde records of singletons came from seven sites, but more than half of the sightings were at Lytham Moss.

Spring passage included one at Heysham Nature Reserve on 8 April, one at Garston Coastal Reserve on 28 March, and one hunting at Myerscough Quarry on 10 May.

On to breeding activity, 2019 was a very poor breeding year; only two pairs held territory on the United Utilities estate in Bowland with no evidence of successful breeding. This was probably linked to the Short-toed Field Vole population, which was found to be very low in a survey conducted at the end of the previous autumn. There was a similar story on the West Pennine Moors with no confirmed breeding and low vole numbers, but the significant loss of suitable habitat there to the large scale fires in 2018 will not have helped matters.

During the late summer-autumn period, one was at Heysham on 18 Oct, one on Mawdesley Moss on 9 Aug and one near Belmont from mid-August to mid-September. Pilling Lane Ends had one on 1 Oct, another was seen at Rossall Point on 17 Oct, and there were records from Starr Gate on 14 & 31 Oct. October also saw records at Knott End, Bodie Hill and Star Hills.

Lunt Meadows remained the premium wintering site of the region with regular reports of multiples, and seven seen there on 28 Dec. Champion Moor also held impressive numbers with three there on 19 Nov and at least six on 9 Dec. Further records came from Lytham Moss, Warton Bank and Marshside, but at a lower frequency than in the first winter period.

HOOPOE* *Upupa epops*
Rare passage migrant.

One was found at Charnock Richard after a local farmer posted an image of it on the Yarrow Valley Appreciation Group Facebook site. The bird was tracked down to Charter House Farm and was well watched by an appreciative procession of birders between 26 and 29 April.

KINGFISHER *Alcedo atthis*
Uncommon but widely-distributed breeding bird, mainly in the east; post-breeding dispersal westwards.

Kingfishers were widespread throughout both coastal and inland regions in both winter periods, with summer records more restricted to the inland waterways, as to be expected.

In the north, the LDBWS winter survey in January recorded them in four 10km squares including three in SD45. Leighton Moss provided regular sightings throughout the year, and particularly from the Eric Morecambe/Allen Pool complex in the winter months, while Heysham had singletons on 24 Aug, 19 Sept and 9-10 Nov.

Three adults were ringed at Brockholes and birds were seen there and on the bordering River Ribble throughout the year, with five recorded on 2 July.

In the south and west, Lunt Meadows had two March records, followed by an individual seen regularly between 27 Aug and 24 Oct. Seaforth also had one in autumn, between 10 Sept and mid-November. One territory was recorded at Carr Mill Dam, and a two kilometre stretch of canal in the Aintree Study Area logged at least one fledged juvenile. Records came from six sites around Liverpool, with two at Sefton Park on 10 Oct. Two juveniles were seen at Mere Sands Wood in May, and a pair fledged two chicks at MMWWT.

In Rossendale, three sites between Rawtenstall and Stubbins produced young, and a pair was seen nesting at Snig Hole, Helmshore

Chorley saw breeding records come in from Yarrow Valley Park, but sadly the pair at Cuerden Valley Park failed due to disturbance.

ELOC received 203 reports this year from across the recording area. The highest count was four at Towneley Park on 23 July, and a juvenile seen at Lower Towneley Scrape on 29 July was the only breeding record.

On the Fylde, Fairhaven Lake, Conder Green, Glasson Basin and Lytham Moss provided regular winter records. Individuals were seen in suitable habitat at a number of sites during the breeding season, but no confirmed breeding records were received.

Kingfishers were noted regularly on reservoirs in the West Pennine Moors (Belmont, Delph, Wards, Ornamental, Springs and Dingle), as well as the usual riparian sightings throughout the year indicating at least one local resident pair, which appeared to have been successful. A bizarre sighting was one perched on top of a road-sign beside the Belmont-Rivington Moor road on 14 Sept, possibly a dispersing bird mistaking the road for a watercourse.

GREAT SPOTTED WOODPECKER *Dendrocopos major*
Common and widespread breeding resident.

Records were widespread geographically and numerous throughout the year for our most visible woodpecker. Its distinctive territorial drumming was a welcome precursor to spring across the county from late January and early February.

In the north, the LDBWS January survey recorded birds in eight 10km squares with eleven in SD57. At Heysham there were four recoveries of individuals previously ringed at the site, and a pair held territory on the EDF land. The RSPB breeding bird survey found birds present in four locations, with three confirmed breeding records in Challan Hall woodland.

Records came in for over 40 sites in Rossendale , mostly singles or pairs, but several breeding records came from the Strongstry and Irwell Valley area. Six woodland sites around Burnley also held breeding pairs.

In the south and west, Seaforth had passage birds in April and October and then a regular wintering bird from November. Pairs were seen at Lunt Meadows, Carr Mill Dam and a nest was located at Kirkdale Cemetery. Most of the Liverpool parks had records during the year and a nest with young was found in Croxteth Park.

The species had a productive breeding year in Chorley with juveniles being seen in June at Great Knowley, Euxton, Brinscall and Heath Charnock.

ELOC had 208 records submitted from across the region, with the highest individual counts six at Foulridge and four at Low Moor and Marl Hill in August. There were 15 possible or probable breeding records, and eight of juveniles from Wycoller, Burnley Kilns, Forest Becks, Marl Hill and Chipping.

Just over 300 records from 81 sites were submitted to the Fylde database, which was slightly down on 2018. Breeding was confirmed by the presence of juveniles at Treales on 23 May and Pilling Lane on 10 June.

GREEN WOODPECKER *Picus viridis*
Fairly common though local breeding bird, mainly in the north and east.

After some isolated sightings from other areas in recent years, in 2019 all the records for this vocal species came from the north and east of the region, its presence often confirmed by its distinctive yaffling.

In the north, the LDBWS January survey picked them up in SD47 & 66, while the RSPB breeding bird survey found presence on Warton Crag. Numerous records from sites within the Warton-Silverdale-Gaitbarrows triangle throughout the year was testament to that area's importance for the species. Elsewhere, Heysham had one from the start of the year until 30 April, and individuals were also seen at Crook O'Lune, Whittington and near Lancaster.

Records came from over 20 sites in the Rossendale area, mostly of single calling individuals, but two pairs were noted cleaning out old nest holes in the Strongstry area on 1 April.

Only a single bird was recorded near Belmont, an individual seen in August.

The Chorley area's first record was one seen flying across Anglezarke Reservoir on 18 Aug. A juvenile was at Hoghton Bottoms on 23 Aug, and three were on Winter Hill on 23 Sept. In October, birds were noted at Lead Mines Clough, Holts Flat plantation, and George's Lane, Rivington. One was seen at Anglezarke Reservoir on 29 Nov.

ELOC received 60 records, slightly down on 2018 (76). These came from 30 different sites, and most related to single vocalising birds. Evidence of breeding was scarce this year, with a pair seen at Hapton Park on 25 March and an adult feeding young at Swinden Reservoir on 11 July.

KESTREL *Falco tinnunculus*
Fairly common breeding resident.

While this is still a fairly common bird throughout the county, the general trend would suggest a decline. Causes of the decline are unclear however one reason maybe the competition posed from other raptors; indeed predation by Buzzards has been previously observed in the West Pennine Moors area.

However, the Over Wyre area had a very successful year where 14 pairs were monitored in nest boxes and 71 eggs were laid from which 49 hatched and all 49 fledged thus giving the average of 5.1 eggs per nest with 3.5 fledging.

Elsewhere, breeding was confirmed on Merseyside at Seaforth Docks, Freshfield Dune Heath and Lunt Meadows. An adult carrying prey in the direction of Fazakerley in June was clear evidence of breeding and in the same month sightings at nearby Croxteth Park and Alt Meadows confirm the Kestrel's presence in this part of Liverpool and in the Docklands area.

In Rossendale breeding was evident at Spring Mill Reservoir. Elsewhere in east Lancashire breeding was scarce with possible sites at Grimsargh and Foulridge but the 369 records from east Lancashire was significantly down on the 627 received in 2018.

In north and central Lancashire a pair was recorded at Warton Crag and further evidence of breeding was seen on 11 July with a family party of six seen at Brockholes. In the Chorley area breeding was evident at Croston Moss and in the West Pennine Moors at Rivington, Belmont and Withnell with both young and family parties seen throughout July and August.

Post-breeding dispersal was evident on the Ribble Estuary where nine birds were recorded at Freckleton Naze Point on 30 July, 21 were counted on the Ribble August WeBS count and five at Alston Reservoirs on 30 September.

The only migration record was a bird flying north north-west at Heysham on 8 March.

MERLIN *Falco columbarius*
Scarce breeding bird, fairly common winter visitor.

This year was another mixed one for this species on the United Utilities estate, where nine pairs set up territory but only six went on to breed, five of them successfully fledging chicks. This compares to five pairs in 2018 and nine pairs in 2017. It is thought that the reason that some of the pairs failed to nest was due to a large amount of heather having been killed by a combination of weather and Heather Beetle in 2018, so it will be interesting to see how this species fares in subsequent years.

On the West Pennine Moors a pair were seen in suitable habitat in the breeding season but no definite territory was found.

Birds were recorded at Bretherton Eyes and Withnell Fold during January with one at Croston Moss on 14 April and up to two in first winter period in the West Pennine Moors. Typically birds have left the wintering area by March but a late spring record at Marshside on 19 April was notable.

East Lancashire had an increase of 55 reports compared to the 41 received in 2018. Distribution of records was more dispersed compared with last year with records received from across the area.

A female hunting by the Heliport at Heysham was a migrating bird and a bird heading north at Clough Bottom Reservoir, Rossendale on 31 March was no doubt moving to its breeding ground. Autumn migration was evident with a Merlin at Starr Gate, Blackpool on 10 Oct and a male along the south wall at Heysham on 22 Nov. Sightings in October came from Bretherton Eyes, two on 12 Oct at Croston Finney and up to two were again seen in the West Pennine Moors in the second period of winter.

It is very difficult to estimate the number of wintering birds in the county, however, at least seven were recorded on the Ribble Marshes along with four at Marshside and Crossens on 30 Dec and three at Warton Bank on 29 Dec. Together with singles reported around Carnforth Marsh, Glasson Marsh, Aldcliffe, Pilling Lane Ends, Brockholes and throughout the south-west mosslands, the population is still estimated to be 75.

HOBBY *Falco subbuteo*
Scarce breeding bird and uncommon passage migrant.

The first on 1 May at Brockholes was followed by an adult migrant in-off the sea at Heysham Head on 10 May.

The wide-ranging and secretive behaviour of the Hobby makes assigning breeding evidence difficult but the two juveniles recorded at Brockholes again confirmed breeding in this area of the Ribble Valley.

An adult and two juveniles together at a site near Eccleston must also represent confirmation of local breeding.

Hobbies were seen regularly hawking for insects over the Bowland Fells and the West Pennine Moors, and while they must be breeding in the very near vicinity, no proof was found of breeding locally. Regular sightings were also recorded at Lunt Meadows and Leighton Moss with perhaps the same bird reported in the Crook o' Lune area. Given the frequency of reports it would also suggest there are also breeding territories in these areas.

Two first-summer birds were seen hunting on Slater Fell, Forest of Bowland on 2 July and another first-summer bird covered Little Singleton, Marton Mere and Skippool Creek on the Fylde in August.

PEREGRINE *Falco peregrinus*
Scarce breeder, uncommon winter visitor.

The general trend in the county over the previous years has been that the number of breeding pairs in rural areas is declining while those in urban settings are increasing.

This year was another very disappointing year for this species in Bowland. Only a single pair successfully fledged chicks on the Bowland SSSI, and yet again, no pairs were found to have laid eggs on any of the private shooting estates. Breeding was confirmed at a site in Rossendale and one site on the West Pennine Moors was occupied by a territorial pair but breeding was unsuccessful.

Away from the rural areas the results were more favourable: breeding was confirmed on Merseyside with the pair on the Anglican Cathedral fledging at least two young, the Tobacco Warehouse pair fledged three and at least one fledged from the pair at Seaforth. On 13 Feb a pair were also seen on territory at St Chad's Church, Kirkby. Further success was recorded at a confidential site in St Helens, Fleetwood Ferry and St. Walburge's Church Preston.

The pair which had bred regularly in Chorley town centre decided to relocate to a site in Wigan, where apparently they had a successful breeding season.

No information was received concerning nesting at Heysham Power Station but birds were certainly on territory. Interestingly, a juvenile was seen on a pylon on the 5 and 10 July.

Further sightings of juvenile birds were evident at Conder Green where three juveniles and two adults were seen on the 19 Aug.

An interesting behavioural observation was made at Preston Dock on 20 July where a male Peregrine caught a Common Tern only then to drop the tern. The entire colony of Terns successfully chased off the Peregrine and the tern survived.

Most winter records were single- or double-figure counts but it would be interesting to know how the county population changes in winter with non-breeding birds migrating. Most Peregrines do not start breeding until they are two or more years of age and therefore newly-independent young birds have a tendency to move.

RING-NECKED PARAKEET *Psittacula krameri*
Rare feral breeder; fairly frequent escape.

South Liverpool, and in particular Sefton Park, remains the stronghold for this gregarious and noisy species. Several double-figure counts came from that site during the period, with the highest being 55 on 27 Jan. There were also regular reports from nearby Princes Park, Allerton, Greenbank Park and Calderstones Park.

In the Chorley area, two were seen flying towards Astley Village on 20 Jan, two were in the Whittle-le-Woods area most of the year, and two were seen in Astley Park on 15 Aug. Two were at Shaw Hill Golf Course on 23 Sept, and four flew over Buckshaw Avenue towards there on 25 Oct. The highest count was a group of eight seen at Whittle on 29 Dec.

Stanley Park was the source of the majority of records In the Fylde recording area, with up to six there throughout the year. Smaller numbers were seen at the long-standing site, Lytham Crematorium, and a singleton was at Freckleton Naze Point on 14 Nov. The majority of records in Preston came from Haslam Park, where up to five were seen regularly throughout the year and nest-building was noted.

In the north of the county, one was at Leighton Moss on 5 Jan, while East Lancashire saw a slight increase in records with 18 reports, the highest, a count of six together at Barrowford.

GREAT GREY SHRIKE *Lanius excubitor*
Scarce winter visitor and passage migrant.

The bird at Leighton Moss in 2018 continued to put in the occasional appearance up until 5 March. What could possibly have been the same bird was seen on Warton Crag on the 29th.

On 9 April, one was found at the top Dean Black Brook on Wheelton Moor where it remained until the 17th.

The only record of the autumn/second winter period was of one on Anglezarke Moor above Lead Mines Clough on 8 & 9 Nov, only a mile from the spring location on Wheelton Moor.

JAY *Garrulus glandarius*
Common resident. Occasional irruptions, some winter dispersal.

The species remains common and widespread throughout the county, being most frequently reported in the Silverdale, Preston and Chorley areas. Maximum counts rarely exceed four individuals. In early January, counts of five were reported from Mere Sands Wood and a feeding station at Strongstry, Rossendale. Five were also noted at Ormskirk on 15 March. Jays were equal nineteenth in the Chorley winter garden survey, down on previous years due to the good acorn crop and, hence, reduced reliance on garden feeders.

Spring vis-mig at Middleton produced seven north on 6 April and odd birds turned up at unusual places such as Freckleton Marsh on the 8th.

There were few confirmed breeding reports – single pairs bred at Freshfield Dune Heath, MMWWT and Challan Hall, Silverdale, as well as a pair fledging young at Jackhouse, Oswaldtwistle and Siddows, Clitheroe. Four pairs were noted around Foulridge with other pairs at Melling (Lune Valley), Lancaster, Ormskirk, Aintree (two) and Wayoh Reservoir. Jays were reported from 33 10km squares during May and June. In July, six were seen at Childwall Woods, south Liverpool, at least five were mobile around Roby Mill and juveniles were seen at Sefton Park in Liverpool.

Autumn, and most notably around mid-October is generally when we get the most records as birds disperse and become really visible. Most larger counts came in this period such as six at Marl Hill, Bowland on 2 Oct, five at Haslingden Grane on the 5th and a total of seven on migration over Middleton on the 12th when there were also flocks totalling twelve birds at Clowbridge Reservoir. Six were at Brindle on the 17th and five at Heysham on the 25th. Eleven Jays were collecting acorns at Cuerden Valley Park during this time.

MAGPIE *Pica pica*
Abundant resident.

In the first winter period there were some significant gatherings of Magpies, the largest of which were in the Liverpool area. Throughout January, up to 126 came into roost at Rimrose Valley and on the 27th, 150 were at a roost in Childwall Woods. Other large roost counts included 72 at Southport Marine Lake on 3 Jan, 40 at Fairhaven on the 2nd, 71 at Devonshire Rock Gardens, Blackpool on the 11th and 67 at Lowerhouse Lodge, Burnley on the 31st. At least 40 were roosting at Buckshaw Village on 5 Feb and 68 were at Speke Alder Woods on 17 March. The CDNHS winter garden bird survey saw this species hold on to its sixth place.

Breeding was widespread and under-reported as usual. Monitored sites reported increases such as MMWWT with eight pairs and five pairs at both Lunt Meadows and Freshfield Dune Heath. There were six nests at Kirkdale Cemetery and eleven in a study area in Aintree.

There wasn't much evidence of autumn movements though 34 at Seaforth on 18 Oct probably included migrants. A roost at Rimrose Valley had 63 on 8 Oct rising to 101 by the 15th with similar numbers remaining through to the end of the month.

Gamekeepers in the West Pennine Moors reported trapping or shooting 576 Magpies during the year, nearly half of the number taken in 2018. The large corvid roost at Egerton was estimated to have 480 – 540 Magpies on 20 Dec. Forty-seven were roosting at Cuerden Valley Park in December, and flocks of up to 20 were at Childwall Woods and Knowsley Safari Park.

JACKDAW *Corvus monedula*
Common breeding resident, some autumn movement.

Jackdaws seem to be doing very well across the county, reported from every 10km square during the year. The Lancaster January Survey clocked up a total of 3149 from nine 10km squares, similar to last year. Up to 300 birds were regularly reported in the Warton Crag/Keer Estuary/Eric Morecambe complex throughout the year.

The largest first winter period counts came from the Stocks Reservoir roost that held 1900 birds on 20 Jan, dropping to 1300 by 1 Feb and 800 by the end of March. Another large roost was near Conder Green with 1800 at Ashton Hall on 20 Jan. Other flocks in excess of 300 birds were reported at Southport Marine Lake (405 on 3 Jan), Childwall Woods (500 on 27 Jan) and Formby (350 on 30 Jan).

Breeding populations were reported to be on the increase around Heysham and Rishton and the colony at Lunt village was described as thriving. In South Liverpool, the species is still rather localised but its range is expanding and numbers increasing. Fourteen pairs bred at MMWWT whilst in Over Wyre, the 44 pairs that were monitored (the vast majority in nest boxes) laid 208 eggs with 117 hatched and 98 fledged. Up to 50 birds regularly fed in and around the Belmont gull colony and were largely tolerated unlike other members of the corvid family. Jackdaws were observed taking emerging dragonflies at Middleton NR in May.

Autumn brought some large aggregations and movements across the region. At Clowbridge Reservoir, there were up to 400 in late September rising to 700 on 6 Oct and 1500 on the 16th. There were 600 at Sawley on 7 Nov and 300 in Burnley on the 11th. Coastal watchpoints saw the usual southwards passage peaking in October. Heysham recorded a total of 535 with a peak of 99 on 23 Oct whilst Seaforth recorded peaks of 870 on the 18th and 660 on the 20th. Observers at Fleetwood Marsh recorded a peak of 482 on 28 Oct and the peak at Fairhaven was of 400 on the 17th.

Winter roosts in the West Pennine Moors were largely devoid of Jackdaws save for 300 at Upper Rivington Reservoir on 14 Oct and 400 at Egerton in December. 350 were at Eccleston on 21 Nov and a similar number were counted into roost at Cuerden Valley Park the same month. The roost at Ashton Hall built from 600 in November to 900 by December. In December, there were also three figure counts from Pilling Lane Ends, Todderstaffe Hall, Waterfoot, Lytham and Eccleston.

ROOK *Corvus frugilegus*
Common resident.

Rook is a species that, although widespread, can be very localised, rarely making long foraging flights unlike other corvids. For instance, contrast records from Haslingden Grane, where the species is rare and three on 14 May was notable, to the number of rookeries in the Rossendale area only a couple of miles away. Similarly, birds are scarce in Hyndburn although small numbers were regularly seen at Jackhouse, Oswaldtwistle with 33 in November a significant high.

The rookery census in the Chorley region found a small increase to 351 occupied nests including a new rookery at Bretherton with 20. More detailed counts from regularly-monitored rookeries are tabulated below but none were received from the Lancaster/Lune Valley area. A small number of nests were reported in the Knowsley region and adults with juveniles were seen on Kirkby Moss and around Rainford in June.

Rookery counts

Chorley & West Pennine Moors	Nests
Astley Park	0
A49 Euxton	36
Howard Arms, Whittle Springs	16
Rawlinson La, Heath Charnock	0
Railway Road, Adlington	37
Prospect House, Wheelton	71
Lower Wheelton	4
Red Cat, Wheelton	24
St Chad's Wheelton	2
Croston Bowling Green	68
Croston Westhead Road	9
North Road, Bretherton	20
Wild Bottoms Wood, Hoghton	Occupied
Town House Farm, Brindle	38
Brindle Village	2
Buckshaw Village	24
Turton/Edgworth (2 rookeries)	112
East Lancashire	
Slaidburn	30
Longridge Fell	33
Nelson Victoria Park	15
Horrocksford	10
Whalley Corn Mills	19
Brungerley Bridge	10
Rossendale	
Crawshawbooth	32
Water	26
Bacup town centre	17
Farmer's Glory	14
Acre	12
Rook Hill	41
Broadclough	35
Lumb	14
Rawtenstall town centre	3

SW Lancs & Merseyside	Nests
Bank Brow, Roby Mill	47
Maghull	15
Kirkdale Cemetery	7
Knowsley Ind. Park	12
Fylde	
Top Plantation, Eagland Hill	51
Skippool	50
Poulton-le-Fylde (4 sites)	31
Catforth (2)	16
Crossmoor	4
Singleton Lodge	67
Little Poulton	46
Singleton, Church Road	36
Singleton Church	13
Little Singleton (2)	14
St Annes, Queensway	114
Lytham Hall	102
St Annes, Hey Houses Lane	92
Lytham, Green Drive	32
Mythop	126
Westby	40
Wrea Green (2)	33
Bryning	26
Wesham	82
Kirkham Railway Station	58
Newton-with-Scales, Dobbies	37
Churchtown	139
Myerscough College	83
St Michael's on Wyre, A586	63
Catterall Hall	52
St Michael's on Wyre, Hall Lane	42

Cuerden Valley Park had around 250 going to roost during both winter periods. The corvid roost at Ashton Hall near Conder Green had the year's biggest count of 350 on 20 Jan and 280 were feeding at Cockerham on 6 Feb. In east Lancashire the peak count was of 150 at Newton-in-Bowland on 24 Jan.

During autumn passage small numbers were recorded flying high over Heysham such as 27 on 19 Oct. Unusually, a total of five migrants were seen over Belmont on three occasions from late October. The second winter period highs were of 250 at the Eric Morecambe complex on 5 Nov, 120 at MMWWT on the 10th and 107 at Ashton Hall in December

A white bird was reported near Abbey Village in early July.

CARRION CROW *Corvus corone*
Common breeding bird. Some southward movement in October.

This common breeding bird was unsurprisingly reported from every 10km square in virtually every month over the course of the year. There were at least 200 reports of flocks in excess of 20; often far more. The roost sites in the WPM that once held very large numbers of crows were occupied by smaller numbers: Delph Plantations had 200 – 250 in both winter periods, Roddlesworth Plantations held 100 in January and Upper Rivington had 100 in January and 150 in October. Away from here, the highest counts of the year were of 160 at Mitton/Winkley in December, 150 at Eagland Hill in January and 100 at Appley Bridge in February. Flocks of 30-50 were seen in Sefton Park, Liverpool during the latter half of the year, many being fed by the public. Seventy were seen gathering on the sandbanks at Oglet before going to roost in Hale, Cheshire.

In the Over Wyre area, seven nests were monitored, 27 eggs laid, from which 19 eggs hatched and 18 young fledged. A total of 54 were counted in two adjacent BBS squares in the Brindle area in April. MMWWT had five pairs breeding and two pairs bred at both Freshfield Dune Heath and Lunt Meadows. One pair bred on the BT Transmitter on Winter Hill.

Some passage was noted in the autumn with Seaforth recording 40 south on 18 Oct, nine past Rossall on the 2nd, 17 over Belmont on the 17th and a total of 202 over Heysham (peak of 55 on the 28th).

Gamekeepers in the West Pennine Moors reported shooting/trapping a total of 427 Carrion Crows in 2019. Two or three territorial pairs at Belmont Reservoir were removed for the benefit breeding waders, gulls and wildfowl. A few hundred were also taken from Upper Hindburn and Roeburndale.

HOODED CROW *Corvus cornix*
Scarce winter visitor or early spring passage migrant; has bred with Carrion Crow.

It is not inconceivable that the following records all relate to the same individual. A bird was reported regularly at Todderstaffe Hall, Poulton-le-Fylde between 13 Feb and 14 April during which period what was probably a different bird was seen at Cocker's Dyke, Pilling on 10 April. One reported at Ainsdale NNR on 14 & 15 April could possibly relate to the Fylde individual, and subsequently was at Freshfield Dune Heath on the 28th and at Cabin Hill NNR on 3 May. Just to add more evidence to this theory of a single roving individual, a bird was seen at Peel on 4 May, Todderstaffe Hall on the 5th, Marshside on the 8th and Rossall Point on the 16th. A hoodie was seen again south of the Ribble over the Municipal Golf Course, Southport on 24 May. There was a gap in records until one was seen at Wesham on 24 June then again two months later on 30 & 31 Aug.

The only record from later in the year was of a hybrid bird at Fazakerley on 25 – 26 Nov.

RAVEN *Corvus corax*
Uncommon resident.

Although, predictably, the larger counts tend to come from upland areas, there were plenty of records from the west of the county. For instance, ones and twos were reported regularly throughout the year on the Fylde with four or more being seen on several occasions. That said, a winter roost in the east of the county contained up to 70 birds in November and up to 39 were roosting in pylons near

Clowbridge Reservoir during September. Eleven were roosting at Cuerden Valley Park in January and 14 were seen leaving a roost at Wymott on 2 Dec.

Two pairs successfully fledged young in Bowland but this level of activity was far below what would be expected in such an area. Two pairs were also successful in the West Pennine Moors. Contrast that with at least six pairs in the Rossendale Valley including one on a Rawtenstall mill. Ravens also probably bred at Nelson and on a pylon at Rishton as well as the regular site at Warton Crag. Young birds were seen at Garston in May and birds were regular at Seaforth throughout the year, the first juvenile seen on 28 May. The largest group in the West Pennine Moors was 14 near Belmont on 1 Aug.

In October, 15 congregated on a carcass north of Ballam and ten were over the Ribble marshes the following day. Four birds moved south over Heysham on 19 Oct.

WAXWING *Bombycilla garrulus*
Fairly common but irregular winter visitor.

There continued to be a thin spread of Waxwing records in the early part of the year as the small number of birds involved moved around the region. The largest flock was of up to 15 on 4-7 Jan near Stanley Road, Bootle.

Up to two remained from 2018 at the Council offices, Chorley to 5 Jan, and two were at Adlington on the 2nd and again from the 12th to the 15th. Singles were in Burnley on 1 Jan and Accrington on the 3rd, three at Colne on 2 Jan and two again in Burnley on 19-20 Jan. Two were found along the A565 at Banks also on 19-20 Jan.

In Lancaster, a single bird was present on 3-5 Jan with eight there for one day on the 9th and then two were at Scotforth from 11-20 Feb.

Four appeared in Wesham on 1 April, increasing to eight the following day which remained to the 4th.

In the second winter period there were even fewer records but not a complete blank. Seven were reported at Euxton on 1 Nov, one at Morecambe on the 8th, three at Fleetwood on the 18th and one at Barrow, Clitheroe the same day. The last reported sighting was of two at Lune Road, Lancaster on 7 Dec.

COAL TIT *Periparus ater*
Common breeding bird. Some irruptive movements in autumn.

The Coal Tit remains a common and widespread member of the county's avifauna. Densities are much higher in the conifer plantations, of course, but in other rural and suburban areas a very rough estimate shows there is probably around one pair of Coal Tits for every five pairs of Blue Tits. A February ringing session near Bashall Eaves near a conifer plantation processed 45 individuals of which 36 were juveniles; a similar number of Blue Tits were caught. The Lancaster January Survey recorded 114 individuals, down on 2018 whereas the Chorley Winter Garden Survey showed them to be once again the ninth commonest visitor.

Breeding status recording on BirdTrack showed evidence from at least 40 sites across the county. In addition, approximately 20 singing males were recorded along Haslingden Grane on 6 April and eight were singing in plantations at Clowbridge Reservoir on 5 May. There was a small number of breeding records in and around Blackpool with adults feeding young on 17 May at Cottam. A juvenile was seen at Gawthorpe Hall, Padiham on 26 May but most fledglings were starting to be seen from mid-June. MMWWT recorded six pairs on the reserve while a study area in Aintree had two pairs. Small numbers were present in woods and parks in south Liverpool and Knowsley.

There was barely any noticeable autumn passage with just seven birds ringed at Heysham, Regular vis mig at Belmont had very few with a peak of seven on 1 Oct. Numbers along Haslingden Grane reached in excess of 50 on 13 Oct but the only other places to regularly record double figures were around Silverdale with a maximum of 18 at Challan Hall on 31 Dec.

MARSH TIT* *Poecile palustris*
Fairly common breeder in the north of the county. Virtually absent south of the Ribble and in the Fylde.

Of the 476 reports received (mostly from BirdTrack) 454 came from SD47 – Leighton Moss and Silverdale area. Of these, 15 were of six or more, the only double-figure count being 20 around Leighton Moss on 12 Sept. Twelve pairs bred at Challan Hall. Along the Lune Valley reports were received of one or two birds from Broomfield, Farleton, Arkholme, Tatham, Melling and Wrayton Wood.

The outstanding record was of one at feeders at Crawshawbooth on 28 July (Craig Bell) and subsequently on several occasions to the end of the year. This was only the sixth record in Rossendale and the first for 18 years.

WILLOW TIT* *Poecile montana*
Scarce breeder in the birch copses of the south-west. Very rare elsewhere.

The most often reported bird was the one that turned up at MMWWT on 18 Aug and continued to be seen every two or three days into 2020; there had been singles there in the first winter period on 31 Jan and 14 Feb. Nearby Mere Sands Wood had regular sightings of single birds throughout the year, including late spring but with no evidence of breeding.

A promising situation developed at Cuerden Valley Park where up to three regularly visited the feeding station near Kem Mill and a pair nested in a specially developed nest box hatching six young. The most northerly records were at Preston Junction on 23 & 27 Feb and Brockholes on 6 Feb.

Around Chorley, there were regular records from Hic Bibi, Whittle Bottoms and Charnock Richard while the Willow Tit survey of several tetrads in the area resulted in additional records from Belmont, Common Bank, Crosse Hall and Yarrow Valley Park. A bird was noted at Wymott on 29 July and again in August and October.

Slightly further south, there were reports of birds from Roby Mill (with two on 13 April) and Beacon Country Park with possibly three birds present on 14 Feb.

Most site records came from the area south of Skelmersdale to Kirkby, Rainford and St Helens. In the spring, records were received from Carr Mill Dam, Stanley Bank LNR, Siding Lane LNR (3), Havannah Flashes, Callen's Farm (2), Moss Farm (Old Coach Road), Ferny Knoll Bog (2), Holland Moss and Kirkby Moss. Two pairs bred at Carr Mill Dam and another along the Goyt Burn.

As detailed in last year's Lancashire Bird Report, the Willow Tit survey, which is currently at the midway point, has so far revealed that the breeding population of the species in the county is similar to that of ten years ago, bucking the national steep downward decline. Perhaps this is due to the more stable habitat in the locations it has retreated to, the series of small local nature reserves that hold many of the breeding pairs and the local management of the habitat that is being championed here and in the neighbouring mosslands and flashes of Greater Manchester.

Autumn records included five at Stanley Bank LNR and singletons from six locations along the St Helens/Sankey Canal, while later in the year there were reports from Bold, Penkford Bridge, Moss Farm and on feeders at Rainford.

BLUE TIT *Cyanistes caeruleus*
Abundant breeding resident.

Blue Tits seemed to do well in 2019 and though there is some evidence of slightly reduced numbers using nestboxes, productivity was quite good. In the Over Wyre area 94 nests were monitored in which 922 eggs were laid, an average of 5.3 young hatched and 4.9 fledged per pair. In the second year of a nestbox scheme at Gawthorpe Hall, Padiham, 14 boxes that had hatched young had an average of 8.6 young per box. A total of 57 young were in Cuerden Valley Park nestboxes. Other well-monitored sites reported the following number of pairs: MMWWT 31, Lunt Meadows three, Aintree eleven, Kirkdale Cemetery six, Bowland Wild Boar Park four occupied boxes and Challan Hall, Silverdale 25 pairs.

In the Chorley winter garden bird survey, the species remained the second most commonly recorded. Numbers were down in the Lancaster January survey to 582. Most larger counts were from feeding sites and regular perambulatory monitoring of sites such as 33 recorded at Challan Hall on 2 Jan, 30 on a walk through Staghills Wood, Rossendale on the 6th and 26 at Brockholes NR on the 3rd.

Fewer birds were ringed at Heysham in October as there was no sign of any irruptive behaviour there.

In the second winter period, a daily count of up to 45 was recorded at a feeder/ringing site at Challan Hall, Silverdale.

GREAT TIT *Parus major*
Abundant breeding resident.

There were no significant changes in the abundance of this very common bird although the Chorley winter garden bird survey has shown a decline in recent years – down to the 9th commonest species. The Lancaster January survey showed numbers much lower than in the previous year (a total of 293) although in some part this was due to lack of coverage in certain areas. Twenty were recorded in Staghills Wood on 6 Jan and 15-20 were regularly recorded around Leighton Moss, Salwick, Jackhouse (Oswaldtwistle) and Brockholes.

However the species seemed to fare well in the breeding season. In the Over Wyre area, from the 64 nests monitored, 502 eggs were laid, of which 310 hatched and 287 young fledged averaging 4.5 fledged per pair. At Gawthorpe Hall, more boxes were occupied than by Blue Tits; 18 boxes had a total of 130 well-developed young averaging a very healthy 7.2 per box. A total of 33 young was counted in nestboxes in Cuerden Valley Park.

As with Blue Tit, this species breeds widely but is generally poorly recorded. However, the strident song of a Great Tit means that breeding evidence from BirdTrack was far more regularly recorded for Blue Tit. Other regularly-monitored sites reported similar numbers to 2018. There were five occupied boxes at Bowland Wild Boar Park, Challan Hall had 19 pairs, MMWWT had eleven pairs and one pair bred at Lunt Meadows. The study area in Aintree recorded eleven territories once again and similarly, five pairs were at Kirkdale Cemetery.

Ringing at Heysham processed 175 new birds which was 50% up on the average of the past five years. Three of the recaptures there were from 2014.

No substantial movement was noted in the autumn and the only counts exceeding 15 in the second winter period were from Crosby (32 on 2 Nov), Scorton Lake (19 on 1 Dec) and Chapel Hill, Rossendale (25 on 15 Dec).

BEARDED TIT *Panurus biarmicus*
Rare breeding resident.

The population at Leighton Moss was estimated to be 30 pairs in 2019 based on sightings and retraps of 27 adult males and 14 adult females, slightly up on recent years but there was a reduced nest-monitoring and ringing effort. There was also probably just one pair on Barrow Scout. Birds were seen in all months with the use of grit trays providing a focal point for the many visitors. There were several counts of 20 with the largest numbers consistently from late September through to November. High-flying eruptive-like behaviour was recorded on several days in October but all returned into the reedbed. Survival rate was estimated to be around 60% for adults and juveniles which was excellent.

The big news this year, however, was of two pairs breeding at MMWWT after eight birds turned up on 21 Feb – possibly from the twelve birds that had previously been at Lunt Meadows from 2018 and last reported there on 19 Feb. Birds were seen in all subsequent months bar August with maxima of six in October and eight in late November.

Sightings were not confined to these sites, however. One was near Heysham on 21 Feb and two were reported in a reedbed north of Burglar's Alley, Fleetwood on 27 Feb and one was seen at Marton Mere on 16 April.

SKYLARK *Alauda arvensis*
Resident breeder, passage migrant and winter visitor.

Numbers were down in the early part of the year compared with 2018 when 350-450 were being reported. Reasonable numbers of birds overwintered around Southport including 100 at Marshside on 14 Jan and some had begun singing by 7 Feb. Twenty were reported at Bolton Le Sands on Jan 1, 35 at Oglet the same day and six were spotted flying east at Roby Mill on 23 Jan.

172 reports were received this year from across the ELOC recording area, the earliest being 6 Feb at Jackhouse but very few came from Heysham with 13 reports in ones or twos between 11 Feb and 8 April.

Relatively few early reports were received across Rossendale and these were mainly lower than ten, although 20 were at Harden Moor on 18 April.

In the Fylde 100 were reported from Bradshaw Lane Head on 2 Jan, 170 were at Birk's Farm on 24 Jan with 30 at New Ridge Farm, Pilling the same day, 150 on Warton Marsh on 28 Jan, 80 on Lytham Moss on 2 Feb and 150 at Out Rawcliffe on 6 Feb. Smaller numbers (peak 70 at Freckleton) were reported for the remainder of February and overall winter numbers were well down on 2018.

Elsewhere, 60 were on Colloway Marsh on 10 Feb, 109 flew over Knott End between 11 Feb and 12 May and low numbers were seen at Brockholes between 16 Feb and 7 July. Further south a flock of 100 was at Bretherton Eyes on 2 Feb.

In the West Pennine Moors the Winter Hill Breeding Bird Survey found approximately 75 breeding pairs over the area burnt in 2018. Over 50 were in song there by 21 Feb and of note was a higher density (approx. 19 birds/km2) in the 2018 burn areas compared with the adjacent unburnt area (approx. 4 birds/km2). Three singing birds were reported on in-bye land at Clough House Farm, Turton in May with a further 17 on adjacent moorland. Approximately ten pairs breed around Belmont Reservoir annually.

Breeding birds were reported in all areas of the county, including 78 pairs at Hesketh Out Marsh, 54 at MMWWT, 51 at Marshside and 25 at The Hile in Rossendale.

Autumn passage movements were unspectacular; 150 at Skitham on 29 Sept which was the last of the larger movements for the year in that area, 50 were at Pilling Marsh on 23 Oct and Warton Bank on the 28th and 368 Flew over Knott End between 7 Sept and 29 Nov, while Heysham had a modest 76 birds between 16 Sept and 31 Oct with a peak of twelve on 29 Oct. Up to 30 were on Pendle Hill on 20-23 Sept, 21 at Croston Finney on 21 Oct increased to 100 by 10 Nov and 50 at Bretherton Eyes on 16 Nov. The largest counts on Merseyside were 60 at Seaforth on 5 Oct with 204 there on the 14th, 60 at Oglet on 14 Nov and 30 at Lunt Meadows on 7 Oct. There were only ten reports in Rossendale from August to the end of the year, none of more than 7 birds

SAND MARTIN *Riparia riparia*
Common breeding bird and passage migrant.

Sand Martin, Fouldridge Reservoir, April (Gary Waddington)

The first were at Leighton Moss on 25 Feb. and the first double-figure report ten at Brockholes on 3 March. Over the following weeks double-figure reports were received from Alston Wetland, Cuerden Valley, Croston Twin Lakes, Preesall, Altham, Foulridge, Dean Clough Stocks and Reservoirs, Carr Mill Dam, Brockholes and MMWWT.

After the first three-figure count at Leighton Moss on 29 March 100 or more were seen throughout the county in spring including at least 800 at Foulridge Reservoirs on 27 April.

Movements slowed during May and records were scarce away from breeding sites in June. Breeding was confirmed across most parts of the county except Merseyside. No information was received from the county's largest colony on the Lune around Arkholme, but sizeable counts of nest-holes included 249 on the Calder at Altham, 234 at Lightfoot Green and 100 on the Ribble at Potter Ford House, with other colonies at Cockerham Quarry, Ightenhill Bridge, Gawthorpe, Ewood Bridge, Brierfield, Townsendfold, Hoghton Bottoms, Brockholes and Alston Wetland.

There were few reports of significant numbers of autumn migrants but they included 150 at the Eric Morecambe complex on 15 July, with 70 there on the 28th and 75 at Glasson on 23 Aug. The last was at Belmont on 30 Sept.

SWALLOW *Hirundo rustica*
Abundant breeding bird and passage migrant.

The earliest reports were a 'probable' at Aldcliffe on 1 March and definites on the 22nd at MMWWT and Alston Wetlands and Brockholes on the 25th. Over the next few days singles were seen around Fleetwood, Eagland Hill, Stalmine, Holden Wood Reservoir and Bretherton while Southport had its first on 8 April.

Thirty at Foulridge Reservoirs on 27 March was the first double-digit count but widespread small numbers were reported in early April with larger counts including 300 at Seaforth on 17 April, 41 at Blackpool on the 19th and 57 at Cocker's Dyke on the 30th. Further spring movements in early May included 173 at Blackpool on the 1st, 65 at Leighton Moss on the 3rd, 200 at Lunt Meadows and 70 at Belmont on the 9th. 377 were reported from Heysham between 1 April and 24 May with a peak of 40 on 11 May.

Typically, there were few significant congregations during June and July, the largest being 35 at Lawson Road, Fleetwood on 7 July and 80 in the Grane area on the 12th. Nor were there any large concentrations of breeding birds, although nesting was extremely widespread throughout the county. The largest breeding groups were 15 pairs adjacent to Belmont Reservoir and twelve in stables next to Freshfield Dune Heath.

Autumn passage was well underway by mid-August with 786 at Bank End the largest count that month and other three-figure counts including 100+ at Withnell Fold and 160 per hour at Belmont on the 16th. The movement accelerated during September right across the county, notably 700 at Charnock Richard on the 6th, 350 at Freckleton Naze and 300 at Cuerden Valley Park on the 7th, 300 at Calderfoot on the 13th, 185 at Belmont on the 14th, 550 at Winmarleigh on the 15th and 220 at Seaforth on the 21st

Numbers reduced rapidly, especially in the north of the county, in October and the only notable counts were 50+ at Lunt Meadows on the 2nd and 4th. The last of the year were singles at Leighton Moss and Cabus on 4 Dec.

HOUSE MARTIN *Delichon urbicum*
Common breeding bird and passage migrant.

The earliest was at Middleton NR on 28 March was followed by MMWWT on 1 April, Altham on the 4th and Chorley on the 7th. Widespread reports of migrants then ensued but most reports were of single figures, exceptions being 200 at Lunt Meadows on 9 May when 50 were also at Foulridge Reservoirs – with 70 there on the 27th and 40 at Pilling on 30 May. The first reports of birds on breeding territories came from Birkdale on 2 May and Clitheroe on the 12th.

Breeding took place throughout the county from Garston in south Liverpool to Tatham in the north-east, but no reports of nesting were received from Rossendale. Birds seen away from breeding sites in June, including 30 at Staining on the 19th, and early July were probably feeding movements, but passage got underway later in July with, for example, 41 at Whalley on 4 July, 30 in the Langdon Valley on the 7th and 60 at Alston Wetland on the 27th. Large August movements included 80 at Seaforth on the 3rd with 120 there on the 16th and 60 on the 28th, 100 over Winter Hill and 125 in Blackpool on the 8th, 150 at Euxton and 200 at White Coppice on the 25th; while September peaks included 150 at Dean Clough on the 2nd, 140 at Lower Wheathead on the 8th, 180 at Seaforth on the 14th with 60 there the next day, and 47 at Jackhouse Reservoir on the 21st.

In Rossendale large flocks of 150 to 200 birds were seen at Cribden Clough, Oakenwood and Reedsholme, many perching on wires in late July and early August, thereafter small numbers were seen until the last on 11 Oct at Haslingden.

The last of the year was at Warton Bank on 12 Oct.

LONG-TAILED TIT *Aegithalos caudatus*
Very common breeding resident.

Information received at bird club level was slightly mixed. There was a slight increase in reports submitted to ELOC and also an increase in double-figure counts but on the other hand it dropped in position in the CDNHS area garden survey.

At a more local level there were six pairs on the EDF properties at Heysham, and the same number in the Aintree Study Area where the population is very stable. Four pairs bred successfully at Cuerden Valley Park.

Autumn passage at Heysham saw 71 birds noted between 2 Oct and 6 Nov, with a peak of 20 on the first date. At Seaforth, where the species is scare at other times, there were regular autumn records including 19 on 29 Sept and 27 on 21 Oct.

Counts of this species are particularly problematic as some people only count the largest single flock seen and others record totals based on multiple groups. Larger totals over 25 birds included 45 at Mere Sands Wood in July, 40 near Belmont in October, 31 at Wiswell in July, 30 at Holden Wood Reservoir in September, up to 30 at Grane in September to November, 30 at Common Bank Lodge, Chorley in December, 28 at Glasson in August and 27 at Blackpool Watson Road Park in October and in Cuerden Valley Park in the second winter period.

CETTI'S WARBLER *Cettia cetti*
Scarce but increasing breeding resident.

Further consolidation at the favoured sites on the Fylde was evident: up to twelve were singing at Marton Mere in April with the now expected birds at other sites in the immediate vicinity also. There were up to five at Fleetwood Marsh Nature Park, where sixteen birds were ringed in total, and others nearby at Burglar's Alley. The only Fylde reports away from these strongholds came from Thornton Marsh Farm in June and Preesall Flashes in October, though presumably some breeding sites are not reported.

There were at least ten pairs on the north Lancashire RSPB properties, comprising six at Leighton Moss and two each at Barrow Scout and Silverdale Moss, and up to five singing males at Middleton NR, while birds only wintered at Heysham NR.

Nine pairs at MMWWT and at least three at Lunt Meadows was further evidence of increases at sites with suitable habitat.. Brockholes had its first confirmed breeding record, with a pair feeding two fledged young on 12 June and three juveniles ringed in total. Birds were singing in the Birkdale area unto April and again later in the year, but it is not known if they bred. There were also several reports from Heysham.

Further consolidation was reflected in sites having their first records. These included one at Seaforth from at least late September into 2020, and the first for the St Helens area in the Sankey Valley in early November.

WILLOW WARBLER *Phylloscopus trochilus*
Abundant breeding bird and passage migrant.

The first appeared at the end of March, at Leighton Moss on the 29th followed by Belmont and Stanley Park, Liverpool on the 30th and Crosby on the 31st. A more widespread arrival was evident at the beginning of April, and subsequently there was some evidence of falls, in particular at Heysham where there were 50 on the 16th and 75 on the 18th.

Around 30 singing males were recorded on Birkdale dunes, with numbers highest away from major paths and disturbance. There were twelve pairs at MMWWT and at Freshfield Dune Heath, an increase of seven. Elsewhere in the south-west up to 25 were singing in the Simonswood Moss area in May, the six pairs in the Aintree Study Area was in line with the recent mean, and there were six territories at Carr Mill Dam.

On the Fylde larger counts at breeding sites included 36 singing males at Winmarleigh Moss on 18 April and up to seven males at Carr House Green Common.

Twenty-two east Lancashire sites had double-figure counts, with peaks of 77 at Bottoms Beck on 12 May during a WBBS count and 62 at both Foulridge Reservoirs and Grindleton Forest; 27 were at Langden Castle on 25 May.. In the Chorley area there were 25 at White Coppice along the Goit on 1 May and ten along the Withnell Nature Reserve track on the 16th, while in the West Pennine Moors there were ten territories around Belmont Reservoir (a small decline), around ten on a nearby BBS square and 13 on the periphery of Winter Hill. Rossendale reported up to 30 in the Cheesden Valley and 25 in the Grane area in late April.

From mid-July to the end of September 70 new birds were ringed at Heysham as local breeding birds moved away and those from other sites moved through; the peak was 18 on 2 Aug.

Identification difficulties make last dates for this species problematic. The last birds reported by bird club regions were 13 Sept in Chorley (Anglezarke Moor), the 19th in Rossendale (Whitworth), the 21st in east Lancashire (Swinden Res), the 23rd in Fylde (Knott End), 25th Belmont and finally 2 Oct at Heysham.

CHIFFCHAFF *Phylloscopus collybita*
Common breeder and passage migrant, uncommon in winter.

Among the birds reported in the first winter period two were seen at both Leighton Moss and MMWWT in February. Elsewhere in the country sewage farms and water treatment works are regularly checked for this species more than in Lancashire, perhaps as the potential rewards increase with more scarce species attempting to overwinter more birders will cover such sites more. The only January report in the east came from such a source, at Ewood Bridge SW on the 13th while one was in the Chorley area at Croston SW on 17 Feb. Clear-cut migrants were noted from early March.

There were 25 pairs at MMWWT, 18 at Freshfield Dune Heath (an increase of six), and 14 in the Aintree study area, which reflected the general steady increase there. Similary, the continued increase in the breeding population at Heysham was echoed with 14 pairs on the EDF land. There were twelve territories in Birkdale Dunes and ten at Carr Mill Dam, St Helens.

The peak count in east Lancashire was 24 on an unspecified date. No detailed information was received from the Fylde but early in the season, when migrants could still have been moving through, there were up to eleven males at Marton Mere and ten at Carr House Green Common; up to seven were singing at Fishwick LNR, Preston in April and May. Five pairs bred in Cuerden Valley Park and there were seven pairs in the Challan Hall woodland in North Lancashire.

A hundred and twenty new birds were ringed at Heysham in September and October; ten at Seaforth on 26 Aug was the peak of autumn movement there.

It can be more tricky to identify wintering birds at the end of the year, as migrants can be coming through well into October and even November. Two at both Belmont and Lower Healey on 19 Oct suggested an inland movement at this time. Up to three were at Stodday in November, this being one of the treatment plants sometimes checked in winter. Otherwise there were up to two at nearby Aldcliffe, two at Seaforth on 15 Dec and widespread reports of singles. Well inland there was a bird at Foulridge Reservoir on 15 and 20 Nov and one was in a garden at Folly Clough, Rossendale on 4 Dec.

SIBERIAN CHIFFCHAFF* *Phylloscopus collybita tristis*
Scarce passage migrant and winter visitor.

There were a couple of reports in the peak late autumn period, but no submissions have been received for what remains a county description species. The autumn of 2019 was a very good one for Siberian Chiffchaffs nationally, and some wintering birds were detected in Lancashire in early 2020.

IBERIAN CHIFFCHAFF *Phylloscopus ibericus*
Vagrant

A singing male spent several weeks at Pilling Lane Ends from 3 May to 23 June in an apparently fruitless attempt to find a mate (D Hall, W Martin *et al*). This is the second record for the Fylde following one in Blackpool in 2011. The record has been accepted by the BBRC.

 This takes the county total to three but the species is becoming more frequent in the country and further records are likely.

Iberian Chiffchaff, Pilling Lane Ends, 19 May (Paul Ellis)

WOOD WARBLER *Phylloscopus sibilatrix*
Scarce and declining breeder and passage migrant.

Migrants were first noted on 23 April at Hackensall Hall (Knott End) and also Brockholes with the latter being only the second site record. Further spring migrants at or near the coast were seen at Blackpool Stanley Park on 24 April, Middleton NR on the 25th, Stanley Park again on 1 May and finally Ainsdale on the 7th. As is usually the case with this species there were no records of outbound autumn migrants anywhere in the recording area.

 Inland records were sparse and strongly suggestive of further decline. One at Tower Lodge on 15 May was the only record from the western part of Bowland. In east Lancashire the only records came from Towneley Park, Burnley on 9 May and Stocks Reservoir on 10 & 28 May and 9 June. In the Chorley area one was at Wheelton Plantation on 9 May with another at Lead Mines Clough the following day; one was reported on territory at one site until at least 25 May and another was in song near Belmont in early June.

YELLOW-BROWED WARBLER *Phylloscopus inornatus*
Scarce but increasing autumn passage migrant.

It was an unusual autumn in that there was an average showing generally, but exceptional numbers in the Heysham area which could not be explained simply by differences in observer effort.

The first was ringed on Middleton NR on 30 Sept and was followed by one with Long-tailed Tits on Heysham Head on 3 Oct. A remarkable arrival probably then occurred entirely on the morning of 13 Oct with birds being detected in improved conditions on the 14th and 15th and a final total of at least fourteen individuals. Lingering birds from this influx were noted on the 16th, 18th and 19th. With none at the same time at Walney or coastal north Fylde it appears that a rain front at dawn, the power station lights and wind direction combined to produced this apparently very localised fall. The only other record in north Lancashire all autumn was at Stodday on the 13th.

Along with the Heysham bird the earliest was at Ainsdale on 30 Sept with another there on 3 Oct and other birds in the south-west at Crosby Coastal Park on the 4th, Blundellsands on the 15th-16th and Crosby village on the 20th.

Fleetwood produced singles records on 3, 11 and 16 Oct and two on the 13-15th (two), Elsewhere on the Fylde there were three in the mid-October influx, at Lytham St Annes NR on the 13th, Knott End Golf Course on the 14th and Watson Road Park, Blackpool on the 14th-15th.

There were two inland records this year: singles at Billinge on 8 Oct and and Cuerden Valley Park the following day.

SEDGE WARBLER *Acrocephalus schoenobaenus*
Common breeding bird and passage migrant.

The first reports of returning birds included MMWWT on 8 April, Marton Mere on the 11th and Heysham and Leighton Moss on the 16th. Seven migrants were ringed at Heysham in the spring.

A census of MMWWT indicated 41 pairs and there were an estimated 37 pairs at Lunt Meadows, a recovery after a poor 2018. The main Leighton Moss population was not censused, there were, however, seven pairs on the saltmarsh, four at Silverdale Moss and four at Warton Mires. On the Fylde up to 23 were singing at Carr House Green Common and eight at Lytham Moss, Marton Mere and Myerscough Quarry. Marshside held ten pairs, Birkdale LNR eight and Hesketh Out Marsh four. At least six singing males were noted at Brockholes. There was one pair on the Heysham EDF properties but Middleton NR wasn't censused.

Sedge Warbler, Lunt Meadows,
21 May (Mike Jackson)

Inland breeding probably occurred at six sites in east Lancashire, Belmont Reservoir had three territorial males and one was at another West Pennine Moors site. There were records from seven other sites in the Chorley area but no records were received from Rossendale.

A number of reports in September included singles at Belmont Reservoir on the 2nd, Leighton Moss on the 7th, Croston Finney on the 15th, Heysham on the 20th and finally Leighton Moss again on the 25th.

REED WARBLER *Acrocephalus scirpaceus*
Fairly common breeder, uncommon passage migrant.

The first arrival was at Leighton Moss on 6 April but it was some time before birds were seen elsewhere, with the next at Marton Mere on the 16th and Heysham, Lunt Meadows and Taggs Island, Birkdale on the 19th. At other well-watched sites arrival was as late as, for example, 4 May at Seaforth.

There was no systematic census at Leighton Moss but there were three pairs on the Inner Marsh. MMWWT was censused with 25 pairs recorded, up to nine were at Marton Mere in the summer, and other Fylde peaks included six at Herons Reach GC and four each at Myerscough Quarry and Fleetwood Nature Park. Seven pairs were noted at Lunt Meadows and five to seven at Marshside. There were nine singing birds at Taggs Island, Birkdale and antoher nearby at Sands Lake. Up to eight were singing along Oglet Shore andt there were at least two pairs at Seaforth. Middleton NR was not censused but there were at least five singing males, with one pair on the EDF properties and more than usual caught after the breeding season.

Further inland at least four singing males were noted at Brockholes, while in the Chorley area up to 15 were recorded on the Rufford Canal at Bretherton, with a couple of pairs in Yarrow Valley Park. The only reports in east Lancashire came from two sites, with nesting only probable at Barnoldswick where a pair were seen on two dates.

Late outward migrants included one at Seaforth on 14 Sept and the last two ringed at Fleetwood Marsh Nature Park on the 18th.

GRASSHOPPER WARBLER *Locustella naevia*
Fairly common breeding bird and passage migrant.

The first was at Brockholes on 5 April, followed by Leighton Moss on the 6th, Anglezarke Moor on the 13th and MMWWT the next day. An 'en masse arrival' was noted in the Belmont area on the 18th and 19th. One at Oglet on 22 April was notable.

There was an interesting east-west divide in population trend assessments. In the central West Pennine Moors 27 teritories were identified from reeling birds, higher numbers than in any of the previous three years and including an increase in the Belmont Reservoir population. It was considered that this was probably due to increasing infestation of in-bye by Juncus. There were records from 22 sites in the ELOC area, which was higher than in any of the previous three years; breeding was thought probable at three sites, while in Rossendale up to four were reeling in the Grane area and there were also records from a couple of other sites.

In contrast, numbers were considered to be down at several sites in the west of the county where an assessment was made. For example, there were four reeling males in the Birkdale dunes, half the total two years ago and with none on the golf course. Two at Middleton NR was also a significant reduction. There were six pairs at MMWWT. On the Fylde up to two were singing at Carr House Green Common, Fleetwood Marsh, Marton Mere and Staining Nook. At least one pair bred at Lunt Meadows and birds were reeling at Brockholes from April to June. One by the canal in Lydiate on 17 June was unusual there.

Few utumn migrants were noted, although one was still reeling at Belmont on 18 Aug. Late August birds included one at Mere Sands Wood on the 25th, while in Sepembert there were birds at Belmont and Leighton Moss on the 1st and finally another at the latter site on the 7th.

BLACKCAP *Sylvia atricapilla*
Very common breeding bird and passage migrant, fairly common winter visitor.

The first winter period provided the usual scattering of birds, particularly at garden feeding stations. There were two together in a Woolton Hill, Liverpool garden and also at Warton, in north Lancashire. Only one was wintering at Birkdale, where there have been several in some winters. Further inland there were three records in the Chorley area and two in the ELOC recording area.

Arrival dates are always subjective due to wintering birds. The first at Seaforth on 31 March was a good pointer. Spring passage was noted at Heysham from 6 to 22 April, with a peak of 20 on the latter date. The first record in Rossendale was on 6 Apilr. Counts elsewhere in the spring included ten at Brockholes and Sefton Park and nine at Marton Mere.

A total of 23 pairs were recorded at MMWWT, 14 territorial males in the Birkdale dunes, eight pairs on Freshfield Dune Heath was an increase of five, six territories at Carr Mill Dam and twelve territories in the Aintree study area, an apparent increase. Similarly, a record eleven pairs were noted on the EDF land at Heysham. Five pairs nested at Cuerden Valley Park.

The breeding population in the Foulridge area was an estimated 44 males, with double-figure counts at four other east Lancashire sites and breeding confirmed or likely at a total of eleven sites. There were eight territories in the Belmont area, and in the ROC area four around Holden Wood Reservoir.

Autumn passage was noted at Heysham from late August to early October, with peak numbers in September when 110 new birds were ringed. There were six at Marton Mere on 9 Sept, and the last in Rossendale was on 22 Sept.

In the second winter period there were again two wintering at Warton. No other site was reported to hold more than one bird but there was the normal distribution of birds across the west of the recording area in particular. There were seven records in east Lancashire and a similar number in Chorley.

GARDEN WARBLER *Sylvia borin*
Fairly common breeding bird and passage migrant.

There were again no records of birds wintering with Blackcaps in the south-west of the county, this unusual but previously regular behaviour seems to have ceased.

The first migrants were on 13 April at Leighton Moss and in the Chorley area at both Copperworks Wood and Withnell. A few scattered reports were received in the rest of the month, before a pronounced arrival at the end of the month including three at Heysham NR on the 30th while increased numbers were reported at a number of inland sites early in May.

Typically for this rather skulking species information on breeding was rather patchy. There were six singing males at Brockholes on 7 May, although it is not known how many of these stayed to breed. Three were singing at Abbeystead in May, two in the Upper Brock Valley and one at Beacon Fell. In east Lancashire there were reports from nine sites in June but success wasn't confirmed from any of them. There were three territories in the Belmont area and two on Winter Hill. Territorial birds were seen at Cuerden Valley Park, Leighton Moss and at least one site in Rossendale.

The last inland report came from New Laithe Farm, Slaidburn on 26 Aug. Autumn migrants were at Heysham from 3 Aug to 14 Oct, with nine ringed at Middleton NR. The only other October report, and the last of the year, was at Freckleton, Fylde on the 25th.

LESSER WHITETHROAT *Sylvia curruca*
Uncommon breeding bird and passage migrant.

A wintering bird was in a Liverpool garden at Garston from 29 March to 10 April. It was considered that this may have been an eastern race bird, but this could not be confirmed without DNA analysis.

Arrival began with two at Heysham NR on 16 April and other early migrants were at Marton Mere and near Kincraig Lake on the 17th. The peak spring migration was noted from Heysham, where there were seven singing males on 20 April. Other counts at this time included four at Freckleton Naze Point on 4 May and Warton Bank the next day.

There were only three reports from east Lancashire – on 23 April at Grimsargh Wetland, up to birds at Alston Wetland between 27 April and 9 July and one at Longridge on 15 May. Singing birds were noted at three sites in the Chorley area, at Bretherton, Ulnes Walton (two) and Tincklers Lane fields, Eccleston (up to three). One was singing on abandoned farmland at Oglet on 25 April, where the species is scarce. There were no reports from Rossendale.

The main autumn passage at Heysham was between 20 Aug and 16 Sept, with 16 birds ringed. A late individual was trapped there on 30 Sept, DNA analysis showed this to be nominate *curruca* and not one of the eastern races. The last of the year was at Carleton, Fylde on 7 Oct.

WHITETHROAT *Sylvia communis*
Very common breeder and passage migrant.

The first arrived at MMWWT on 15 April with others at Crosby on the 16th and Bispham and Hightown on the 17th before a widespread influx on the 18th including further inland, although none were noted in the LDBWS area before one at Heysham on the 20th. Fifteen were at Middleton NR on 24 April There were 24 singing at sites in the Garston and Oglet area on 12 May, the same day there were 12 at Jackhouse in East Lancs.

There were 25 pairs at Lunt Meadows. There were 24 singing males in the Oglet area in mid May. At least 20 singing males were noted across the Birkdale Dunes area. At the Aintree Study Area there were nine territories which was in line with a five year mean. There were 15 pairs at Marshside and and 14 pairs at Hesketh Out Marsh. Twelve pairs at Freshfield Dune Heath was an increase of six, while there were eight pairs at MMWWT.

On the Fylde no breeding totals were reported but there were at least 13 at Carr House Green Common in June. Breeding was considered probable at eight sites in the Chorley area and in east Lancashire breeding was confirmed at seven sites and thought probable at a further five. There were reports from more sites in east Lancashire (40) than in any of the previous three years. In the north there were six territories on the Heysham EDF land and four at Warton Mires, and in Rossendale breeding was confirmed with three singing males at Holden Wood Reservoir.

The total of 142 ringed at Heysham was in line with recent totals, and included a typical late autumn spike in numbers. Small numbers of migrants were seen through to mid-September, among the last of which were singles at Lunt Meadows and and Jackhouse Reservoir on the 16th, Crosby on the 17th, Marton Mere on the 19th and finally one at Heysham on the 25th.

Whitethroat, Rawtenstall, 11 May (Craig Bell)

FIRECREST *Regulus ignicapilla*
Uncommon passage migrant, scarce in winter.

All records this year came in the latter part of the year starting with one accompanying a tit flock at Carr House Green Common, Inskip on 1 Oct. This was followed by one at Oglet on 20 Oct. A first-year male was ringed at Heysham NR on 4 Nov, swiftly followed by one along the Causeway at Leighton Moss on the 6th.

GOLDCREST *Regulus regulus*
Common breeding bird, especially in the east. Common double passage migrant and winter visitor in variable numbers.

In contrast to 2018, Goldcrests were widespread and numbers good throughout the year. In the first winter period, birds were reported from most 10km squares with records weighted to the east and the Silverdale area. Most reports were of ones and twos but six were at Spring Wood, Whalley and four at Low Moor, Clitheroe on 1 Jan. Approximately 15 were feeding low to the ground at Calf Hey Reservoir on 20 Jan and counts of six were at Stocks Reservoir on 25 Feb and Haslam Park, Preston on 19 March.

A bird was singing at Liverpool Hope University in Childwall from the very early date of 2 Jan. A singing bird was present at Waterfoot, Rossendale on 20 Jan and one at Little Singleton on 10 Feb after which a lot more reports of singing birds were received as spring migration got into full flow. The spring passage at Heysham consisted of 71 (of which 42 were trapped and ringed) between 28 Feb and 7 April with a noticeable peak of 23 at Red Nab on 20 March. This influx was also noted at Birkdale LNR but there was no evidence of any staying to breed in the area.

Singing birds were noted from 28 sites on the Fylde including three at Cuddy Hill on 14 Feb. Singing males were recorded widely in south Liverpool and Knowsley including three at Sefton Park. Just single pairs bred at MMWWT and Aintree, whereas there were five territories scattered around Cuerden Valley Park. The most densely populated site was at Challan Hall with 16 pairs. Thirteen singing birds were noted along various site on Haslingden Grane, seven territories were logged around Foulridge and forested upland areas held many but were generally unquantified.. There were still singing birds well into June and July at several sites.

Autumn passage started on 27 Aug at Heysham NR with 135 birds recorded, including 98 ringed, and continued to mid-October with no particular peak. A similar pattern was noted at Birkdale and elsewhere. Ten were at Pilling Lane Ends on 30 Sept and Seaforth recorded its first of the autumn on the 29th.

At Calf Hey Reservoir, a minimum of 25 were present on 15 Sept, increasing to 45 by 13 Oct and then down to 15 on the 27th. Twelve were grounded at Belmont on 15 Oct and birds were noticeably widespread throughout Croxteth Park on 13 Nov.

WREN *Troglodytes troglodytes*
Abundant breeding resident, passage migrant and winter visitor.

Wrens are benefitting from a series of mild winters having survived the beast from the east in 2018 with numbers generally increasing across the county. Regular recording at Carr House Green Common had maxima between 17 and 26 in most months apart from a drop off in activity in July and August. A similar pattern was developing at Low Moor, Clitheroe with 30 in February and 39 in May and numbers at Jackhouse were generally around the 20 mark with a peak of 27 in June. Many regularly-watched and recorded sites showed a similar pattern but with smaller totals with birds most noticeable from March to July. Being less obtrusive in January accounts for the low ranking in the Chorley winter garden survey (17th place) and the Lancaster January survey (just 107 recorded).

MMWWT recorded 85 pairs breeding, a huge increase in numbers or perhaps better monitoring. Twenty-one pairs bred at Challan Hall, Silverdale and 38 birds, mostly singing males, were noted in two adjacent BBS squares at Brindle and 25 were counted at Lower Burgh Meadow in May. A breeding survey on Winter Hill realised seven territories with another five immediately adjacent to the survey area. Heysham had 23 breeding territories, which was similar to previous years. Lunt Meadows, however, recorded just eight territories. Dataset submissions from Birdtrack, Fylde, ELOC, LDBWS and ROC showed 155 sites with breeding evidence.

There was a typical autumn passage at Heysham and an influx of ten birds was noted at Seaforth on 2 Nov.

NUTHATCH *Sitta europaea*
Fairly common and increasing breeding resident.

As last year, Nuthatches are consolidating their position in all areas of the county. The species has climbed to 14th place in the Chorley Winter Garden Survey visiting 14 out of the 23 gardens surveyed. In Cuerden Valley Park 17 singing males were counted and there were three territories in Longworth Clough. Its presence in Over Wyre increased where three nests were monitored around Preesall in which 22 eggs were laid, 21 hatched and 18 young fledged.

The species is common in the Silverdale area and up through the Lune Valley. Fifteen pairs bred at Challan Hall and daily counts of up to seven were regular in the Silverdale area.

In east Lancashire, there were reports from 76 sites with breeding evidence in many of the wooded cloughs leading down to the Ribble, Hodder and Calder. Four nestboxes were occupied at Gawthorpe Hall, Padiham in which 29 young were ringed (a very healthy average of 7.3 per box). One box was occupied at Bowland Wild Boar Park. The

Nuthatch, Leighton Moss, 1 December (Paul Ellis)

species is commonly encountered at Jackhouse, along the Haslingden Grane woodlands down to Stubbins and west to Wayoh Reservoir.

In Liverpool, birds were present throughout the year in all the major parks such as Sefton and Croxteth Parks as well as woods around Speke and in Knowsley. Seven pairs were present at Carr Mill Dam. The species is now resident in the pinewoods of Formby up through Ainsdale NNR and Ainsdale village as well as Hesketh Park and the Botanic Gardens in Southport.

The species has reached most suitable corners of the Fylde, most regularly at Stanley Park/ Salisbury Woodland in Blackpool and Lytham Hall , and in July birds were being seen in Pilling and Out Rawcliffe.

TREECREEPER *Certhia familiaris*
Common breeding resident.

Treecreepers are, like Nuthatches, a widespread resident of woodlands and parks but their population is rather more stable. Although resident and breeding in the Formby pinewoods and Ainsdale NNR, there were very few reports in the area as a whole. In Rossendale, it was encountered sporadically with the only regular records from the Haslingden Grane area with five at Calf Hey on 15 Dec notable. In the Chorley winter garden survey, it only appeared in six

Treecreeper, Leighton Moss, 1 December (Paul Ellis)

out of the 23 monitored. In Over Wyre the species is scarce, so records at Hackensall Wood, Preesall were note-worthy.

The rich woodland habitat around Leighton Moss had the highest density with 15 pairs breeding at Challan Hall and a daily peak of nine seen in April. Fours and fives were occasionally recorded elsewhere in the county at locations such as Knowsley Safari Park, New Laithe Farm, Newton, Mere Sands Wood and Calf Hey Reservoir.

Four pairs bred in Cuerden Valley Park, three pairs at Carr Mill Dam and pairs were present at several sites along the Hodder, Calder and Ribble in east Lancashire. Two pairs bred at Foulridge and two at Cut Wood, Rishton.

Three new birds were caught and ringed at Heysham in mid-September, probably dispersing from farther afield as the only other record in the area was from Heysham Head.

The species is widespread in south Liverpool and Knowsley with regular reports from Sefton Park, the woodlands between Croxteth and Knowsley village, Speke Mill Wood and Tarbock Farm. Birds were also present at Sherdley Park, St Helens and plantations and copses on the mosslands north to Skelmersdale.

STARLING *Sturnus vulgaris*
Abundant breeding bird, double passage migrant and winter visitor.

Monthly Peak Counts

	Jan	Feb	Mar	Apr	May	Jun	Jul	Aug	Sep	Oct	Nov	Dec
Leighton Moss	130000	10000	45	200	16	150	150	250	120	150	35000	10000
Stocks Reservoir	30000	30000	40							1000	30000	40000
Marton Mere	400	30	0			1000		1000	3000	4000	11000	4000

The stand-out counts in the first winter period were the roosts at Leighton Moss and Stocks Reservoir as summarised above with the peak at the former counted on 10 Jan. Numbers dropped off very quickly during February at both sites. Elsewhere, 12500 were seen heading to roost over Blackpool 6th Form College on 16 Jan, 4000 at Elswick on the 4th, 3877 (in 28 flocks) going to roost in the Seaforth docks over Crosby on the 1st, over 3000 at Belmont on 27 Feb and lower four-figure counts at Jackhouse, Gressingham, Cockerham, Lower Thurnham, Lytham Hall, Hesketh Out Marsh and Thursden Valley during February. There were still a few four-figure flocks in March, the largest being 2500 at Thursland Hill, Cockerham on the 17th and 2000 at Freckleton on the 4th.

Away from Stocks Reservoir, numbers reported any distance inland were generally less than 100 with the largest flocks being 300 at Charnock Richard on 12 Jan and 500 at Bretherton Eyes on 16 Feb. It was a similar story in south Liverpool where 220 at Oglet on 1 March was the largest count.

During the breeding season birds were seen in generally small numbers across the county, being reported in virtually every 10km square. A pair was noted taking in nesting material to a box in Roby Mill on 24 Feb and feeding young on 21 April. Most early reports of fledged juveniles were received from mid-May onwards but the first were at Eccleston on 6 May, Rainford on the 8th, Waterloo on the 12th and Belmont on the 15th. In the Pilling-Preesall area, 22 nests were monitored in which a total of 98 eggs were laid, from which 83 hatched and 75 young fledged (average 3.4 fledged per pair).

Feeding flocks of adults and juveniles are a common sight from late spring and early summer, most numbering in double figures but some larger congregations of between 100 and 3000 noted at several locations including Clitheroe, Altham, Belmont, Warton Bank and Glasson Marsh. A thousand roosted at Marton Mere on 16 June and 1000 were in a flock at Marshside on 6 July. A roost at Fleetwood Marsh had 1000 birds on 14 July, rising to 10000 by 26 Aug and then down to 6000 in early September. At Seaforth NR there were 700 on 23 June rising to over 2000 by 24 July.

In September, numbers in the Marton Mere roost reached 3000 but it wasn't until October that larger flocks were noted around the county. Up to 4000 roosted at Lunt Meadows reedbed on 16 Oct, three flocks totalling 5000 birds were noted around Eagland Hill on the 26th and 800 were noted in the Gisburn Forest at the end of the month. Feeding flocks in the hundreds were noted widely such as 130 stripping Whitebeam berries in Speke on the 10th. November brought the highest counts with

4500 roosting at Heysham on the 6th, 11000 at Marton Mere on the 10th, 25000 at Leighton Moss on the 1st increasing to 35000 by the 20th, and a minimum of 30000 at Stocks Reservoir on the 18th. December peak counts were at least 40000 at Stocks Reservoir and 18750 at Blackpool North Pier as numbers at Marton Mere and Leighton Moss receded to maxima of 4000 and 10000 respectively. Four-figure counts were noted at Braides, Belmont and Lunt Meadows in December.

RING OUZEL *Turdus torquatus*
Rare local breeding bird on the hills; uncommon double passage migrant.

As with last year, spring arrivals started slowly with only one March record in the Langden Valley, Bowland on the 28th. However, once into April passage was well underway with a good spread of reports throughout many of the upland sites in particular.

On the West Pennine Moors a good return of 31 birds was recorded between 3-23 April, including seven on 14 April. In Chorley the first were four on Withnell Moor on 6 April and included a peak of six on the 17th. Likewise, sites in east Lancashire enjoyed an excellent spring passage through mid- to late April with nine birds in the Hareden Valley on the 11th, six at both Dean Clough and Higher Wenshed on the 16th, up to 14 on Pendle Hill on the 18th and six at Thievely Pike on the 20th. In total there were reports from 20 sites in the ELOC area, in line with recent years – 18 in 2018, 22 in 2017 and 16 in 2016.

On the coast spring records included sightings at Ainsdale on multiple dates between 30 March and 17 April, mainly of singles but peaks of seven on 6 April and six on the 14th. A few more single records were received between the same dates along the coastline from Crosby, Formby and Hightown. Further north there were two at Fleetwood on 6 April, one at Pilling Lane on the 7th and two at Hesketh Out Marsh on the 14th.

The only breeding records came as usual from Bowland where birds seemed to arrive back later than usual, but once they had returned it was another good breeding season on the United Utilities estate; no systematic surveys were carried out in 2019 but 13 territories were identified. This is lower than in the last few years, however, as some areas that held birds in recent years were not covered adequately. Several pairs successfully raised second broods and one possibly raised a third.

Autumn Bowland records included a single in the Langden Valley on 4 Oct, and three birds were feeding on Rowan berries in Smelt Mill Clough in Bowland on 14 Oct. Elsewhere in the uplands eight were at Haslingden Grane on 13 Sept, while passage through Belmont included seven between 7 Sept and 12 Oct with one on 5 and 19 Oct at Winter Hill.

On the coast a male was near Poulton-le-Fylde on 15 Oct and a juvenile was at Middleton NR on the same day. Further south a single at Speke-Garston Coastal Reserve on 18 and 21 Oct completed the year's sightings.

BLACKBIRD *Turdus merula*
Abundant breeding resident and winter visitor; common double passage migrant, more evident in autumn.

The Lancaster and District January survey counted 647, lower than the 2018 total and the five-year mean. Over 30 were recorded near Belmont on 1 Feb and there were up to 30 coming to a feeding station in the Rossendale area on 4 Feb.

A light spring passage included 20 on 20 March at Heysham NR while 17 flew over Knott End on 19-27 March including nine on the 20th.

Breeding records were received from many locations throughout the county. No substantive trends can be determined from the available data, but a typical year would be a reasonable assumption. Some highlights and summaries from the records received included nest-monitoring in Over Wyre of five nests, recorded 21 eggs laid, twelve hatched and eight fledged resulting in productivity of 1.6 fledged per pair. In Chorley surveys of two adjacent BBS squares totalled 23 birds in April and 16 were counted during a survey of Lower Burgh Meadow in May; nine pairs also bred at Cuerden Valley Park. Three territories were recorded during a Winter Hill breeding bird survey. In Rossendale records were received from 31 sites and at Heysham up to 20 pairs bred on EDF properties. There was a count of eleven in Moor Park West, Preston on 11 May.

On Merseyside 19 territories were located in an Aintree study area and six in Kirkdale cemetery, 16 pairs at Freshfield Dune Heath – in line with the long-term mean, at least six pairs at Lunt Meadows, while 34 pairs were reported from MMWWT, a big increase on the 14 reported in 2018.

The main autumn movement began in October and peaked in the first half of November with no significant totals reported after mid-month. On 1 Nov 32 were recorded at Southport Marine Lake and 40 in the Haslingden Grane area. Twelve were at Seaforth in the first week of November and 20 on the 15th. At Heysham 131 on 30 Oct, 104 on 4 Nov and 145 on 6 Nov were notable autumn peaks and part of a passage between 13 Oct and 10 Nov which included 736 birds., There were 21 at Singleton 5 Nov and double-figure counts reported were from at least 25 other sites across the Fylde during the year. At Knott End, 113 flew over between 2 Oct and 29 Nov including 30 on 29 Oct. Inland, 60 were at Stocks reservoir on 18 Nov.

Few notable early winter records were received but 105 were at Aldcliffe on 18 Dec and 10+ in a Belmont garden on the same day, while at Singleton 28, 33 and 32 were recorded on 2, 15 and 25 Dec respectively.

FIELDFARE *Turdus pilaris*
Common to abundant winter visitor and passage migrant.

At the start of the year a flock of 120 was at Bretherton Eyes on 2 Jan which was the first of several three-figure counts reported in January. Other large flocks that month included 150+ at Medlar on 9 Jan, 100 at Elswick on 19 Jan, 105 at Treales on 21 Jan, 220 on 26 Jan and 260 on 28 Jan both at Inskip. In February, 100+ were at Bryning on the 16th, 250+ at St Michaels-on-Wyre on 27th, while in east Lancashire 300 were at Salterforth on the 27th. The Lancaster winter survey recorded 344 across the eleven squares surveyed in January.

Departing birds were seen until April including 13 at Mawdesley on the 15th, two at Belmont on the 20th, nine on Pilling Moss on the 22nd, 30 in the Cheesden Valley on the 19th and five at Snigholes on the 27th. The last to depart east Lancashire was on 25 April at Dean Clough.

Autumn followed a similar pattern to usual with the first arrivals in late September to early October with two detectable peaks – the first pulse around the third week of October and the biggest movement around 29 October with a 1000+ report from the Fylde where the greatest number of three-figure counts came from.

Fieldfare, Pilling Lane, 31 December (Paul Ellis)

Arrivals began on the last day of September at Belmont with 200 there on 29 Oct and a visible migration peak of 446 in the first hour after sunrise on 9 Nov. Chorley arrivals began with two at Lead Mines Clough on 4 Oct increasing to more than 600 over Anglezarke Moor on 21 Oct. Other three-figure counts included 200 on Croston Moss on Nov 15 and 300 at Hoghton on 26 Nov.

In east Lancashire 150 were at Stocks Reservoir on 20 Oct and 250 at Longridge on 31 Oct although across east Lancashire there were records from fewer sites and fewer counts of 100+ than in 2018. In Rossendale, the first of the autumn were 20 on 20 Oct and some winter movement on 19 Dec saw multiple flocks totalling 3-400 birds over Deeply Vale.

At least 932 passed through Heysham between 20-31 Oct with a peak of 350 on 20 Oct. The Fylde returned two four-figure counts including over 1000 mainly heading south at Newton-with-Scales on 29 Oct and 1500+ at Medlar on 29 Dec. There were many three-figure counts across the Fylde with the first of the autumn on 21 Oct with 180 at Carr House Green Common and 190 at Pilling Lane.

REDWING *Turdus iliacus*
Abundant double passage migrant and winter visitor.

The year turned out to be a remarkable one with an unprecedented roost recorded in east Lancashire at Longridge Fell in November, but this was preceded in the earlier months of the year by fairly typical late winter and migration periods.

The Lancaster and District January survey recorded 406 Redwings across the eleven squares surveyed, while the Chorley peak was 40 at Eccleston on 14 Jan.

The last of the spring in Chorley was at White Coppice on 13 April. On the Fylde 381 flew over Knott End from 14 Feb to 18 April, including 112 on 20 March. The last at Belmont was on 18 April and in east Lancashire at Jackhouse on the same date.

The timing of autumn arrivals mirrored that for Fieldfares with the first on 17 Sept and migration getting going in earnest in the first week of October. Vis mig at Belmont included 1112 in the first hour after sunrise on 5 Oct and at Clowbridge one session noted 350 in one hour on the same day when there were also multiple double-figure flocks over. Chorley counts included 350 at Cuerden Valley Park on 17 Oct, while the peak autumn count on the Fylde was 600 at Marton Mere on 20 Oct with several three-figure counts at various sites during December. Autumn passage at Heysham totalled 2658 birds between 4 Oct and 6 Nov with a peak of 1300 north on 20 Oct.

However, the year ended in spectacular fashion at Kemple End on Longridge Fell when completely unprecedented numbers were discovered roosting at dusk from 5 Nov into 2020 (see separate article).

SONG THRUSH *Turdus philomelus*
Common breeding resident.

On Merseyside a bird at Speke and three at Oglet were singing on 1 Jan and at the other end of the year three were singing on Princes Park on 30 Dec. The Lancaster winter survey recorded 29 birds, a little lower than 2018's 38.

On the Fylde records came in from over 50 locations during the year including over 20 during the breeding season. The first report of a male singing was at Carr House Green Common on 24 Jan, followed by two at Catforth on 11 Feb and one at Cuddy Hill on the 14th. The first song was heard in east Lancashire on 26 Jan at Marl Hill and in Rossendale on 10 Feb.

There were records at 43 sites in Rossendale during the year, while in east Lancashire there were two double-figure counts – 14 at Jackhouse on 23 Feb and an estimated breeding population of 22 pairs in the Foulridge area.

The only evidence of spring passage was at Knott End where 33 flew over from 14 Feb to 7 May including five on 14 Feb.

In Chorley 15 males were singing in Cuerden Valley Park in March and seven birds were in two adjacent BBS squares in the Brindle area in April. A continuing downward trend in breeding was noted at Heysham where only a single territory was located on EDF properties. Three territories were found on Winter Hill and six pairs bred at MMWWT.

In autumn, a typical light passage with a coastal bias included 72 at Heysham between 2 Oct and 6 Nov with a peak of 16 grounded on the latter date. At Knott End, 169 flew over between 14 Sept and 24 Nov including 20 on 5 Oct, while six were recorded at Seaforth on 2 Nov and 13 on 16 Nov.

MISTLE THRUSH *Turdus viscivorus*
Common breeding resident; some autumn dispersal/passage.

Early reports of singing males came from east Lancashire at Marl Hill on 8 & 25Feb, Wilpshire on the 14th & 23rd and Dean Clough on the 25th, on the Fylde at St Michaels-on-Wyre on 13 Feb with a pair at the same location on 27 Feb when a male was also singing at Out Rawcliffe. The Lancaster January survey recorded 41 birds in eight of the eleven squares surveyed, with a maximum of 20.

In east Lancashire there were double-figure counts at Grindleton Forest of 31 on 27 June , and 28 at Forest Becks on 6 Aug. A flock of 25+ was at Belmont on 9 June and ten were at Croston Moss on 10 July.

There was only a single confirmed breeding record in east Lancashire at Twiston, but it was possible or probable at five other sites and was almost certainly under-recorded. In Chorley three were found in two adjacent BBS squares in the Brindle area in April, while Rossendale records came in from 40 sites including breeding evidence from several. The only double-figure count there was at least 20 on 13 Sept at Haslingden Grane. Three pairs bred at MMWWT.

Autumn movements were noted from September to November. In Chorley 20 were at Shaw Hill on 19 Sept and on Croston Moss on the 21st. Twenty-five were at Aldcliffe were on 30 Sept and 23 flew over Knott End from 30 Sept until 19 Nov including four on 29 Oct. Twelve flew south at Lunt Meadows on 18 Oct, while autumn passage at Heysham accounted for 14 birds between 14 Oct and 6 Nov with a peak day-count of nine on 4 Nov. The last record of the year was one on 30 Dec singing at Princes Park, Merseyside.

SPOTTED FLYCATCHER *Muscicapa striata*
Fairly common but declining breeding bird and double passage migrant.

Arrivals followed the expected pattern with the first few records in the second week of May – the first of which was at Knott End on the 8th, and the peak arrival over the two-week period from the 11th. Records were then received every week for the next 20 weeks until the last of the year on 21 Sept.

Spotted Flycatchers were reported at 31 sites in east Lancashire with breeding confirmed at six. The first at Wycoller on 11 May was followed by Cross of Greet Bridge the following day and the peak count of the year was twelve at New Laithe Farm on 3 Aug. The only other breeding records received came from Chorley where the first were at Anglezarke and Hoghton Bottoms on 15 May with breeding possibly occurring at both sites, with further singles at Eccleston on 18 May and White Coppice on the 29th. A pair made a failed breeding attempt in Lead Mines Clough and one bred near Wheelton plantation. However, the presence of six at Tower Lodge in north Lancashire also suggested at least attempted breeding as did a pair by the canal at Salwick – where they nested in 2018 – on 17 May,

Heysham had only a single spring record on 19 May but the passage was more productive on the Fylde with records at 13 locations with the at Knott End bird quickly followed by singles at Stanley Park on 10 May and Staining Nook the next day. Records were received until mid-June with a gap before the first of autumn at Fairhaven Dunes on 8 Aug. A few more mainly coastal records were seen through into September until the last record at Newton Marsh on 20 Sept.

The last of the year was at Syd Brook, Eccleston (Chorley) on 21 Sept.

ROBIN *Erithacus rubecula*
Abundant breeding resident, autumn passage migrant and winter visitor.

The Lancaster January survey recorded 321 birds across the eleven squares with a maximum count of 71. On the Fylde double-figure counts were made of 14 at Haslam Park in January, 15 at Marton Mere in February and 13 at Ingol in March, while in east Lancashire there were multiple 20+ counts from Low Moor in February, March and April. Ten were ringed at Heysham on 20 March.

Widespread abundance on the Fylde was demonstrated by records from 117 locations with many reports of breeding between April and August. Nest-monitoring in Over Wyre returned the following data from five nests: 27 eggs laid, 13 eggs hatched,13 young fledged resulting in productivity of 2.6 young fledged per pair. In Chorley 32 were recorded in two adjacent BBS squares near Brindle during April 19 were at Lower Burgh Meadows in May and three territories were identified on Winter Hill.

Elsewhere, 31 breeding pairs were recorded at MMWWT, 20 at Freshfield Dune Heath equalling last year's record total, but only one pair was at Lunt Meadows down from five last year.

Autumn reports included 40+ on 25 Sept at Leighton Moss, ten at Tatham Hall Farm on 13 Sept, and eleven at Burglars Alley on the 14th. Seaforth experienced a marked influx from mid-October with numbers peaking at 45 on 2 Nov, while "typical numbers" passed through Heysham between August and early November. Double-figure counts were made at multiple sites in east Lancashire in September and October, including a peak of 33 at Jackhouse on 15 Oct.

PIED FLYCATCHER *Ficedula hypoleuca*
Uncommon breeding bird and passage migrant.

A female ringed at Heysham on 18 April and was the only record there for the year. One was at Hesketh Out Marsh the same day, while on the Fylde one was singing at Tatham Hall Farm on the 19th with three in Fleetwood on the same date. The first spring arrival at Belmont was on 2 May and a single male was seen at Seaforth on 4 May.

A positive year was reported In the species' upland breeding stronghold. Pied Flycatchers were reported at 13 east Lancashire sites with the first from Moor Piece on 7 April, a new earliest date for the area. 2019 was described as "a brilliant year" in Bowland in the woods above Stocks Reservoir where there were 19 pairs compared to twelve in 2018. Of the 18 pairs that could be monitored, 17 fledged 100 chicks, compared to 55 chicks in 2018. A nesting female that was ringed as a chick near Edmondbyers in County Durham nested above Stocks Reservoir again for her third season. Bowland Wild Boar Park had ten occupied nest boxes with at least 30 eggs on 11 May. Two other sites in east Lancashire had double-figure counts with ten at Great Slush/Birkett Woods on 1 June and twelve at Moor Piece on 15 May. In summary, breeding across nine monitored sites in Bowland was excellent with nest success of 84%.

In the Lune Valley 109 nests were monitored across 20 sites. Of these, 81 were successful with 494 nestlings recorded. This represents a nest success rate of 74% which is an increase on the 63% in 2018 when 451 nestlings were recorded from 68 successful nests of 108 monitored, although not bettering the 83% success rate of 2017.

No data were provided on the cause of nest failures in any of the years in either Bowland or Lune Valley, but if available in future this would provide some useful context to these excellent projects.

Further south, one active nest was located in the Belmont area and in Chorley the first of the year was on 19 April at Anglezarke, where a breeding attempt was later recorded, but a second pair failed. A male was singing on 4 May at Wheelton plantation.

Autumn records were limited. One at New Laithe Farm on 27 July and another there on 4 Aug, along with one at Champion Moor on 28 July were the returns for Bowland, while another single was recorded further north at Leighton Moss on 3 Aug. No records were received after 4 Aug.

BLACK REDSTART *Phoenicurus ochruros*
Rare breeding bird; uncommon double passage migrant and winter visitor..

Reports were received for most months of the year of one or two birds.

On the Fylde a single was at Cockers Dyke on 14-15 April with another at Pilling Lane on the 14th. A male on 6 April was the sole spring record at Heysham, while in east Lancashire one was at Waddington on 25 June while there singles on Pendle Hill, mainly in the landslip area above Pendleside Farm, on 20-23 Aug and up to two on 10-23 Sept.

One singing on the Liverpool Tobacco Warehouse on 21 June and one at the same location on the 24th suggested probable breeding.

A pair was on Winter Hill from 21 Sept to 20 Oct and one at Tatham on 24 Oct, while Heysham had females on 27 Nov and 12 Dec. A male was at Seaforth between on 15-16 Nov and one was on Banks Marsh between 29 Nov and 2 Dec. Fylde, winter records were one at Fleetwood on three dates on 9 & 20 Nov and 20 Dec. Further north, one was at Hest Bank on 11 Dec and the last of the year was at Bolton-le-Sands on 21 Dec.

REDSTART *Phoenicurus phoenicurus*
Fairly common breeding bird and double passage migrant.

The first were at Freckleton on 7 April – with further spring singles on coastal Fylde on the 20-24th, and on the 11th at Heysham with further singles there on 17, 18 & 24 April. The first in Chorley was on Chorley golf course on 18 April and one was back at Belmont on the 26th. The Merseyside coast produced a male and female at Seaforth on 20 April and one at Formby on the 23rd. The first of three males in Rossendale was seen at Holden Wood Reservoir on 11 April.

At least four pairs bred at traditional sites in the Anglezarke area, two breeding territories were noted at Belmont with another at Roddlesworth and an additional singing male was at Clough House Farm, Turton. A juvenile was at Belmont on 24 Aug.

In Bowland eight pairs nested in the woods above Stocks Reservoir, compared to six in 2018. All nests were successful, with 49 chicks fledging. Elsewhere in east Lancashire there were reports from 31 sites. The first spring records were three males at New Laithe Farm on 12 April and with eight there on the 20th. In addition to Stocks Reservoir breeding was reported from seven other sites. A newly-fledged juvenile was near the quarry in Croasdale on 2 July, several kilometres from the nearest breeding areas. Breeding was confirmed in Fylde at Tatham Hall Farm and Proctors Farm in July.

The few autumn records received included two at Heysham on 26 Aug, one at Hightown on 16 Sept and a female at Bodie Hill, Fylde on 30 Sept.

WHINCHAT *Saxicola rubetra*
Scarce and declining breeder on eastern hills; uncommon double passage migrant.

Spring movements got going in the third week of April. Heysham spring passage totalled eleven between 21 April and 16 May, with a peak of three on 8 May. There was only a single spring record from MMWWT on 10 May but on Merseyside singles were at Seaforth on 22-23 April and Crosby on the 20-26th. Chorley's first was at Bretherton Eyes on 6 May with another at White Coppice on 23 July. Spring passage on the Fylde saw records of singles between 19 and 21 April at predominantly coastal sites, then a gap to the remaining ones between 2-12 May.

In east Lancashire there were reports from 20 sites with the first on Longridge Fell on 17 April and two May records at Alston and at Croasdale, where two males were singing in the same areas as in 2018.

Successful breeding was recorded at Hareden, Cross of Greet Bridge and Lower Wheathead. A Birdtrack record of six from Whitendale on 12 July suggests likely breeding too in the valleys north of Dunsop Bridge. A sighting at Littledale on 17 July, and one at White Coppice on 23 July were the only other potential breeding season records. Perhaps a slight improvement over last year, but no significant upturn in the species' fortunes to speak of.

Autumn reports were received from eleven sites in the ELOC area in August, eight in September and at Clowbridge Reservoir on 6 Oct and Parsonage Reservoir the following day. The only autumn record at Heysham was two on 26 Aug. One was at Leighton Moss on 9 Sept. Autumn migrants in Chorley included one at Croston Moss on 25 Aug with two more there on 24 Sept. Remaining migrants at Winter Hill included ten on 14 Sept, six on the 17th and one on the 20th, and one was at Great Knowley on 28 Sept.

Return passage on the Fylde saw singles at Glasson Marsh on 26 Aug and Fairhaven Dunes on the 27th, followed by a few more singles in the third week of Sepember, the last of which was at Ballam on the 21st.

Whinchat, Cocker's Dyke, 12 May (Paul Slade)

STONECHAT *Saxicola torquata*
Fairly common, increasing breeding bird in upland and coastal areas; fairly common passage migrant and winter visitor.

Records were received for every week of the year across Lancashire and every month had a peak site count from somewhere of five or more birds with the exception of September where several sites had counts of up to four.

The clear majority of winter records were from coastal areas, including ten on Lytham Moss in December but there is a regular overwintering population in the uplands, no doubt benefiting from the typically milder winters of late (late winter 2018 being a recent exception).

Up to four were seen on several dates at MMWWT in January when wintering birds were also at Croston Moss and White Coppice in January. However, the Lancaster January survey recorded only a maximum count of two birds from a single square. Stonechats are present widely on the Fylde especially in winter with records from around 40 predominantly coastal sites in all months except June of mainly one or two birds. Early in the year six were at Lytham Moss on 4 and 8 Jan with five there on 6 Feb. Later in the year there were ten at the same location on 22 Dec.

Spring passage seemed to get under way a week or two earlier than usual with a peak in the second half of February but an apparent lull in the first two weeks of March – perhaps triggered by the exceptionally warm weather in late February and the notably wet early March. Records picked up again in mid-March and held steady through the middle of April before tailing off again, where breeding records began to take over.

Passage through the Fylde was light with records of mainly one or two birds predominantly from coastal sites. Passage at Heysham included 13 between 18 and 28 Feb with a peak of five. The last record of the winter at MMWWT was a single bird on 11 Feb but at least five were at Lunt Meadows on 20 March.

Breeding reports were widespread with reports from the uplands indicating the successful recolonisation of the last decade is at least consolidating or expanding further. Breeding was confirmed at eleven sites in east Lancashire and three sites there had double-figure counts – Croasdale on 21 June, Langden on 17 July and Cross of Greet Bridge on 17 Aug.

Twenty-two territories were recorded in the west/central West Pennine Moors with many pairs multi-brooded. Successful breeding was also reported from Anglezarke Moor, Wheelton Moor, White Coppice, Great Hill Farm and Dean Black Brook between May and September, again suggesting successful multi-brooding. At least five family groups with 19+ birds were observed around Belmont in mid-August, where number built to around 24 in September.

Juveniles were recorded on the Fylde on 7 July at Warton Bank and 29 Aug at Fairhaven, and at Garston Shore, in south Liverpool on 12 Aug.

Autumn passage was protracted; reports increased gradually from September through to the winter with a shift towards more of the sightings being coastal from November onwards. There were many reports of parties of up to four, including eight at Twiston Moor and Pendle Hill, seven at Crosby and four at New Laithe Farm – all on various dates in September.

From November coastal records predominated with sites on both sides of the Ribble and on the Wyre featuring especially but with few from further north around Morecambe Bay.

WHEATEAR *Oenanthe oenanthe*
Fairly common though local breeding bird; common double passage migrant.

Unsurprisingly, the warm end to February brought the first Wheatears of the year with singles at Torrisholme on the 26th and Winter Hill the next day. There was then a pause in early March, when the weather turned wetter and cooler, before the main arrival began in the week commencing 16 March.

Two at Belmont on 19 March heralded a heavy period of passage with at least 166 birds recorded including a group of 23 on 17 April. At Heysham, 199 birds passed through between 18 March and 9 May with a peak of 40 on 8 May.

The first on the Fylde were at Blackpool and Cocker's Dyke on 20 March with almost daily records up to 20 May from at least 49 locations. On the south side of the Ribble two were at Marshside on 23 March. Spring sightings at Seaforth began on 18 March with a peak of 30+ on 19 April. East Lancashire produced records from 43 sites, the earliest record at Hapton on 20 March and almost daily records through to mid-May with a peak count of 38 at Dean Clough on 2 April. Eleven on Darwen Moor on 16 April. The reporting rate across the county peaked in the week commencing 13 April before tailing off rapidly through to the end of May.

Confirmed breeding occurred at Cross of Greet Bridge and Parsonage Reservoir with probable breeding at Dean Clough, Langden Valley and Pendle Hill. One territory was identified on Winter Hill with a juvenile noted in early July. A displaying male was also seen at Belmont Reservoir in late Apr while four were at Salter Fell on 2 July.

An uptick in the reporting rate in the last week in July signalled the start of autumn movements, which built up momentum to peak in the last week of August before declining through to mid-October.

Return passage in east Lancashire saw birds reported from ten sites in August, 15 in September and three in October, including twelve at New Laithe Farm on 8 Sept and the last on Pendle Hill on the 22 Oct, where there had been ten the previous day.

At Heysham autumn passage totalled 58 birds between 17 July and 19 Oct with a peak of 16 on 26 Aug.

Compared with spring, autumn was relatively quiet at Belmont with only 17 recorded but visible migration at Winter Hill saw 44 Wheatears over on 7 Sept and 30 on the14th with the last there on 12 Oct.

Return passage on the Fylde got going on 2 Aug with one at Cockersand and a few more coastal records in the first half of the month before almost daily sightings between 19 Aug and 6 Oct including nine at Lower Ballam on 16 Sept, three Rossall Point on the 30th and one at Bank End on 16 Oct. The last at Seaforth was on 24 Sept.

EASTERN BLACK-EARED WHEATEAR *Oenanthe melanoleuca*
Vagrant.

An adult female was found with a group of Northern Wheatears on the coast near Fluke Hall on the Fylde on 1 Sept where it stayed until the 16th. (P. Ellis, P. G. Slade).

It stood out immediately and examination of the tail pattern quickly established its identity as either a Black-eared or Pied Wheatear. As more observers and more detail observations became possible during its obliging stay opinion consolidated around it being an Eastern Black-eared Wheatear – and it was submitted as such to the BBRC.

However, at the time of writing BBRC has not agreed this identification, no doubt due to the difficulties of diagnosing this species in this plumage.

If accepted it will become Lancashire's first record of Eastern Black-eared Wheatear. We have one record of Pied Wheatear, at Seaforth in October 1997.

Eastern Black-eared Wheatear, Fluke Hall, 16 September (Paul Ellis)

Eastern Black-eared Wheatear, Fluke Hall, 8 September (Craig Bell)

DIPPER *Cinclus cinclus*
Uncommon breeder, mainly in the east.

Records were widely received from suitable habitat across the county with no out-of-context sightings of note.

The Lancaster and District winter survey recorded 13 with an unsurprisingly uneven distribution with records from only four squares and nine of the total from a single square in the Bowland uplands.

In east Lancashire reports were received from many suitable rivers and streams across the area. The first singing bird was at Wood End Sewage works on 9 Jan, and breeding was confirmed at eight locations. In Bowland there were two pairs in Hareden, where one nest was found and fledging observed, in the Langden and Dunsop Valleys and at Slaidburn.

Breeding was confirmed at five sites in Chorley, including a pair which fledged two chicks on the River Darwen at Hoghton Bottoms, and with further suitable sites suspected to hold breeding pairs. Four territories were recorded on Belmont Brook with another territory on Broadhead Brook upstream of Wayoh Reservoir.

The widespread distribution of Dippers in Rossendale is evident in the data showing records from at least 34 sites across 25 one km grid squares, many of which reported evidence of breeding. Birds were reported in all months of the year.

Fylde records included sightings of one or two birds at Brock throughout the year, one at Fulwood on 18 Feb, two at Ashton on Ribble on two dates in early April and three at Myerscough on 6 May.

Birds were singing in November at Ightenhill Bridge and Hoghton Bottoms and on 12 Dec at Foulscales Brook. A peak of 16 was reported in the Jackhouse area on 2 Dec.

HOUSE SPARROW *Passer domesticus*
Abundant breeding resident. Red list (breeding decline).

As usual the most comprehensive information came from nestbox monitoring in the Pilling-Preesall area, where 23 nests were monitored and 105 eggs laid, from which 72 hatched and 64 young fledged.

In east Lancashire it was considered that the apparent small recovery of 2018 may not have continued, with half as many double-figure counts being submitted compared with the previous year and confirmed breeding at only one site. In contrast there was some range expansion in the Belmont area with the resettlement of a farm, and also good productivity with 40 plus in one garden in September. Similarly, an improved showing in the garden survey suggested some recovery in suburban Chorley.

Notable concentrations included 70 at Marshside in December, 60 at Bilsborrow in November, 51 at Newton-in-Bowland in January, 50 at Bolton-le-Sands in July and similar numbers at Oglet in September and Glasson Dock in October. In the Aintree study area there were seven distinct flocks and a total population in excess of 200 birds, while the species remains common, but patchily distributed, throughout Liverpool. The maximum in the Rossendale area was 40 at Whitworth in September.

This species generally doesn't move very far, and whilst in most years some evidence of local movement is reported at well watched sites there was no evidence of this during the year save for a male at Belmont Reservoir on 2 Aug.

TREE SPARROW *Passer montanus*
Common breeding resident. Red List (breeding decline).

As with House Sparrows the most comprehensive breeding information came from the Over Wyre area. From the 542 nests by 262 pairs that were monitored 2629 eggs were laid, from which 1474 hatched and 1368 young fledged. There were 21 nests at Todderstaffe Hall; at all of these Fylde sites supplementary feeding by birders has helped sustain the population. There were 22 pairs at MMWWT.

Peak counts on the Fylde included 80 at Eagland Hill feeding station in March, 74 at Ridge Farm on 22 Sept, 65 at New Lane feeding station in January and 50 at Eagland Hill on 2 Feb, while away from these strongholds there were up to 30 at a feeding station at Wesham Marsh towards the end of the year. In the Lancaster area the peak count was 25 at Aldcliffe on 21 Oct which may have included some passage birds, there were no large assemblies around Cockersand this year but up to eleven were at Hare Tarn in January and ten at Potts Corner in February.

Thirty-seven reports were received from eleven sites in east Lancashire which were both down on 2018. Up to 40 at Hodder Foot on 13 Aug included a high proportion of fledglings. The other large count was 16 at Calder Foot also in August which may have reflected successful breeding, which was confirmed only at Brownsills in addition to Calder Foot. At Brockholes eleven on 21 Jan was a notable number by recent standards, reflecting apparent declines in the east of the county. Comfortably the peak count in Chorley was 15 on Coppull Moor in December, while up to six were regular all year in Eccleston.

The peak count In the south-west was 70 at Hesketh Out Marsh on 11 Jan, with up to 30 the same month at Burscough Moss. Up to eight were noted in the St Helens area at Rainford.

As with breeding information the majority of passage records came from north Fylde, in this case analysis of sound-recordings revealed 200 over Knott End between 14 Feb and 14 May, then 118 from 24 Aug to 19 Nov. There was barely any other spring movement reported. Autumn passage was not particuarly evident either, although to some extent this may have been due to lower visible migration coverage in some areas. At Heysham 24 birds moved over between 20 July and 28 Oct, with a peak of seven on 25 Oct.

DUNNOCK *Prunella modularis*
Abundant breeding resident. Amber list (breeding decline).

Peak counts of this species are generally difficult to interpret as they are as much a reflection of the way in which observers record and collate counts as any actual peaks in distribution. Larger totals reported included 18 at Jackhouse in February, twelve at Brockholes in March, eleven at Leighton Moss in November and ten in the Cheesden Valley, Rossendale in April, at Whalley in May and at Aldcliffe in October.

The species dropped from fifth most abundant to seventh in the CDNHS area winter garden survey, while the number of territories on the EDF properties at Heysham was above average at 22. Eight territories in the Aintree study area was reflective of a general decline there and this was also the case at Lunt Meadows where there was only one pair, but six pairs on Freshfield Dune Heath was stable. There were seven pairs at Warton Mires. In the West Pennine Moors birds were reported nesting in atypical bracken-bed habitat up to 325 above sea level.

The sedentary nature of this species was reflected in very little visible evidence of migration. At Heysham it was considered a poor year for dispersal and the only concrete record concerned two on 18 Oct. The same month five were seen to leave high south apparently migrating at Gynn Gardens, Blackpool on the 16th with a single doing the same at Fleetwood Cemetery on the 23rd.

YELLOW WAGTAIL *Motacilla flava flavissima*
Scarce breeding bird, fairly common passage migrant

This is a declining species which is now on the edge of its north-west England breeding range, exacerbated by the intensive animal husbandry, including multiple silage cuts, in recent 'strongholds' such as Wenning Foot in the north of the region. Consequently it varies from being an individually notifiable species in the Lancaster area, to regular passage bird with occasional breeding evidence in the Fylde and to a regular breeding and passage migrant south of the Ribble in the favourable crop-growing areas. There is a similar pattern of northern scarcity in the east of the county with, for example, gradually decreasing numbers east Lancashire and Rossendale down to single figures in 2019, including a lingering male at Holden Wood Reservoir on 7-9 May.

The only spring record from Heysham was two on 22 April. Other northern records were limited to singles over the Stone Jetty on 30 April and 11 May, one at Aldcliffe on 10 May and one with Pied/White Wagtails at Wenning Foot on 26 April. In contrast, the north Fylde vis mig was excellent with 69 recorded over Knott End between 12 April and 23 May with peaks of ten on 22 April and eleven on 7 May; Rossall vis mig saw a total of 47 between 16 April & 15 May with peaks of seven on 22 April, five on 21 April, four on 1 May, while at Blackpool vis mig produced ten between 19 April and 11 May with half of these on 30 April. Off-passage birds included up to six at Aggleby Pits on 21-22 April and three at Ream Hills on 22-23 April and at Pilling Lane Ends on 21 April.

South of the Ribble, there were no regular spring vis mig data, simply routine recording, especially at coastal sites and on the south-west mosses. Seaforth experienced its best spring passage since 1987 with 17 bird-days between 18 and 28 April, including seven on the 22nd. There was no evidence of spring passage as such in the east of the county with a spring blank at Winter Hill, for example.

Despite monitoring of former sites, there was no evidence of any territorial individuals in the north of the county and just one in the Fylde, a female feeding young near Union Lane, but many extensive crop fields were difficult to access. In the Chorley area, there appeared to be at least attempted breeding at Bretherton Eyes and at least one bird lingered at Croston Finney during late April. There was no breeding census of birds south of the Ribble, but Paul Slater's detailed observations give a snapshot for a small proportion of the area: suggestive breeding pairs were present in spring-sown cereal, sprout and potato fields in the Rainford Old Coach road area and breeding season registrations came from Catchdale Moss Lane, Ferny Knoll Road and Kirkby Moss. Other breeding records included five recently fledged young at Hesketh Out Marsh.

In the ELOC area there were just eight casual records between 19 May and 26 Sept with half of these over Clowbridge Reservoir. In addition, Ewood Bridge sewage works held low single figures in

August. Autumn records from the north of the region saw just singles south over Sunderland Point on 27 July and 12 Aug and two over Middleton NR on 3 Aug. Autumnal gatherings on the Fylde may have reflected local breeding success in the case of three juveniles at Freckleton Marsh on 23 July, but all the rest could equally have been off-passage birds from a distant source. The main site, Bank End, peaked at four on 15 Aug with the last on 6 Sept and there were reports of ones and twos from five other sites with the last at Peel Hill on 16 Sept. Vis mig at Rossall saw eight singletons on six dates between 4 Aug and 19 Sept and three on 24 Aug, and Knott End also saw a sharp contrast with spring with just three recorded between 8 July and 26 Aug..

South of the Ribble by far the largest numbers were reported from MMWWT with '20+' on 18 & 26 Aug and 3 Sept, while single-figure counts came from a wide variety of sites, mainly coastal, but including daily counts of up to four at Croston Moss 18-31 Aug.

BLUE HEADED WAGTAIL *Motacilla flava flava* (and hybrids/intergrades with *flavissima*)
Scarce migrant, occasionally one or both parents of breeding pairs

Males were seen at Hesketh Out Marsh on 20 April, Seaforth on the 22nd, Fleetwood golf course on the 30th, Bank End on 13-14 May and Banks Marsh on 17 May. Perhaps surprisingly, there were no reports found of 'Channel' Wagtail, the hybrid..

GREY WAGTAIL *Motacilla cinerea*
Fairly common breeding bird, common passage migrant and winter visitor

Winter period records were widespread, with many lowland sites in the Fylde and south of the Ribble supporting birds in areas where they do not breed. In contrast, upper clough breeding sites were evacuated with many inland winter records limited to lower altitude sewage works, village ponds or along the floodplain stage of rivers

Spring passage was, as usual, a bit before many vis miggers get going, so there were just odds and ends of single figures from most sites. The exceptions were at Rossall where 55 were recorded between 25 Feb & 5 May with peaks of nine on 25 Feb and eight on 2 March, and Knott End where 81 were recorded between 15 Feb and 22 May, peaking at nine on 8 March.

Plenty of breeding data received indicated that even in the core range of upland cloughs and inland river valleys, there was often a close nesting association with bridges, waterworks buildings or other man-made structures. This even included use of a nestbox on the West Pennine Moors, and sewage works were utilized at, for example, Colne. Lowland or near-lowland records west of OS line 50 used a wide variety of breeding locations, mainly close to water, but also including sewage works, culverts such as at Croxteth, waterside structures such as Carr Mill Dam and Damside Mill Yard and structures associated with a parkland lake at Stanley Park., Blackpool. Persistent sightings in the summer from Gynn Gardens and central Blackpool might be related to a single urban breeding pair (possibly on a small cliff). See ringing report. Other western lowland records were predictably along rivers such as the Alt, Yarrow, Wyre and Conder.

2019 provided some visual evidence to support the indications from the Heysham ringing programme that visible migrants at perceived 'long haul' flight- height are presumably up there avoiding the likes of Sparrowhawks and in fact the 'migration', as regards distance travelled in Lancashire, is frequently little more than a short-stage dispersal with many ringed vis mig birds wintering in the county, often within a handful of kilometres.

Several September mornings of cloud-bound Lake District saw the NW to SE vis mig limited to this species, presumably just hopping across the Bay, with the longer distance, usually far more numerous, migrants such as Meadow Pipit completely absent. As befits the 'partly migrant' status, some movements were lengthy with, for example, a 2019-ringed bird wintering in Yeovil. Autumnal vis mig saw some decent counts of: 201 over Knott End between 6 June and 4 Nov, peaking at 18 on 19 Sept; 159 over Rossall between 20 Aug and 30 Oct with peaks of 13 on 8 Sept and 14 on 16 Sept; 149 over Heysham between 27 Aug and 31 Oct, peaking at 19 on 16 Sept. In contrast, just 23 over Winter Hill between 3 Sept and 14 Oct with a peak of four on 14 Sept..

PIED WAGTAIL *Motocilla alba yarrelli*
Common breeding bird, very common passage migrant and probable winter visitor

This is by no means an entirely resident species, being (like Skylark) a summer visitor to many inland areas, including upper river valleys and the lower fell slopes. In the absence of any current ringing we are not sure how many of our wintering birds come from further north.

Winter feeding maxima were in near-coastal lowlands with 35 near Croxteth Brook on 15 Feb, 30-40 at Little Knowley in November-December, 27 at Todderstaffe Hall on 27 Dec and 33 at Bank End on 31 Dec. Winter roosts we were informed about included 40-50 at Fishmoor Reservoir in the first winter period, up to 113 in Liverpool City Centre in the first winter period but only 19 there in the second period, 55 at Greenfield NR Colne in the second winter period and 20s and 30s at Stocks, Spade Mill and Belmont, mainly in autumn

SD66 provides a good example of the inland difference between breeding and wintering numbers. Only six were found during eight hours of survey work in winter, all of these were predictably around sewage works or lowland villages/farmyards covering the five northern tetrads. In summer, every tetrad was occupied by breeding pairs with many of these on upland barns and stone walls. At the other extreme, it was one of only two known breeding species in coastal SD36V (Heysham north wall) and one of six in nearby SD35Z. In the remainder of the county, it was absent only from moorland without rocky outcrops with no obvious concentrations or favoured habitat, providing there were buildings, stone walls or natural riparian cliffs

In the absence of large roosts being reported, the real number-crunching was with the vis mig data. Spring passage saw 656 at Rossall between 25 Feb and 14 May, peaking at 42 on 19 March, 791 registrations on the recorder at Knott End between11 Feb and 23 May with again the peak, 86, on 19 March. Less well-recorded were Heysham with 120 between 18 March and 18 April, peaking at 25 on 20 March and Winter Hill with 16 between 26 and 30 March peaking at five on 26 March. Off-passage gatherings in spring of note included 73 at Preesall on 18 March, 80 at Ewood Bridge sewage works on 31 March, 41 at Aggleby's Pit on 22 April. Autumn passage at Rossall saw 432 between 24 Aug and 10 Nov, peaking at 31 on 20 Sept and 38 on 30 Sept. Knott End saw 669 between 18 June and 29 Nov peaking at 25 on 30 Sept. Winter Hill saw 676 between 8 Sept and 6 Nov with a large day-count of 215 on 12 Oct. Other vis mig included 194 over Heysham between 8 Sept and 29 Oct, peaking with 34 on 18 Oct and 26 flew over Belmont Reservoir in just one hour on 9 Oct. Autumnal gatherings of note included 140 at Ewood Bridge sewage works on 6 Sept, 83 at Bank End on 11 Aug, 60 at Little Knowley on 30 Oct, 50 at Barrowford Reservoir on 26 Sept and 40 at Jackhouse on 9 Oct.

WHITE WAGTAIL *Motacilla alba alba*
Common passage migrant

This section deals with sightings of off-passage birds in spring – autumn sightings seem to have slipped into the realms of uncertainty! Obviously a fair chunk of the spring vis mig, especially April birds and autumnal vis mig, especially mid-September birds, are of this form but cannot be identified as such.

The Sefton Coast status in spring was tersely categorized as 'a dreadful passage' and there were few reports above low single figures. However, Seaforth experienced a more or less average spring including 50+ on 15 and 19 April. Further north just the one site produced the goods. Aggleby's Pit recorded 35 on 21 April, 41 on 22nd and 12 on 23rd. Fifteen other Fylde sites recorded between one and nine and six north Lancashire sites saw low single figures. Further east there were low single figures at Bretherton, Croston, Stocks Reservoir, Alston wetlands, Ightenhill Bridge and Rishton Reservoir.

RICHARDS PIPIT* *Anthus richardi*
Vagrant

One was at Rossall School on 30 Oct (AS Disley) and another at Mythop on 1 Dec (F Bird). These are the 35th and 36th acceptable records for the county.

MEADOW PIPIT *Anthus pratensis*
Common breeding bird, abundant passage migrant

Winter records received were typically scattered, perhaps most regular as a notebook 'also ran' at well-recorded coastal fields and saltmarshes with a peak of 90 at Staining on 11 Dec. Inland records came mainly from reservoir edges such as 50+ at Parsonage on 21 Dec, 16 at Spade Mill on 1 Jan and 15+ at Dean Clough on 25 Feb. It is especially difficult to find in winter in north Lancashire away from the agricultural fields around Cockersand and the saltmarshes with irregular single figures on flood-plain fields and around small open sewage works

The spring passage was generally very good this year but autumn coastal passage fell foul of westerlies during the peak period while the east coast/Pennine vis mig stations 'filled their boots',.

In spring, Rossall recorded 9358 between 25 Feb and 3 May with peaks of 1042 on 30 March, 861 on 6 April and 770 on 7 April; 5926 flew over Knott End between 11 Feb and 14 May including a peak of 369 on 7 April; Heysham saw 2247 between 26 Feb and 23 April with a peak of 431 on 6 April. and 1105 were recorded at Pilling Lane on 7 April. Therefore the peak passage came slightly later than usual.

Autumn passage saw just 3886 between 30 Aug and 10 Nov over Rossall with peaks of 597 on 28 Sept and 449 on the 30th. Nearby Starr Gate had a peak of 1560 on 30 Sept, while 1363 flew over Knott End between 24 Aug and 29 Nov and Heysham saw just 760 between 7 Sept and 6 Nov with a peak of 140 on 30 Sept. Several days during the usual peak autumn passage saw seemingly suitable conditions at Heysham but a migration diverting synopsis further north, including heavy cloud over the Lake District (see Grey Wagtail). The Lancashire/Greater Manchester border on Winter Hill, on the western edge of the Pennines, on the other hand, saw a decent autumn passage with 25564 between 5 Sept and 20 Nov, with September peak counts of 3127 on the 18th, 1814 on the 20th, 1618 on 23rd, 2146 on the 26th and 1774 on the 30th. Perhaps unusually, October counts there were unremarkable with the notable exception of the highest count of the year of 3550 on the 12th. Elsewhere, there was an early high count of 500 over Grane on 13 Sept.

The most significant breeding data saw a complete absence in large swathes of floodplain and low altitude agricultural land in north Lancashire, notably silage fields and heavily-grazed pasture where *Juncus* had been removed/was very scattered. This follows the same pattern as Skylark and it is not until the *Molinia*-dominated lower moorland or *Juncus*-filled pasture (which is not mown during the breeding season) is reached that these species can be found. Here and on nearby heather moorland, including grouse moors, Meadows Pipits can be very common and difficult to count. The

Meadow Pipit, Cocker's Dyke, 30 October (Howard Phillips)

Winter Hill BBS detected 200 pairs with an arrival in mid-March, about a month after Skylark. A farm at Clough Hill, Turton registered 22 singing males. Lowland breeding concentrations occur on the extensive saltmarshes, mosses and dune systems with, for example, ten pairs on Birkdale dunes and 17 pairs on Hesketh out-Marsh.

TREE PIPIT *Anthus trivialis*
Scarce breeding bird and passage migrant

The data search suggested that we could perhaps do with a year of 'please submit all breeding records'. Records received seemed to suggest a significant reliance on the clearfell/early stages of the conifer industry cycle with other records from more permanent scattered upland tree cover. There were 50 reports sent in to ELOC of breeding records or early autumnal gatherings/vis mig. The latter category saw the largest counts with 15 at/over Crown Point on both 24 and 27 Aug. New Laithe Farm recorded 5-8 on seven dates in late August/early September.. Scattered breeding records came from other upland sites, including Docker Moor (3-4 pairs), Beacon Fell (at least two pairs) and the Belmont area

The regular flight-height/audibility of this species means that records are missed if background noise is an issue or vis mig coverage is not in the form of single-minded stationary concentration. They are also out of audible range for several would be recorders. The outstanding datasets were from Rossall and Knott End. At Rossall, 150 flew north between 10 April and 15 May with peaks of 13 on 18 April, twelve on 22 April and ten on 11 May. At Knott End, 184, including some nocturnal registrations, flew over between 7 April and 23 May including 20 on 19 April and 18 on 30 April. At Heysham, just 13 were recorded between 6 April and 8 May with a peak correlating with the above of four on 18 April.

Compared to Crown Point (see above), coastal autumn passage was poor with 24 over Knott End from 1 Aug to 16 Sept including ten on 25 Aug, 18 over Fairhaven during 24 Aug-21 Sept with a peak of eight on 24 Aug, 16 over Rossall from 23 Aug-14 Sept with a peak of six on 24 Aug and just two singles over Heysham. It doesn't appear there was much vis mig in August at Winter Hill with just four right at the back end between 7 and 14 Sept. Scattered casual submissions from many other coastal and inland sites on passage and the recorder is to be commended for managing to hear an overhead migrant at Vauxhall on 24 Aug!

ROCK PIPIT *Anthus petrosus*

Anthus petrosus petrosus
Very rare breeding bird, first confirmed in 2018

Following regular sightings in winter 2018/9, plumage details suggested the same pair as 2018 double-brooded in two separate holes in the south harbour at Heysham. One young survived from the first brood and two from the second – the latter benefited from a Painted Lady invasion-inclusive diet! The Heysham Head pair produced at least two young seen together on 14 June and was probably single-brooded as in 2018. At least one extra bird frequented Red Nab during the breeding season and up to six between Red Nab and Heysham Head during winter 2019/20 were probably local birds.

There were no other definite sightings of the nominate race.

Anthus petrosus littoralis or unspecified
Fairly common passage migrant and winter visitor, presumably almost exclusively littoralis

Supported by colour-ringed sightings in previous winters as well as temporal occurrence pattern, the mainly 'salt-marsh winter population' is thought to comprise exclusively of Scandinavian birds. They are most regularly recorded on the high spring tides as a by-product of Water Pipit searches and 2020 was no exception. There were plenty of site counts from all our saltmarshes of one to four individuals but the only reports of more than five together were '6+' at The Heads on 24 Jan, 13 at The Heads on 22 Feb, eight at Barnaby Sands on 13 Oct and six at Cockersand on 29 Dec. The Rossall data provided the most comprehensive vis mig records with a single spring bird on 26 Feb and eleven between 2 Oct and 9 Nov with peaks of two on 2 Oct and 6 Nov. Departure in spring is often very early and, in this area, very few reports of the distinctive summer plumage. One Knott End on 8 Sept was early with most arrivals not until early October.

WATER PIPIT *Anthus spinoletta*
Scarce winter visitor and passage migrant

Usually out of sight on extensive saltmarshes, this species is well-recorded when displaced by the highest spring tides.. Therefore the largest counts are during high tides related to the spring equinox. The autumnal high spring tides mainly occur prior to this species' arrival and the mid-winter spring tides are too low for more than, at best, partial counts.

By far the best area was the north Ribble Freckleton/Warton section where record counts were obtained. Maxima were 20 on 9 Feb, 30 on 11 Feb, 40 on 13 Feb, 30 on 15 Feb, 30 on 2 March (all Warton), 30 on 2 April, 43 on 8 April, 34 on 9 April, 27 on 13 April, 32 on 14 April, 12 on 15 April and the final one on 19 April (all Freckleton). Counts at other seasons saw presence at Warton from 13 Nov with a peak of four on 18 Nov and a peak of two at Freckleton on 29 Dec.

Water Pipit, Freckleton, 6 April (Paul Ellis)

At another favoured site, The Heads on the Wyre, where the tides do not have to be quite as high to reveal presence, the peak count was 15 on 24 Jan and all the usual spring peak counts were of five (22 Feb) or less. Two were at Conder Green on at least 24 Feb with singleton(s) on three other February dates. Singles were at Pilling Lane Ends (23 Feb) and Fleetwood (1st Jan, 3rd & 10th Nov). South of the Ribble, up to three were regularly recorded on Crossens Outer Marsh from the start of the year until 1 April and a singleton was recorded a number of times in the same location from 3 Nov onwards.

The only inland records which could be unearthed were one on Middleton NR on 22 Feb and one in a flooded field at Belmont on 25 Nov.

CHAFFINCH *Fringilla coelebs*
Abundant breeding bird, passage migrant and winter visitor.

The Chaffinch population seems to be stable at present, although perhaps somewhat reduced from a number of years ago in some areas as evidenced from observations in the Chorley region where it remained 12th in the Winter Garden Bird Survey (down from 6th a few years ago), and from Brindle where, in two adjacent BBS squares, only 22 were noted in comparison to a peak of 58 in 2006. However, it is still a very common and regularly-recorded species with the incessant song of the males ubiquitous in spring.

In the first winter period the largest counts came from the Eagland Hill-Pilling area where regular feeding sites drew in the birds and the watchers. The peak count was of around 100 at Bradshaw Lane on 2 Jan but the more consistent sites were at New Lane (with 70-80 recorded regularly into mid-March after which numbers dropped to single figures as birds dispersed), and Thompsons Fold (with 30-40 on most occasions but over 60 on 16 Jan). Several other locations on the Fylde had counts in excess of 40 but elsewhere there were few significant assemblies: a feeding site at Strongstry, Rossendale held at least 40 on 18 Jan, 50 were at Windle Farm, Eccleston on the 19th and 38 at Newton-in-Bowland on the 24th. A roost at Belmont held at least 40 on 14 & 28 Jan and 30 on 23 Feb. A total of 853 flew over Knott End between 11 Feb and 15 May including 99 on 28 March.

The odd snippet of song was heard in late January at Sowerby and early February at Wood End SW and Clitheroe but from 10 Feb there was an explosion of singing males reported from all corners of the county. Counts of singing males and breeding pairs were roughly similar to last year: eleven pairs at Freshfield Dune heath was around the average as were five territories around Aintree, six at Carr Mill Dam and two at Kirkdale Cemetery. Thirty-two pairs at MMWWT was significantly more than in 2018 and 15 pairs in Birkdale Dunes was again around the norm. Eleven males were singing at Cuerden Valley Park and a survey of Winter Hill found five territories on the periphery of the area that suffered from fires in 2018. In the Over Wyre area, 542 nests of an estimated 262 pairs were monitored in which 2629 eggs were laid, 1474 eggs hatched and 1368 young fledged. Sixty-three singing males were recorded in a tetrad with Foulridge in the centre. Seven pairs bred at Challan Hall, Silverdale and over 130 sites reported singing males.

Autumn passage was broadly similar to last year with totals seen at Fairhaven numbering just 257 (peak of 104 on 3 Oct) and Heysham recording 1723 with a peak of 297 on 25 Oct. Sound recording at Knott End recorded 2,373 peaking at 407 on 28 Oct. These numbers are more like a daily total on east coast sites but in Lancashire birds pass through on a broad front; passage monitored in the first hour after sunrise at Belmont recorded 367 in a fairly consistent passage over 21 mornings including a peak of 42 on 5 Oct. The largest daily count was of 303 at Rossall Point on 23 Oct and 198 passed south over Formby Point on the 14th. Peak count at Seaforth was 40 on 5 Oct.

Things were generally quiet in the second winter period save for a flock of around 800 feeding on a harvested Maize field at Newton-with Scales on 20 Nov. A flock of at least 100 was Buckden Wood, Stubbins on 28 Nov, 120 were at Hoghton Bottoms on 2 Dec and 130 were feeding near Belmont on the 31st. Numbers at the Fylde feeding sites peaked at around 50-60,

BRAMBLING *Fringilla montifringilla*
Winters in variable numbers. Fairly common double passage migrant, mostly in autumn.

Brambling is a species that is well recorded when present in the county and 2019 proved to be another good year. The hangover of the 2018 influx was much in evidence in the early part of the year with birds moving to gardens as the beech mast crop became exhausted. In this period, birds were recorded from 61 sites across 25 10km squares with most records coming east of the M6 corridor. In Rossendale there were some impressive counts at the Strongstry feeding station with birds present daily from 29 Nov 2018 through to 20 April 2019 with peak counts of 37 on 3 Jan and over 60 on the 18th. Counts in the teens were regularly present at Calf Hey and Folly Clough, Goodshaw. Further north, birds were regular at Marl Hill with a peak of 28 on 11 Jan as well as Shireburne Park, Clitheroe with 25 on 3 Feb. Birds were present in a Belmont garden through to 14 May with 20-30 seen on several days, peaking in mid-March through to mid-April after which most birds departed. Of the four known roost sites nearby, the only one counted produced 58 birds on 14 Jan. The only other large count was of 40 at Yarrow Reservoir on 13 Jan.

Further towards the coast, numbers were far lower. Two were visiting a feeding station at Eagland Hill in January and up to four were present through February. March and April saw more widespread sightings of mostly single passage birds at places such as Birkdale, Stanley Park, Blackpool, Fleetwood, Pilling Lane, Rainford, White Moss, Higher Walton, Bashall Eaves and Brockholes with two or more from Hoghton Bottoms (6 on 20 March), Mitton, Rishton, Clitheroe, Gisburn Forest and West Bradford. Eighteen flew over Knott End between 24 Feb and 20 April including three on 31 March.

The first of the autumn passage were at Folly Clough in Rossendale on 11 Oct and Fluke Hall on the 12th. Passage monitored over Belmont recorded 703 over ten days from 15 Oct to 9 Nov with a peak of 244 on 27 Oct coinciding with a flock of 330 feeding in nearby beech-woods. Heysham recorded just 35 with a peak of 15 on 17 Oct whilst 82 flew over Knott End between 17 Oct and 18 Nov including 29 on 28 Oct. Six passed south over Rossall Point on 23 Oct, 20 were noted at Tower Lodge on the 30tht and seven NE over Rimrose Valley the same day. One or two were noted at MMWWT, Kew, Poulton-le-Fylde, Ridge Farm, Roeburndale and New Laithe Farm throughout this period.

There followed an influx into the more upland areas during November with 10 at Kemple End on the 8th, 50-100 at Shedden Wood on the 13th and 19 at Stocks Reservoir on the 15th. Numbers at Shedden Wood increased to 300 by 16 Dec, at least 70 were in a large finch flock at Marl Hill on the 20th and approximately 60 were at Dean Black Brook above White Coppice on the 26th. Roost counts at Belmont increased from 99 on 10 Nov to 258 on the 22nd and 394 on 22 Dec. In the rest of the county, Bramblings were rather thin on the ground with surprisingly no great numbers noted in Rossendale.

HAWFINCH *Coccothraustes coccothraustes*
Rare and localised breeding resident.

Records of this species reverted to type with all but three records coming from the Silverdale area. There was a single report from the formerly regular site at Woodwell on 5 Jan; that was followed by a series of records of up to five from an undisclosed site in the Silverdale area during March and April including display and six later in August. Birds also turned up at Leighton Moss in May and July hopefully indicating a breeding presence nearby.

Single migrants were noted away from this area. A bird frequented a feeder at Banks on 8 April and in late October there were birds reported at Crook O' Lune (a semi-regular site) on the 28th and Ainsdale NNR on the 31st. At Knott End, sound recordings indicated singles flew over on 6 April and 18 Oct.

BULLFINCH *Pyrrhula pyrrhula*
Common breeding resident.

Bullfinches continue to do rather well in the county with the highest density around Silverdale but also plenty of records from central Lancashire and a broad swathe of locations through the middle of the county, up through the Ribble Valley and associated tributaries. The Chorley Winter Garden Survey saw Bullfinch move up to 16th place whilst the Lancaster January Survey clocked up 61 with 42 in the Silverdale area alone. The species remains notable on the Fylde with records from just 21 locations during the year and only regular at Carr House Green Common, Marton Mere (in the winter periods) and Myerscough Quarry.

In the first winter period, Bullfinches were commonly seen at garden feeders in some numbers. Peak counts of seven were obtained from Marl Pits, Folly Clough and Strongstry in Rossendale, and in east Lancashire, counts of seven or more were noted at Jackhouse, Stocks Reservoir and Low Moor (Clitheroe). Up to 30 were seen in four discrete flocks around Belmont in late January. Leighton Moss and Challan Hall, there were regular daily totals in high single figures but with some days reaching twelve individuals.

Birds were regularly seen in a Rishton garden with no more than six at any one time but 19 new birds were ringed and 27 were retrapped in the course of spring passage, most notably in March.

There were few records in the Liverpool area but birds were present in spring at a few locations between Kirkby and Rainford in St Helens with young seen in hedges along Dairy Farm Road in June.

There were three territories at Aintree, a pair at Freshfield Dune Heath and the usual 4 – 5 pairs at Birkdale Dunes. A single pair nested at MMWWT and young were seen at three location around Cuerden Valley Park. Breeding was reported in Skelmersdale, Ormskirk and at several locations around the south and east of Preston. Two pairs were located on Winter Hill and a pair fledged young at Belmont Reservoir. Young birds were noted at Rishton, Burnley, Swinden Reservoir, Clitheroe, Longridge and Lower Wheathead in east Lancashire. In addition, a survey of the tetrad around Foulridge indicated seven pairs in the area. Three pairs successfully raised young at Stubbins and pairs were seen at several suitable locations elsewhere in Rossendale. Six pairs were located at Challan Hall and the surrounding woodland whilst the breeding population at Heysham seems stable at four pairs.

At Heysham, 32 migrants were noted during the autumn with a peak of ten on 23 Oct. Otherwise there was little evidence of passage.

In the second winter period, double-figure counts away from Leighton Moss consisted of ten at Waterfoot on 18 Dec, ten at Jackhouse on the 21st and twelve at Stocks Reservoir on the 31st.

GREENFINCH *Chloris chloris*
Common but declining breeding resident. Some autumn movement.

The decline of the Greenfinch has been well documented over recent years but hopefully the nadir has been reached and there are some shoots of recovery. The species was 18th in the Chorley Winter Garden Survey (where it was once 10th when the annual survey started in 1998) but BBS at Brindle produced the best count for ten years. On the other hand, the Lancaster January Survey produced an all-time low of 54. Even so, the species seems to be most commonly reported from the Fylde and northwest of the county.

Peak counts in the early winter period were up to 42 gathering pre-roost at Marton Mere during January and 25 going to roost in conifers at Warbreck Hill. There were very few other double figure counts in a disappointing period: eleven at Marl Hill on 20 Jan, 14 at Poulton-le-Fylde on the 28th, eleven at Burnside (near Slaidburn), 20 at Crook O'Lune on 11 Feb, 20 at MMWWT on 13 March and 12 at Rawtenstall on the 23rd.

An early singing male was noted at Roby Mill on 19 Jan, otherwise it was mid-February when singing birds were more noticeable such as at Pilling on 6 Feb, Catforth and Warbreck Hill on 11 Feb, Greenbank Park, Liverpool on the 14th and Rawtenstall and Whitworth on the 24th.

There was a slight spring passage with 19 new birds ringed at Heysham and 13 at Rishton.

Breeding evidence was supplied from around 80 locations. It was reported as still fairly common around Southport with at least four pairs on Birkdale Dunes, two in Birkdale village and several singing around Kew. MMWWT recorded 16 breeding pairs whilst numbers at Freshfield Dune Heath recovered to five pairs. Just three pairs were noted at Aintree and two pairs nesting at Stubbins was considered a local success. A flurry of juveniles ringed at Heysham in late July – August would have been of local origin.

Autumn passage started around mid-September and vis-miggers noted 182 over 14 days at Crosby, 63 over Belmont on 9 days and 275 over Heysham with a peak of 67 on 25 Oct. Thirty-nine birds were ringed at Fleetwood Marsh NP on 19 Oct and 20 on the 28th. A flock of 18 was at Marl Hill on the 13 Sept and at least ten were in a Belmont garden from late August to the end of the year peaking at 17 on 7 Oct. Greenfinches were irregular at Seaforth NR with a late peak of 20 migrants on 15 Nov. Other passage flocks of note were 50 at Aldcliffe on 23 Oct and Hest Bank on the 26th, 40 at Cockersand and 50 at Barrow Scout on the 28th, 30 at Lytham on 5 Nov, 70 at Birkdale Dunes LNR on the 6th and 20 at Mitchell House Reservoirs on the 13th.

A good flock was present at Cockersand through to the end of the year, peaking at 80 on 11 Nov. The largest count of the year was 108 at a pre-roost gathering at Pine Lake on 26 Nov. December's peak counts included 50 at Pilling Lane, 29 at Warton Bank, 25 at Aldcliffe, 45 at Todderstaffe Hall and 27 at Prince's Park, Liverpool.

TWITE *Linaria flavirostris*
Rare and decreasing breeder. Common winter visitor on coasts.

A regular delight of winter birding on the Lancashire coast is the sight and sound of flocks of Twite as they busily feed and circulate around their favoured areas. The flocks at Knott End and Southport were particularly well documented with the former often giving excellent views.

Monthly Peak Counts

	Jan	Feb	Mar	Apr	May	Jun	Jul	Aug	Sep	Oct	Nov	Dec
Southport	163	35	127	34						82	150	60
Banks Marsh			35							52	42	80
Knott End	92	90	63	34						24	48	60
Cockersand	80	52	120	40						12	0	2
Bolton-le-Sands	140	68								1		41
Whitworth Quarry				6	8	6	4	1	15			
Cant Clough					2	2	6	20	7			

As can be seen from the summary table above, the largest counts came from the Southport flock that was generally seen in both winter periods in the environs of the pier north to the yacht club though occasionally fragmenting with birds seen once at a former site at the end of Weld Road and several times up towards the former sand-winning plant compound at Marshside Road. Similarly at Knott End, the birds were most often reported at their favoured feeding site on the ferry slipway but there were occasional reports from the other side of the Wyre at Fleetwood and then east to Cocker's Dyke which may refer to separate flocks. They were last reported in numbers at the slipway on 21 March, so 13 passing Rossall Point on 31 March and eight on 7 April were passage birds as were up to 34 at Mount Park, Fleetwood on 6 – 7 April. The last bird was on at Knott End on the 19 April.

Other flocks were present further north with 140 on the saltmarsh at Hest Bank on 1 Jan decreasing to 68 by the 6 Feb, 50 at Middleton Sands on 24 Jan, 16 at Glasson on 23 Feb and up to 120 at Cockersand. Heysham had few reports with just three in spring.

The first birds were back at breeding sites in Rossendale in early April; Lee Quarry on the 2nd and Whitworth Quarry on the 7th. Two colour-ringed birds were present early in the breeding season and on 8 Sept, two pairs and a flock of eleven (probably two family parties) were seen. Two birds were seen near Worsthorne on 13 April and thereafter Cant Clough on 13 May when a male was singing. Family groups were seen in July but in August, several more were present with 17 – 20 seen on the 22nd – 25th. Twenty were also noted at Swinden Reservoir on 18 Aug and two were there on the late date of 29 Nov.

Twite flock, Southport, November (Charlie Lowe)

In the West Pennine Moors, it was a promising year starting with two birds on Great Hill and another nearby on 16 April. Two birds were feeding on Winter Hill on 21 May (suggestive of breeding close by) and one was seen above Belmont on 11 July. A flock of five were seen above Belmont on 8 Sept and 1 Oct, one was at Winter Hill on 20 Sept and small flocks were noted on Wheelton Moor on 1 Oct and Rivington on the 27th.

The first returning birds were singles at Knott End on 2 Oct and Church Scar, Lytham on the 13th followed by six at Knott End on the 15th and Cocker's Dyke on the 16th. Small numbers of autumn migrants were noted at Pilling Lane Ends, Heysham and Carnforth Slag Tips. Flocks reached double figures on 23 Oct at Cockersand, 28 Oct at Knott End and Old Hollow Farm, Banks and 31 Oct at Southport.

LINNET *Linaria cannabina*
Common but declining breeding resident. Double passage migrant, common winter flocks in the west.

This is a species that needs some attention as though the population seems stable year to year following the population crashes of 40 years ago, there is still a slow and steady decline as shown in the BBS analysis. Anecdotal evidence from correspondents is supporting this.

As a breeding bird, the numbers reported were low, especially in the southwest of the region. At Seaforth NR, no pairs bred, there were just two pairs at MMWWT, one pair at Aintree and the three pairs at Lunt Meadows NR was the lowest ever total there. At Freshfield Dune Heath there were just four pairs, well below the recent average of 15 pairs. One success story was at Mere Sands Wood where two pairs were the first to breed there this century through the establishment and maintenance of young scrub with gorse in the dry heath area of the reserve.

In south Liverpool, Knowsley and Rainford the species was widespread with breeding season presence around Speke Alder Woods, five sites around Oglet, three at Garston, Kirkby Moss, Simonswood Moss, Croxteth Brook, Knowesley Safari Park, Holland Moss, Dairy Farm Road and Old Coach Road, Rainford. It was present in small numbers on farmland by the Yarrow between Croston and Eccleston and two young were noted at White Coppice in June.

In the Southport area, there were at least six pairs in Birkdale Dunes, 14 pairs at Marshside and 36 pairs at Hesketh Out Marsh. Breeding evidence on the Fylde was scant with singing males noted at Marton Mere, Cocker's Dyke, Cockersand, Treales and Inskip. Heysham recorded five territories on EDF property and six pairs bred on Carnforth Marsh.

The species presence in the uplands and upper stretches of the Ribble and Lune is generally limited to passage and the breeding season. In East Lancashire a flock of ten at Parsonage Reservoir on 2 March was early but more typically birds started turning up from the 20th at Alston, Sunnyhurst, Swinden Reservoir and Ightenhill. The first record for Rossendale was of six at Cribden Clough on 26 March.

On Winter Hill, the breeding survey for UU produced ten territories with a further two nearby. Four territories were located at Ward's Reservoir, Belmont. Four pairs were located near Cant Clough Reservoir with a further pair at Hurstwood. Linnets were reported from over 80 sites in the east during the summer months but never in any great concentration, just the odd pair or two. Eight pairs were located around Arkholme but otherwise, reports from the Lune Valley were few.

In the early winter period there were three figure flocks noted at several sites including 300 at Thurnham Moss on the 2nd, up to 220 at Glasson Marsh from the 20 Jan to 20 March, 160 at Wrampool on 27 Jan and 17 Feb, 160 at Church Scar, Lytham on 20 Jan, 120 at Bretherton Eyes on 1 Jan, 225 at Croston Moss on 1 Feb, 172 at Birk's Farm, Eagland Hill on 5 March and 190 at Aggleby's Pit (Preesall) on the 24th. The largest count of the year was 335 at Downholland Moss on 3 Jan and the peak counts in Liverpool were 132 at Croxteth Brook on 15 Feb and 120 at Aintree on 26 March. Sixty-two roosting at Hardshaw Brook in St Helens centre on 6 Feb was an unusual record.

Spring passage at Heysham recorded 139 birds between 20 March and 1 May with a peak day count of 24 on 18 April. On 7 April total of 243 flew east over the sea wall at Pilling Lane, 46 were recorded over Rossall and 58 were recorded at Crosby.

Several post-breeding flocks were noted in August with the largest being 250 at Lytham Moss and 100 at Carnforth Slag Tips. A flock of 60 at Haslingden Grane on the 17th was the largest gathering recorded in the east of the county in 2019. Numbers in the east decreased markedly in September with occasional reports from around Oswaldtwistle up to 10 Oct and one at Cliviger on the 11th.

Autumn passage at Heysham consisted of 212 birds between 12 Sept and 30 Oct with a peak of 134 on 5 Oct. None were ringed for the first time since 1980. At Crosby, 738 were counted over 24 days from 1 Aug to 3 Oct with a peak of 106 on 25 Sept.

The peak counts in the second winter period were at Todderstaffe Hall with 150 on 8 Nov through to 23 Dec, Warton Bank with 160 on 6 Oct, Halsall Moss with 150 on 11 Dec and Glasson Marsh with 100 on the 29th. A flock on Croston Moss had 50 birds on 25 Aug, increasing to 100 by 24 Sept and then 200 at the end of the year. Winter records in the east are uncommon so one at Dean Clough on 9 Dec and 13 at Martholme on the 18th were notable.

MEALY (COMMON) REDPOLL* *Acanthis flammea*
Scarce winter visitor.

The bird that was found in Oswaldtwistle on 25 Dec 2018 was seen again on 3 Jan. What was presumably this bird turned up in a Rishton garden on the 6th when it was trapped, ringed and aged as a first-winter male (D Bickerton). This bird was subsequently seen later the same day back in Oswaldtwistle (with ring!) and subsequently at Rishton on several occasions until at least 3 April.

There then followed a flurry of new birds in Rishton during what would be considered the spring passage period with a good numbers of Lesser Redpolls. A second first-winter male was trapped and ringed on 4 March and retrapped on the 24th. A third first-winter male was caught on 23 March and a fourth on 24 March, retrapped on 1 April. Ringed birds were still at the feeders up to 20 April (D Bickerton). No other records were submitted.

LESSER REDPOLL *Acanthis cabaret*
Fairly common but decreasing breeding bird. Common double passage migrant and winter visitor.

It was another mostly disappointing year for this species with few double figure counts away from particular hot-spots. Indeed, during January the species was recorded from only 16 sites, mostly in the east of the county, with maximums of 15 at Brinscall on 7 Jan and ten at any one time in Rishton where 19 birds were trapped during the month. In February, there were fewer birds from a similar number, but mostly different, locations than January.

March saw the start of a good passage of Lesser Redpolls with several garden feeding sites such as ones in Freshfield, Longridge, Wilpshire and Clitheroe attracting up to three birds. Feeders at Rishton attracted large numbers with maxima of 25 on 23 March and 30 on 3 April. Between 4 March and 1 May, 62 new individuals were trapped and ringed out of a total of 86 birds processed including seven controls from elsewhere in the UK. March reports came from 38 sites whereas in April it was from 91 as migrating birds called overhead and dropped into feeders. There was a better spring passage at Heysham with 104 between 28 March and 30 April with a peak of 35 on the 20th. Just 24 were counted on vis-mig at Crosby and around 80% of the annual Fylde sightings for this species came at this time with 19 at Fluke Hall and 12 at Pilling Lane Ends on 21 April the only double figure counts. Over Knott End, 342 were recorded between 14 Feb and 13 May including 66 on 20 Apr. Three flocks totalling 22 birds were noted over Rossendale School on 19 April.

There were regular small numbers reported at Birkdale and at six sites around Simonswood Moss in May suggestive of local breeding but the bulk of the summer records were from the east of the county. Displaying males were noticeable especially across Bowland, Hyndburn, the West Pennine Moors and at several locations in Rossendale. Two females with brood patches were trapped in Rishton in June with breeding probably taking place in copses on the adjacent Rishton and Accrington Golf Courses. A clear-felled plantation near Belmont had three territories and there were four around Belmont Reservoir. In Belmont village itself, three pairs regularly visited gardens and young were seen from 15 June. A breeding bird survey of Clough House Farm, Turton found at least three territories whilst on Winter Hill, one was found in the burnt area but a further eight were charted on adjacent land. Family groups were noted at White Coppice and Anglezarke in July.

It was a generally poor autumn passage with just 15 noted at Heysham, 25 over Knott End and only five sightings elsewhere on the Fylde in the period. In east Lancashire, no birds were seen in Rishton though small numbers were still at Jackhouse. The bulk of the birds remained at higher elevations with over 30 over Crown Point, Burnley on 27 Aug, 20 at Lee Clough, Rossendale on the 8th and 50 at Stocks Reservoir on the 15th. Numbers at Stocks Reservoir increased to 100 on 3 Nov and 200 on the 7th with 80-100 present to the end of the year.

Other winter flocks in double figures were 15 at Shedden Clough on 13 Nov, 35 at Belmont on 14 Dec, 20 at Anglezarke Reservoir on the 15th and 15 at Leighton Moss on the 18th.

COMMON CROSSBILL *Loxia curvirostra*
Rare breeding bird. Occasional irruptive movements.

Crossbills were rather scarce this year with only five January records: two at Clough Head Quarry, Haslingden on the 13th, at least nine at Barley on the 15th, eight at Moor Piece on the 18th, Three at Lead Mines Clough on the 19th and one at Saunders Height, Rawtenstall on the 30th. On 1 Feb, 25 were at Lead Mines Clough followed by eight at Roddlesworth Reservoirs on the 4th and at least ten at Belmont on the 9th. Ten flew over calling at Marl Hill on the 12th and small numbers were seen regularly around Stocks Reservoir and Haslingden Grane.

Two over Formby Beach on 22 Feb, two in Formby on 17 March, one on 23 April at Cabin Hill and six there on 4 June were the only records during the year from that area. A flock of birds was mobile at Birkdale LNR in April with seven seen on the 5th. Occasional birds in the area subsequently were suggestive of breeding on Hillside GC. The coastal strip had very few sightings all year: two at Lytham Hall on 24 March, one over Starr Gate, singles over Knott End on 27 Feb & 21 April with two over on 28 March and finally three over Freckleton Naze on 11 April were the only records on the Fylde. One was at Marshside on 22 April and none were seen at all at Heysham.

April and May brought records of two to four birds from Belmont, Long Mynd, New Laithe Farm, Stocks Reservoir, Calf Hey Reservoir, Moor Piece and Longridge Fell. Breeding was only confirmed at Belmont where a pair was seen feeding three young. Through the summer and early autumn virtually all the (very few) records came from Bowland.

Late October saw birds a little further afield with one at Warton Crag on the 19th and ten near Belmont on the 29th. November was a little busier with one at MMWWT on the 1st, sixteen at Longridge Fell on the 12th (with one male singing), two at Docker Moor on the 16th, seven at Calf Hey Reservoir on the 17th, and one at Challan Hall Allotment on the 19th. In December up to 20 birds were seen and heard around Hesbert Hall in Gisburn Forest and two to three birds were noted at Moor Piece, Kemple End and Lead Mines Clough.

GOLDFINCH *Carduelis carduelis*
Common breeding resident and passage migrant. Flocks in winter.

Probably getting near to becoming the most commonly encountered finch and beats Chaffinch in the number of submissions through website databases. It was, once again, the most commonly reported finch in the Chorley Winter Garden Survey moving up from 9th to 5th place (it was 17th in 1998) whilst in the Lancaster January survey, an above-average 333 were recorded. There were few large flocks though in the first winter period, the only count above 100 being 124 at the Belmont roost site on 10 & 28 Jan. The next largest was 61 at Fleetwood Memorial Park on 26 Jan, 50 at Kincraig Lake on the 13th and 53 at Stone Jetty, Morecambe on 24 March. Forty birds at Stocks Reservoir was the highest count from the east of the county and 30 at Calf Hey Reservoir the largest from Rossendale.

Spring passage at Heysham consisted of just 57 between 25 March and 14 April with a peak of 23 on the 6th. On 7 April, 62 passed east during the morning at Pilling Lane. A total of 195 were counted over Crosby between 18 March and 24 April with peaks of just 23.

Breeding birds were widely reported and on the whole the population seems stable. In the Aintree study area, ten territories were located which has been the same for the past few years. Five pairs bred at Freshfield Dune Heath, six pairs at both Lunt Meadows and Kirkdale Cemetery and three pairs at Cuerden Valley Park, Belmont and on the edge of the Winter Hill survey area. MMWWT had 20 breeding pairs whilst at Marshside there were 13 and 21 at Hesketh Out Marsh. At least five pairs bred at Heysham.

The first juveniles of a protracted breeding season were seen at Brook Vale, Waterloo on 21 May and in Rishton on the 25th but it wasn't until July when larger numbers of juveniles were being seen and small flocks forming. No large flocks were reported in July but during late August there were flocks of around 100 birds at Lytham Moss on the 19th, Horncliffe Quarry, Rawtenstall on the 24th and New Laithe Farm on the 26th. There were 200 at MMWWT from 28 Aug and into September, over 300 at Belmont in late August and 350 at Lunt Meadows on 3 Sept, the highest count of the year. Two-hundred were at Croston Moss on 28 Sept. Other three-figure counts were 100 at Pilling on 14 Sept, Lytham Jetty on the 15th, and Pendle Hill on the 20th. Counts of 120 were reported from Seaforth NR on the 21st, Carr House Green Common and Conder Green from the 25th through into early October and Marl Hill on 18 October. A flock at Clowbridge numbered 130 on the 25th.

Heysham counted 387 on autumn passage with one flock of 80 on 30 Oct. At Belmont, 432 were counted with a peak of 87 in an hour on 3 Oct.

Peak numbers decreased thereafter though there were still plenty of large flocks numbering up to 50 in most parts of the county throughout November and December including sites in Rossendale and east Lancashire. Seventy birds roosted at Belmont on 14 Dec.

SERIN* *Serinus serinus*
Vagrant

One was identified flying over Knott End through a sound recording on 21 April. (C Batty) This is only Lancashire's 5th record, the previous being on 20 April 2013 and before that May 1994. Only the very first record was of a bird that was seen to perch up as all the rest have been fly-overs. Another sound-recorded diurnal migrant at Knott End is still under consideration by the records committee.

SISKIN *Spinus spinus*
Uncommon breeding resident. Common double passage migrant and winter visitor.

It was another similar year to the previous, perhaps a little better with widespread reports of Siskins from across the county in both winter periods, retreating to records from the upland areas in the summer. Many reported Siskins vising garden feeders, a distinct aid to recording this widely appreciated small finch.

Double-figure counts in January were restricted to Leighton Moss with up to 40 being reported quite regularly, twelve at Bailrigg on 11 Jan and up to 18 at Lytham Hall. February brought 20 to Boilton Wood, Brockholes on the 10th, 15 at Crow Wood Farm, Bashall Eaves on the 16th and 15 at Belmont on the 19th. Flocks of around 50 birds were noted in Cuerden Valley Park during February and March in which time 89 birds were caught and ringed. A garden in Rishton had a flock of at least 25 briefly on 3 March and a total of 36 birds were ringed later the month.

March and April saw many small flocks move through the county on passage with the larger ones being 12 over Oglet on the 1st, 30 at Crook O'Lune on 3 March, 14 at Stone Jetty, Morecambe on the 24th, 15 at Stocks Reservoir on the 27th, 14 at Birkdale Dunes on the 30th, twelve on feeders in Longridge on 2 April, twelve at Mount Park, Fleetwood on the 7th and 66 east in three hours over Pilling Lane the same day. There were 14 at Teal Bay also on the 7th, 14 at Singleton on the 9th, 14 at New Laithe Farm on the 12th and 35 at Crow Wood Farm on the 14th. Heysham recorded a poor spring passage with only 14 birds and vis-mig at Crosby had a total of 24. Sound-recording migrants at Knott End revealed a passage of 1044 between 11 Feb and 10 Jun with 83 on 27 Feb.

There were a few migrant stragglers in early May but the emphasis shifted towards the breeding population predominantly in areas of plantations and mainly in Bowland with birds present at a minimum of 17 sites. Birds were also present at Crook O'Lune and Brookhouse where recently fledged young were present, a couple of sites along Haslingden Grane, Entwistle Plantations (where there were an estimated 20 pairs) and Wayoh Reservoir. In the West Pennine Moors, two displaying males were at Clough House Farm, Turton, five territories were mapped adjacent to the Winter Hill survey area, two pairs bred at Belmont (with juveniles seen from 22 May) and birds were present at Wheelton Plantation. Two juveniles were seen at Great Knowley in June suggestive of local breeding success and a juvenile was ringed in Rishton in July.

Completely out of the blue, a large flock of 150 appeared at Stocks Reservoir on 15 Sept only to disappear again in a period when only small numbers of birds were being seen anywhere in the county. It was October before migrants were being noticed elsewhere. Vis-mig at Belmont produced 233 over 21 days with a peak of 86 on 3 Oct. A total of 341 flew over Knott End between 21 Jun and 29 Nov including 61 on 18 Oct. Heysham recorded just 53 with a peak of 22 on the 18th, 30 flew south over New Laithe Farm on the 12th and on the 14th, 90 were at Fluke Hall and 65 flew east along the sea wall at Pilling Lane. There were 30 near Wymott on the 19th, 25 at Lead Mines Clough on the 21st, eleven at Marton Mere on the 21st, 15 over Burnley Central Station on the 22nd and 19 over Rimrose Valley on the 22nd also. There were 20 at White Coppice and 40 near Belmont on 26 Oct, 14 over both Fairhaven Dunes and Pilling Marsh on the 28th and 20 at New Laithe Farm on the 29th.

November brought 20 to Lancaster on the 3rd and 100 appeared again at Stocks Reservoir the same day. Twelve were at Docker Moor on the 16th, 16 at Calf Hey Reservoir on the 17th, eleven at Leighton Moss on the 22nd, 21 at Briercliffe on the 24th and 11 at Birkdale on the 27th. A flock of 25 at the Bowland Wild Boar Park on the 30th increased to 42 by the end of December.

Peak counts in December were 30 at Anglezarke Reservoir on the 15th, 80 at Hoghton Bottoms on the 23rd and 60 in Roddlesworth Plantations on the 25th. At least 20 birds were present much of the time at Mere Sands Wood.

LAPLAND BUNTING* *Calcarius lapponicus*
Rare autumn passage migrant and winter visitor to coasts.

Only one record was submitted and accepted, that of a female calling and flying at eye-level west on Newton Fell on 6 May. (S Dunstan)

SNOW BUNTING *Plectrophenax nivalis*
Fairly common winter visitor to summits and coasts.

Two birds from 2018 were regularly reported on the beach between St Annes and Squires Gate up to 19 Feb. The only other records in the first winter period were of one at Scout Cairn, Pendle Hill on 2 Feb, two at Fair Snape Fell on 5 Feb and one on the beach at Fleetwood on 11 March.

The first of the autumn were seen at Blackpool and Rossall point on 14 Oct, followed by two at Starr Gate, one over Heysham and one at Cockersand all on the 17th. The last bird remained to the 22nd. On 31 Oct, two flew south over Hightown, one was at Rossall Point and two were on Fair Snape Fell. Singles over Knott End on 30 Oct and 10 Nov were identified from sound-recordings.

Single birds were seen at Heysham and Church Scar, Lytham on 5 Nov, Red Nab, Blackpool and Great Hameldon on the 10th, Cockersand on the 12th, Pendle Hill on the 13th and Formby Point on the 14th. Two were seen at Birkdale Beach on 15 Nov and eleven were found at Ainsdale Beach on the 17th whilst conducting a WeBS count. These were also reported on the 18th, then four were seen at Crosby on the 19th.

A total of eight were seen on Pendle Hill on 20 Nov but none were seen after that. One was at Great Hill, Anglezarke Moor on 27 - 28 Nov and two were nearby at Redmond's Edge on the 9 Dec with one there on the 30th. One was on Fair Snape Fell again on 3 Dec.

Back at the coast, one was at Sunderland Point on 26 Nov, one on Crosby Beach on the 27th, eight at Hightown on the 29th and one at Ainsdale Beach on the 30th. From a single bird on 3 Dec, a flock of up to four birds established themselves on the beach at Fleetwood Marine Lakes through into 2019. Finally there was a single bird near the Eric Morecambe complex at Leighton Moss on 13 Dec.

Snow Bunting, Cockersand, 19 October (Paul Ellis)

CORN BUNTING *Emberiza calandra*
Common but declining breeding resident in the south-west and Fylde.

Regular monitoring of the feeding sites at Eagland Hill had relatively few birds over the first winter period with none being seen at Bradshaw Lane. However at Birk's Farm, in between the two feeding sites, double-figure counts of birds could be seen regularly as they sat on overhead wires on into February with a maximum on 53 on 2 Jan, 62 on 5 Feb, 81 on the 28th. And 22 on 26 March. Slightly away from Eagland Hill, but still in the SD44 hot-spot for this species, 14 were seen at Cockerham Moss Edge on 9 Jan, 11 at Cockersands on 6 Feb, 25 at Pilling Moss on the 23rd and 28 at Stalmine Moss on 9 March.

The mosses of south-west Lancashire are another regular spot for this species with winter flocks especially notable at MMWWT where there were 33 on 2 Jan and 20 still on 30 March. In the Croston area, 30 were at Bretherton Eyes on 20 Jan, 50 at Croston Finney on the 20th, 40 at Croston Twin Lakes on 2 Feb and an exceptional count for the area of 78 at Bretherton Eyes on 6 March. There were also counts of 23 at Hesketh Out Marsh on 2 Jan, ten at Windle Farm, St Helens on the 19th, 14 on Jacksmere Lane, Scarisbrick on 14 Feb and 20 at Lunt Meadows on 8 April. Single figure counts were also received from Banks, Red Cat Lane (Burscough), Halsall Moss, Plex Moss, Formby Moss and Hightown. The only out of range passage bird was noted at Crosby on 24 April though sound-recording at Knott End produced six between 8 April and 15 May including three on the latter date.

From early April to mid-July, singing males could be heard across mossland sites in the county though they were quite thinly scattered. On the Fylde, singing birds were noted at Lytham Moss (four), Weeton, Stalmine, Bone Hill (two), three sites around Pilling. Cockerham, Eagland Hill (three), Jarvis Carr, Stake Pool, Stalmine Moss (four) and Brock, the most easterly site in the county. In the south-west there were five pairs at MMWWT, two at Curlew Lane (Rufford), four singing males on Mawdesley Moss (where continued removal of hedgerows and small trees degrades the potential habitat further), four at Plex Moss, two at Scarisbrick and singles noted at Hesketh Out Marsh and Lunt Meadows. In the Rainford – St. Helens area there were two at Ferny Knoll Road, five along the length of Catchdale Moss Lane and two along Dairy Farm Road.

There were hardly any records submitted for August and none for September. In October there were one or two birds reported at Northwoods Farm (Eagland Hill), Lytham Moss, Dairy Farm Road (Rainford), Plex Moss, Burscough and Banks The first flock at Eagland Hill was ten on 3 Nov with 32 there on the 16th and up to 53 at the end of December. During December, numbers on Burscough Moss reached 40, 35 were on Halsall Moss on the 11th, 20 were at Mawdesley on the 9th, 23 at Banks on the 22nd and 18 at Bretherton Eyes on the 31st. One at Warton Bank on 28 Dec was an unusual find there.

YELLOWHAMMER *Emberiza citrinella*
Fairly common but decreasing resident, mostly in the south. Scarce autumn passage migrant.

The distribution of Yellowhammers is somewhat similar to Corn Bunting in Lancashire in that it is almost entirely found in the lowland west of the county but is a little more widespread preferring to nest in the more vegetated areas.

In the winter period, few large flocks form and although they use feeding sites on the Fylde, for example, there were only ten sites that had double-figure counts and only four with counts over 15. Out of the three Over Wyre winter feeding sites, only New Lane had any appreciable numbers of visitors with peaks of 14 on 11 Jan, 16 on the 30th, 26 on 19 Feb and ten on 4 April. There were twelve at Windle Farm, Eccleston (St Helens) on 19 Jan, eleven at Halsall Moss on the 23rd, 14 at Eccleston (Chorley) on 12 Feb, 30 at Roby Mill on 3 March, twelve at Plex Moss on 26 April and 12 at Gorse Hill NR on 18 May. Regular sightings were to be had from January to mid-April at Wesham Marsh where food was being provided and numbers getting up to 18 individuals by 11 March. Some passage was noted over Knott End with four singles between 27 Mar and 1 May.

The first song was heard in mid-February but more widespread come March. The majority of records for singing males came from Knowsley and West Lancashire. Around Halewood, singing males were noted at Speke Millwoods, Finch Lane, Brook Farm (two), Tray Ashes Farm and Springfield Farm. There was a good concentration of singing males around Kirkby Moss with four at Moss Plantation, seven along Cut Lane, three at Spencer's House and one at Simonswood Moss. In the Rainford to Skelmersdale area there were territories at Reed's Farm, Old Coach Road (two), Holly Farm, Ferny Knoll Farm (three), White Moss, Bickerstaffe Moss, Holland Moss (four) and Windle Moss (two). Three were singing upon the western side of Billinge Hill and three along Lafford Lane, Roby Mill.

Smaller numbers were noted at Formby Moss, Downholland Moss, Haskayne Cutting, Gorse Hill (Ormskirk), MMWWT, Hic Bibi, Croston and Eccleston whilst ten singing males were on Bretherton Moss and seven on Croston Moss.

On the Fylde, singing birds were heard at Elswick (three), Eagland Hill (two), Bone Hill (two), Churchtown, Skitham (three) and Out Rawcliffe. One completely unexpected report was of one singing at Cocketford Car Park, Tockholes on 9 June which is the first in east Lancashire since 2015.

There was a small autumn passage noted with two east over Fairhaven Dunes on 19 Sept and singles over Middleton NR on 5 Oct and Heysham NR on the 18th.

A flock of 28 at Coppull Moor on 16 Dec was the largest count of the second winter period followed by 16 on Bretherton Moss on the 31st. Several were seen along Old Coach Road and Dairy Farm Road, Rainford on 21 Dec and four were present at Speke Millwoods at the end of the year. Very few birds used the feeding sites on the Fylde in this period with a maximum of seven recorded in November.

REED BUNTING *Emberiza schoeniclus*
Common breeding bird and winter visitor. Double passage migrant.

This widespread bunting seems to be holding its own across the county with populations showing a degree of stability after some turbulent years. Reports of Reed Buntings came from all parts of the county with very few particularly large concentrations in the winter months. In fact even double-figure counts were hard to come by - 35 coming to roost at Leighton Moss on 11 Jan was the largest count in the first winter period followed by 30 at Belmont on the 20th, 20 at Wesham Marsh on the 1st, 15 at Barnaby's Sands on the 20th and 16 on the island at Stocks Reservoir on 1 March. Very few birds (maximum of six) used the feeding sites around Eagland Hill and the Lancaster District January Survey recorded just 15 birds – well down on the norm. Spring passage was largely unnoticeable with an average of three birds a day over Crosby and none at Heysham.

It is pleasing to note that we received a lot of breeding data for this species, most of it positive. The large areas of reedbeds at many of our major reserves hold a good population of Reed Buntings. Leighton Moss is clearly a stronghold with 54 pairs breeding on the main reserve and another ten on Barrow Scout. Similarly at MMWWT, there were 54 pairs but 17 pairs at Lunt Meadows was low in comparison to recent years. There was just a single pair at Freshfield Dune Heath, two at Seaforth NR and 15 territories along the Birkdale coast. Ten pairs were counted at Marshside and another seven at Hesketh Out Marsh while north of the Ribble, ten singing males was the maximum count at Marton Mere, six at Carr House Green Common and five at Winmarleigh Moss.

The species is a common breeding bird on upland pastures and moors. Fifteen pairs around Belmont Reservoir was the equal highest figure (along with 2014) in the 25 years of monitoring. Breeding bird surveys at Clough House Farm, Turton produced eight territories and there were a similar number on Winter Hill. Five singing males were at Lower Burgh Meadow and also along the Yarrow west of Eccleston. A minimum of ten pairs were located around Dean Clough Reservoir on 4 April, eight singing males were along the Grane Road in June and four were around Clowbridge Reservoir. Three pairs bred at Grove Lane Marsh, Padiham and at Whitebirk Marsh, Blackburn despite significant loss of habitat and encroachment of buildings in both areas.

In the Aintree study area, there were the usual three pairs, four territories were located around Simonswood Moss, two at Ferny Knoll Bog, nine around Halewood, three on Garston Shore and ones and twos at several other sites from Croxteth Park east to Rainford.

Autumn passage was slight with a total of 161 over Crosby between 2 Aug and 3 Oct (peak of 42 on 23 Sept), 179 over Knott End between 15 Jul and 27 Nov including 15 on 14 Oct and 63 at Heysham between 7 Sept and 30 Oct but never in double figures, in common with other watchpoints such as Seaforth NR, Rossall and Fleetwood Marsh. October brought 70 to Belmont in four discrete flocks and 110 in five flocks on 10 Nov including 30 mobbing a perched Hen Harrier. A moorland feeding site had six birds still at the end of the year. Thirty birds were on Anglezarke Moor also on 10 Nov with numbers there rising to over 50 by 27 Dec. Further east, there was a flock of 15 at Shedden Clough on 13 Nov, eleven at Marl Hill in Bowland on the 27th and 30 at Swinden Reservoir on 17 Dec.

ESCAPES

REEVES'S PHEASANT *Syrmaticus reevesii*
A male was again seen at Eagland Hill on 16 Feb and 20 March and one at Preesall Flashes on 21 March. Another was on Croston Moss on 3 May.

INDIAN PEAFOWL *Pavo cristatus*
Once again, birds were reported all year at the Clitheroe household waste disposal centre, with a maximum count of nine (5males, 2 females and 2 juveniles) on 18 Oct.

BAR-HEADED GOOSE *Anser Indicus*
As in the past few years Bar-headed Geese were widespread in low single figures throughout most of the year but how many individuals were involved remains uncertain.

The only east Lancashire record was one reported at Upper Foulridge Reservoir on 14 June, 14 & 27-28 July and 2 Aug; the Fylde had one on 7 Sept at Copthorne and two on Warton Marsh/Bank on 14-15 Oct and up to three were at the Eric Morecambe complex/Leighton Moss during late April May. In the south-west single(s) were at Marshside on 27-28 March and 16 April, and at MMWWT on 4 May.

BLACK SWAN *Cygnus atratus*
The majority of this year's records came from the coastal west with the exception of a single at Upper Foulridge Reservoir on 23 Dec.

The Fylde had the lion's share with records in every month from at least ten sites and with a peak count of three at Lytham on 29 July and Eagland Hill on 20 Oct. Further south two were at HOM, Banks Marsh and Marshside during September and a pair at Seaforth from 19 April to 25 July.

EGYPTIAN GOOSE *Alopochen aegyptiaca*
Up to three were close to Alston Wetland from 1-14 Jan and another three at Conder Green from 1 Jan to 6 Feb with one remaining until the 17th.

Two to three (presumably those that had been at Alston) were in the Warsdley/Little Bowland area in east Lancashire from 13 March until 10 May.

The final records were 14 on Banks Marsh on 24 Oct with twelve still there on 2 Nov and one at Leighton Moss on 20 Nov.

Egyptian Geese, Conder Green, 5 February (Stuart Piner)

RUDDY SHELDUCK *Tadorna ferruginea*
There was a small but marked influx in summer, perhaps originating from the feral population in continental Europe. This began with three juveniles flying over Cockersand on 7 Aug and up to four moving between Marshside, Banks and Hesketh Out Marshes and on the north side of the Ribble at Freckleton and Fairhaven Lake between 8 Aug and 9 Sept.

Presumably five different birds flew over the Sankey valley, St Helens at Haydock on 18 Aug and there was one last record of a first-winter at Banks Marsh on 2 Nov that was relocated at Cocker's Dyke on the 3rd.

Ruddy Shelduck, Cocker's Dyke, 3 November (Paul Slade)

MUSCOVY DUCK *Cairina moschata*

Muscovy Ducks were reported from several regions throughout the year, including Victoria Park, Nelson (maximum 15) and Ball Grove Park in east Lancashire, Brinscall in Chorley (four) and Greenbank Park, Liverpool

WOOD DUCK *Aix sponsa*

There were three records in Burnley, all of a single female: at the Deer Pond, Towneley on 14 March and Rowley Lake on 29 March and 4 April. The only other record was a male at Eagland Hill on at least 26 March and 5 May.

HARRIS'S HAWK *Parabuteo unicinctus*

Singles were seen at Burscough Bridge on 14 May and Taylor Park, St Helens on 9 Nov.

GYRFALCON *Falco rusticolous*

A white morph female was seen at Slipper Hill Reservoir near Foulridge on 18 Feb; it has been submitted as a wild bird to the BBRC but has not yet been adjudicated.

KESTREL *Falco tinnunculus*

One with jesses was seen regularly in Eyes Lane, Bretherton during the second winter period.

EAGLE OWL *Bubo bubo*

An escaped or released individual was seen in the Prescot area on 9 Jan. No records were received from the feral breeding population in the Bowland area.

CRIMSON ROSELLA *Platycercus elegans*

One was at Heysham from late September until 10 Nov when it was recaptured.

GALAH COCKATOO *Eolophus roseicapillus*

One was at Marton Mere on 11 Feb.

BUDGERIGAR *Melopsittacus undulatus*

One was at Knott End on 1 April.

VILLAGE WEAVER *Ploceus cucullatus*

A male was photographed on a feeder at Harwood Lane, east Lancashire on 22 Sept.

Ringing Report 2019-20

Pete Marsh

Welcome to the 2019 ringing report which covers the 12 months of ringing recoveries received July 2019 to July 2020.

Once again, 90 per cent of the assembly time was spent on the likes of deciphering small print on the life-history attachments received concerning what are often multi-observed colour rings – many of which are not cut and paste-friendly! It would be really helpful if next year people could possibly set the recoveries out in the way they are published here before sending to me. Please also include the straight line distance. Thanks very much.

If you are ringing significant numbers of a species which is likely to see its legs examined by a wandering telescope or long lens, have a think about a colour-ringing scheme. In this respect, one species which has been colour-ringed in Lancashire since the last century has been Twite and there cannot be many more difficult species on which to observe the legs in the field! Despite moaning and groaning about them being impossible, especially along the Sefton Coast, a fair amount of information was obtained from the colour rings, especially when they went to the western Highlands and Islands of Scotland where the grass is shorter and they were on territory, not in skittish flocks!

My own Grey Wagtail study, a much easier species to observe on its solitary winter circuit or as a breeding bird, has produced over 50 sightings of colour-ringed birds but only two (dead) birds which would have been reported using metal-only. It was one of the few aspects of ringing to benefit from Covid-19 as the 'walks from home' resulted in an unprecedented spike of breeding season sightings

However, the Knot leg flag recording has taken the discrepancy of reporting between field-observable marks and metal rings to a new level. Peter Knight explains: "You might be interested to know that in the Sept 2017 Sefton coast catch we fitted 519 Knot with Orange-flags, and a further 636 with just a metal ring. The only information from all those metal ringed birds was when we re-trapped some in the subsequent catch in March 2018 and one in the small March 2019 catch (they were all then fitted with flags) – none have been caught by other ringers or recovered elsewhere. Contrasting this with about 7000 sightings of the Orange flags just emphasises how much more we learn with respect to certain species from colour marking compared to metal-only".

The first half of this report consists primarily of ringing recoveries related to 'in the field' observations whilst the recoveries depicted in the second half, including most of the passerines, often show the value of the work of various ringing groups throughout the country catching each other's birds. Also valuable are tide-line checkers such as Mike Standing (with a significant contribution to those analysing ringing recoveries from Puffin Island, Anglesey!) .

Hopefully, many of you have managed to negotiate some ringing during Covid-19 over and above the obvious garden-net-catching of the likes of Goldfinches. The problem so far seems to be understandable nervousness by large organisations where ringers perhaps oddly come under the 'volunteer' umbrella and have been furloughed along with paid staff and most recording activities.

Thanks to all for your help compiling this report including Rob Robinson (BTO), Peter Knight, Rose Maciewitz, Peter Alker, Jon Greep, Ian Walker, Tony Conway, Steven Grimshaw, Bill Aspin, Chris Batty, Bob Danson, Craig Bell, Hugh Jones, Mark Breaks, North Lancs RG, Ian Hartley, Malcolm Downham, Howard Stockdale, Janet Packham, Janice Sutton, Mark Nightingale, Tim Vaughan, Gavin Thomas, Stuart Darbyshire, Mike Standing, Charlie Liggett, Kane Brides, Pete Kinsella, Richard du Feu, Paul Ellis, Paul Slade, Stephen Dunstan, South west Lancs RG, Merseyside RG, Steve White, Pete Crooks, Jon Carter, Nick Godden, Shaun Coyle and Tony Cooper.

PALE-BELLIED BRENT GOOSE

The pair of Canadian-Arctic-ringed birds which usually winter on the Furness peninsula targeted the gutweed crop at Heysham in late winter 2018/9. The life-histories were fully documented in the 2018 report and the same pair reappeared again off Heysham in early 2020.

PINK-FOOTED GOOSE

1482658	Adult Male	16/04/2016	Rashierieve, Newburgh: 57°17'N 2°3'W (Aberdeenshire)
	Seen	24/04/2016	Brekka, Fljótsdalur: 65°4'N 14°49'W ICELAND 1,100km NNW
	Shot	19/10/2019	Scarisbrick: 53°36'N 2°56'W (Lancashire) 413km S
1499001	1st Y F	22/03/2018	Martin Mere: 53°37'N 2°52'W (Lancashire)
	Seen	20/11/2019	Manor Farm, Carthorpe: c. 54°14'N 1°34'W (North Yorkshire) 110km N

WHOOPER SWAN

ZY0934	Adult Female	10/02/2010	Martin Mere Swan Pipe: 53°37'N 2°52'W (Lancashire)
	Seen	03/11/2019	Myroe Levels, Lough Foyle: 55°6'N 7°0'W (Londonderry) 315km WNW
ZY0960	Adult Male	16/03/2010	Martin Mere Swan Pipe: 53°37'N 2°52'W (Lancashire)
	Caught	13/02/2013	Martin Mere
	Seen	15/12/2016	Martin Mere
	Caught	19/11/2018	Martin Mere
	Seen	25/4 & 04/05/19	Þveit, Nes: 64°19'N 15°16'W (Austurland) ICELAND 1,381km NNW
A10012	1st year M	16/08/2015	Hyannamostjorn Myvatnsheid1 ICELAND 65 22N 17 15W
	Seen	22/01/2018	Byall Fen Pymoor (Cambridgeshire)
	Seen	18/01/2019	Purls Bridge RSPB (Cambridgeshire)
	Seen	08/11/2019	Leighton Moss 1481km SE

SHELDUCK

GN81532	Adult Female	03/02/2016	Newton Farm, near Cardiff: 51°29'N 3°6'W (Cardiff)
	Seen	24/02/2017	Martin Mere: 53°37'N 2°52'W (Lancashire) 237km N
	Seen	21/02/2019	Martin Mere
	Seen	15/02/2019	Martin Mere
	Seen	08/03/2019	Martin Mere
GR60540	Adult Male	19/01/2015	Slimbridge Swan Pipe: 51°44'N 2°24'W (Gloucestershire)
	Seen	07/12/2015	Martin Mere: 53°37'N 2°52'W (Lancashire) 211km N
	Seen	09/11/2016	Martin Mere
	Seen	13/11/2017	Martin Mere
	Seen	09/01/2018	Slimbridge
	Seen	19/11/2018	Martin Mere
	Seen	30/10/2019	Martin Mere
BLB H167331	Adult Male	17/02/2013	Rieme: 51°10'N 3°46'E (Oost-Vlaanderen) BELGIUM
	Seen	24/11/2015	Martin Mere, Burscough: 53°37'N 2°52'W (Lancashire) 526km NW
	Caught	25/12/2019	Martin Mere Swan Pipe
BLB H179589	First-year Male	16/02/2016	Rieme: 51°10'N 3°46'E (Oost-Vlaanderen) BELGIUM
	Seen	07/01/2019	Martin Mere: 53°37'N 2°52'W (Lancashire) 526km NW

PINTAIL

FH04868	Adult Female	30/01/2019	Slimbridge Swan Pipe: 51°44'N 2°24'W (Gloucestershire)
	Caught	25/11/2019	Martin Mere Swan Pipe: 53°37'N 2°52'W (Lancashire) 211km N
	Caught	03/12/2019	Martin Mere Swan Pipe
FH19979	Adult Male	09/01/2018	Slimbridge Swan Pipe: 51°44'N 2°24'W (Gloucestershire)
	Caught	17/12/2019	Martin Mere Swan Pipe: 53°37'N 2°52'W (Lancashire) 211km N
FH00143	Adult Male	17/12/2018	Martin Mere Swan Pipe: 53°37'N 2°52'W (Lancashire)
	Shot	13/01/2019	Hauteville-Sur-Mer: 48°58'N 1°31'W (Manche) FRANCE 526km S
J39026	1st Y Male	17/12/2019	Martin Mere Swan Pipe: 53°37'N 2°52'W (Lancashire)
	Shot	21/12/2019	Colombières: 49°16'N 0°58'W (Calvados) FRANCE 500km S
FH00110	1st Y Male	31/10/2018	Martin Mere Swan Pipe: 53°37'N 2°52'W (Lancashire)
	Shot	16/05/2019	Tom, Izhemskiy Dist.: 64°30'N 53°22'E (Komi) RUSSIAN FED. 3,303km NE
FH00191	Adult Male	26/02/2019	Martin Mere Swan Pipe: 53°37'N 2°52'W (Lancashire)
	Shot	10/05/2019	Alexandrovsky Dist.: 60°19'N 78°22'E RUSSIAN FED. 4,661km NE
FH00194	1st Y Female	28/02/2019	Martin Mere Swan Pipe: 53°37'N 2°52'W (Lancashire)
	Long dead	18/05/2019	Nes Hecb: 66°34'N 44°40'E (Nenets A.O.) RUSSIAN FED. 2,904km N

An excellent series of informative self-explanatory recoveries.

TEAL

ES55426	Adult Male	08/11/2018	Martin Mere Swan Pipe: 53°37'N 2°52'W (Lancashire)
	Shot	15/01/2019	Derries, Lower Killashandra: 54°0'N 7°32'W (Cavan) 310km W
ER09840	1st Y Male	11/10/2018	Martin Mere Swan Pipe: 53°37'N 2°52'W (Lancashire)
	Shot	26/01/2019	High Buston, Alnmouth: 55°21'N 1°38'W (Northumberland) 209km N

LITTLE EGRET

GV75204	Nestling	22/05/2018	Rossmere Park, Hartlepool
	Seen	to 05/07/2018	Rossmere Park, Hartlepool
	Seen	19/07/2018	Dorman's Pool, Teeside
	Seen	03/11/2019	Red Nab, Heysham, Lancs c125km SSW
	Seen	22/01/2020	Old Moor RSPB Reserve, Yorks
	Seen	21/03-22/03/20	Old Moor RSPB Reserve
GR19702	Nestling	16/07/2015	Penryhyn Castle, Bangor, Gwynedd
/CRs	Seen	04/03/2018	Freckleton Naze Point, Fylde
	Seen	27/02/2019	Freckleton Naze Point, Fylde

We need to see what happens to our young birds - any of the breeding sites suitable for ringing young?

SHAG

1496688	Nestling	10/06/2019	Puffin Island: c. 53°18'N 4°1'W (Isle of Anglesey)
	Freshly dead	18/12/2019	Rossall: 53°53'N 3°2'W (Lancashire) 91km NE

CORMORANT

5282643	Nestling	22/06/2019	Puffin Island: c. 53°18'N 4°1'W (Isle of Anglesey)
	Shot	22/09/2019	Trout Fishery, near Garstang: 53°52'N 2°44'W (Lancashire) 105km NE

Not all inland miscreants are sinensis.

OSPREY

JC1	Nestling	2016 breeding season, Monymusk, Aberdeenshire	
	Seen	05/09/2019	Dean Clough Reservoir, nr Gt Harwood

HEN HARRIER

FH61035	Nestling female	22/06/2017	Roan Fell (Borders)
	Seen	07/06/2020	nr Slaidburn (Lancs) 145 kms

One of the breeding females.

RED KITE

ZP wing tag	Nestling	01/06/2017	Site confidential, Co Wicklow, Ireland
	tideline wing only	05/04/2020	Keer Estuary, Millhead

Presumably originally a watery grave, but where from? Quite an inland location for an open sea death.

OYSTERCATCHER

FV53387	Adult	17/10/2001	Heysham, near Lancaster: 54°1'N 2°54'W (Lancashire)
	Fresh dead	06/07/2019	Hoxa, South Ronaldsay: 58°49'N 3°0'W (Orkney) 532km
J06118	First-year	07/09/2016	Sandy Haven: 51°43'N 5°5'W (Pembrokeshire)
	Seen	28/04/2018	Dawlish Warren, Exe Estuary: 50°36'N 3°26'W (Devon) 171km SE
	Seen	21/07/2019	Cockersands, near Glasson: c. 53°58'N 2°53'W (Lancashire) 290km NNE
CR 'J2'	Adult	04/02/2018	Dawlish Warren NNR (Devon)
	Seen	4/7/18-19/2/19	Dawlish Warren
	Seen	17/9-3/12/19	Dawlish Warren
	Nesting (1 chick)	02/05/2020	Tarnbrook, Abbeystead, Lancs 381 NNE

AVOCET

EY98059	Nestling	24/05/2015	Seal Sands, Teesmouth: c. 54°37'N 1°12'W (Stockton-on-Tees)
	Seen	28/05/2015	Seal Sands
	Seen	19/07/2015	RSPB Blacktoft Sands (East Yorks) 106 km SSE
	Seen	17/07/2015	Alkborough Flats: c. 53°41'N 0°40'W (North Lincolnshire) 109km SSE
	Seen	22/04-26/04/17	Leighton Moss RSPB, Carnforth: 54°9'N 2°48'W (Lancs) 115km WSW
	Seen	03/01/2019	Lytchett Bay, Upton: c. 50°43'N 1°59'W (Dorset) 436km S
	Seen	18/02/2019	Martin Mere: 53°37'N 2°52'W (Lancashire) 155km SW
	Seen	08/04/2020	Aldcliffe Marsh, Lancaster c120km SSW

Several other recoveries containing similar information but not as all-inclusive as this (eg lacking midwinter sighting).

GREY PLOVER

DT10521	Adult	30/03/2018	Altcar Rifle Range Foreshore, Hightown: 53°31'N 3°5'W (Merseyside)
	Seen	01/05/2018	Altcar Ranges
	Seen	03/12/2018	Bull Island: 53°22'N 6°8'W (Dublin) 203km W
	Seen	14/02/2019	Bull Island
DD82885	Adult	22/03/2018	Altcar Rifle Range Foreshore, Hightown: 53°31'N 3°5'W (Merseyside)
	Seen	29/08/2019	Donabate Beach: 53°29'N 6°6'W (Dublin) 199km W
	Seen	25/10/2019	Donabate Beach
DT10530	Adult	30/03/2018	Altcar Rifle Range Foreshore, Hightown: 53°31'N 3°5'W (Merseyside)
	Seen	27/09/2018	Altcar Ranges
	Seen	12/10/2018	Hoylake: 53°22'N 3°11'W (Merseyside) 17km SSW

	Seen	11/02/2019	Unnamed Site: 47°35'N 2°43'W (Morbihan) FRANCE 660km S
	Seen	10/04/2019	Ainsdale: 53°38'N 3°1'W (Merseyside) 14km NNE
	Seen	29/08/2019	Altcar Ranges
	Seen	22/12/2019	Altcar Ranges
DD82893	Adult	22/03/2019	Altcar Rifle Range Foreshore, Hightown: 53°31'N 3°5'W (Merseyside)
	Seen	24/11 & 23/12/19	Plage de Kerler: 47°51'N 4°3'W (Finistere) FRANCE 635km S
DD82895	Adult	22/03/2019	Altcar Rifle Range Foreshore, Hightown: 53°31'N 3°5'W (Merseyside)
	Seen	17/04/2019	Altcar Ranges
	Seen	14/12/2019	Unnamed Site: 48°50'N 3°10'W (Cotes-d'Armor) FRANCE 521km S
DD82833	Adult	22/03/2019	Altcar Rifle Range Foreshore, Hightown: 53°31'N 3°5'W (Merseyside)
	Seen	03/05/2019	Ainsdale: 53°38'N 3°1'W (Merseyside) 14km NNE
	Seen	26/12/2019	Unnamed Site: 47°53'N 3°58'W (Finistere) FRANCE 630km S
PLG	Adult Male	23/08/2018	Ujscie Wisly, Mikoszewo: 54°21'N 18°57'E (Pomorskie) POLAND
GN35848	Seen	06/04 & 10/04/19	Southport: 53°36'N 3°1'W (Merseyside) 1,433km W

Now we need some breeding season sightings

RINGED PLOVER

NW52932	Adult Female	17/06/2016	Camperdown, South Dundee: 56°27'N 3°3'W (Dundee)
	Seen	21/06/2016	Camperdown
	Seen	13/06/2017	Hilbre Island: 53°22'N 3°13'W (Merseyside) 344km S
	Seen	13/08/2017	Crymlyn Burrows: 51°36'N 3°51'W (Neath Port Talbot) 542km S
	Seen	27/02/2018	Charleston, Dundee: c. 56°27'N 3°3'W (Dundee) 0km
	Seen	10/09/2018	Crymlyn Burrows: 51°36'N 3°51'W (Neath Port Talbot) 542km S
	Seen	24/02/2019	Silverdale Moss: 54°11'N 2°48'W (Lancashire) 254km S

Not an easy one to analyse!

NOS	First-year	10/09/2019	Makkevika, Giske: 62°30'N 6°1'E (More og Romsdal) NORWAY
8B80982	Seen	14/10/2019	Southport: 53°38'N 3°0'W (Merseyside) 1,117km SSW
CRs	Nestling	05/06/2018	Beltringharder Koog, Schleswig-Holstein, GERMANY
	Seen	12/06/2018	Beltringharder Koog, Schleswig-Holstein, GERMANY
	Seen	04-05/09/2018	Richel, NETHERLANDS
	Seen	09/10/2018	Vlieland, NETHERLANDS
	Seen	23/11/2018	Knott End, Fylde
	Seen	27/12/2018	Formby Point, Merseyside
	Seen	04/03/2019	Hightown, Merseyside
CRs	Nestling	20/06/2018	Beltringharder Koog, Schleswig-Holstein, GERMANY
	Seen	03/07/2018	Beltringharder Koog, Schleswig-Holstein, GERMANY
	Seen	14/09/2018	Schlüttsiel, Schleswig-Holstein, GERMANY
	Seen	12/11-05/12/18	Knott End, Fylde
	Seen	28/06 & 03/07/19	Beltringharder Koog, Schleswig-Holstein, GERMANY
	Seen	08/05-21/05/19	Beltringharder Koog, Schleswig-Holstein, GERMANY
	Seen	03/07 & 23/07/19	Beltringharder Koog, Schleswig-Holstein, GERMANY
	Seen	06/10/2019	Rossall Point, Fylde
897531	Nestling male	16/07/2012	Bolungarvik, NW ICELAND
	Incubating	09/06/2015	Bolungarvik, NW ICELAND
	Nesting	02/06/2018	Bolungarvik, NW ICELAND
	Seen	07/04/2019	Ainsdale
8110113	Nesting Ad F	03/07/2018	Langarvatn, SW ICELAND
& geolocator	Seen	06/04/2019	Southport

LITTLE RINGED PLOVER

T31778	Adult Female	01/07/2015	Murton, near Forfar: 56°38'N 2°49'W (Angus)
	Caught	27/05/2016	Murton
	Seen	20/04/2017	Murton
	Seen	02/04/2019	Silverdale Moss: 54°11'N 2°48'W (Lancashire) 274km S

Unsurprisingly the first one from Scotland to our area

| CRs | Juvenile | 03/08/2019 | Tancat de Milia, Sollana, Valencia, SPAIN 39°18'N 0°21'W |
| | Seen | 21/06-30/06/20 | Alston Wetlands, nr Longridge, Lancs |

CURLEW

FJ23789	Adult Female	24/09/2017	Llanrhystud, near Aberystwyth: c. 52°17'N 4°10'W (Ceredigion)
	Mammal predation	22/03/2019	Altham, near Accrington: 53°47'N 2°21'W (Lancashire) 205km NE
FA95811	Adult	15/12/2015	nr Usk Lighthouse, Newport, Gwent
&CRs	Seen	to 15/01/2016	nr Usk Lighthouse, Newport, Gwent
	Seen	30/03/2019	Alston Reservoir 256km N

BAR-TAILED GODWIT

| DT10585 | Adult | 30/03/2018 | Altcar Rifle Range Foreshore, Hightown: 53°31'N 3°5'W (Merseyside) |
| | Seen | 28/05/2018 | Dublin Port: 53°21'N 6°11'W (Dublin) 206km W |

	Seen	19/01/2019	Bull Island: 53°22'N 6°8'W (Dublin) 203km W
	Seen	28/02/2019	Blackrock: 53°18'N 6°10'W (Dublin) 206km W
NOS	First-year	29/09/2017	Revtangen, Klepp: 58°45'N 5°28'E (Rogaland) NORWAY
K04742	Seen	18/11/2017	Hunstanton Cliffs: 52°56'N 0°29'E (Norfolk) 716km SSW
	Seen	22/12/2018	Heacham: 52°54'N 0°28'E (Norfolk) 721km SSW
	Seen	18/05/2019	Seaforth: 53°27'N 3°1'W (Merseyside) 789km SW
	Seen	14/09/2019	Ainsdale Beach: 53°36'N 3°4'W (Merseyside) 778km SW
NOS	First-year	06/09/2017	Revtangen, Klepp: 58°45'N 5°28'E (Rogaland) NORWAY
7218378	Seen	01/01/2018	South Gare, Redcar: 54°37'N 1°7'W 610km SW 0y 3m 26d
	Seen	26/04/2018	Leighton Moss RSPB Reserve, Carnforth: 54°9'N 2°48'W (Lancs) 721km SW
	Seen	13/04-14/04/19	Leighton Moss

Some extra sightings of a bird published last year

ICELANDIC BLACK-TAILED GODWIT

EW64394	Adult	12/10/2015	Harty marshes, Kent
YGR RNR	Seen	14/10/2015	Oare marshes, Kent 2km (24 scattered sightings outside breeding season)
	Seen	05/11/2016	Marshside Southport, Lancashire 367km NW
	Seen	03/12/2016	Oare marshes (4 times outside breeding season)
	Seen	09/10/2017	Caldy, Dee Estuary, Wirral, Merseyside 355km NW
	Seen	12/10/2017	Marshside Southport, Lancashire
	Seen	09/02/2018	Lytham Hall, Fylde Coast, Ribble Estuary, Lancashire 372km NW
	Seen	12/07/2018	Oare marshes (17 scattered sightings)
	Seen	25/03/2019	Vogalækur, Mýrar, ICELAND 1986km NNW
	Seen	03/07/2019	Oare marshes (19 scattered sightings)
	Seen	29/12/2019	Freckleton Pool Lane, Ribble Estuary, Lancashire 368km NW

Recent status suggests moulting in Kent and wintering in Lancashire

RG-OH	Adult	29/09/2019	Evoa Tagus Estuary(Setubal) PORTUGAL
	Seen	10/04/2020	Aldcliffe Marsh, Lancaster

KNOT

There are four main Knot ringing schemes using colour rings; Norwegian (Arctic north-west), Iceland, Netherlands and our Sefton Coast. A team of ring-readers, notably Peter Knight and Rose Maciewitz, have resulted in a phenomenal number of readings, mainly Lancashire but also eg Dublin area. The total number of readings of Orange Sefton coast leg flags is now around 7,000, involving over 90% of the birds that were fitted with flags. The other schemes have also seen large numbers of observations producing a fascinating web of movements, involving breeding, moulting and wintering grounds and also food-rich staging posts such as Porsanger in Arctic Norway.   Other sightings include 119 readings of 43 Icelandic birds and 9 readings of 7 Norwegian birds. Papers are in preparation so it would not be fair to hijack the data and go into detail here other than to mention Norwegian-ringed birds only seem to be present in our area in mid-winter and return early to feed up in the Norwegian fjords. Note the 'lost bird in the Azores', published in the 2018 report. was seen at Formby on 13/8/19 by Peter and Rose.

N3NPNP	Adult	31/08/2016	Moëze-Oléron, FRANCE 45.53.34N 1.05.02W
	Seen	26/02/2017	Formby Point
	Seen	20/12/2017	Thurstaston, Dee Estuary
	Seen	20/01/2018	Thurstaston, Dee Estuary
	Seen	16/05/2018	Lambastadir, ICELAND 64.28.20N 22.05.54W
	Seen	29/10/2018	Thurstaston, Dee Estuary
	Seen	08/03/2019	Ainsdale Beach
	Seen	27/07/2019	Midholt, ICELAND 64.47.56N 22.27.27W
	Seen	06/11/2019	Thurstaston, Dee Estuary
N5YPNY	Adult	18/10/2015	Schiermonnikoog, NETHERLANDS 53 28N 6 15E
	Seen	14/02/2016	Southport
	Seen	26/04/2016	Island Föhr, GERMANY 54.40.50N 08.29.80E
	Seen	14/08/2016	Wad ten noorden van Griend, NETHERLANDS 53 16N 5 15E
	Seen	11/03/2016	Formby Point
	Seen	25/3-26/3/17	Southport
	Seen	28/12/2017	Thurstaston, Dee Estuary
	Seen	13/03/2018	Marshside, Southport
	Seen	06/04/2019	Southport
12N	Ringed	22/05/2017	Straumfjordur, SW ICELAND 64 29N 22 13W
791928	Seen	30/8-15/10/17	Griend, NETHERLANDS 53 16N 5 15E
	Seen	2/8-16/10/18	Griend, NETHERLANDS 53 16N 5 15E
	Seen	15/9-24/9/19	Griend, NETHERLANDS 53 16N 5 15E
	Seen	13/01/2020	Heysham old Heliport
	Photo	23/02/2020	Heysham old Heliport
84N	Ringed	24/05/2017	Skogranes, SW ICELAND 64 46N 22 36W
791996	Seen	17 & 20/5/18	Skogranes, SW ICELAND 64 46N 22 36W
	Seen	02-03/02/2019	Heysham old Heliport

| | Seen | 11/01-11/02/20 | Heysham old Heliport |
| | Seen | 13/02/2020 | Ainsdale, Merseyside |

Note the movement to Ainsdale.

12N	Ringed	22/05/2017	Straumfjordur, SW ICELAND 64 29N 22 13W
791928	Seen	30/8-15/10/17	Griend, NETHERLANDS 53 16N 5 15E
	Seen	2/8-16/10/18	Griend, NETHERLANDS 53 16N 5 15E
	Seen	15/9-24/9/19	Griend, NETHERLANDS 53 16N 5 15E
	Seen	13/01/2020	Heysham old Heliport
	Photo	23/02/2020	Heysham old Heliport
48C	Ringed	20/05/2017	Skogarnes, SW ICELAND 64 46N 22 36W
786865	Seen	20/8 & 26/8/17	Weld Road, Southport
	Seen	02/12/2017	Walney Island, Cumbria
	Seen	09/04/2018	Southport, Merseyside
	Seen	12/5-19/5/18	Skogarnes, SW ICELAND
	Seen	07/04/2019	Weld Road, Southport
	Seen	17/04/2019	Formby Point, Merseyside
	Seen	08/02/2020	Heysham old Heliport
	Photo	12/02/2020	Heysham old Heliport
AT	Ringed	21/05/2019	Mårnes, Porsanger, NORWAY 70 24N 25 32E
	Seen	30 & 31/07/2019	Hitarnes, ICELAND 64 59N 22 21W
	Seen	16/08/2019	Snettisham, Norfolk 52 52N 0027E
	Seen	27/02/2020	Heysham old Heliport
N8GPYG	Ringed	27/08/2017	Griend, NETHERLANDS 53 15N 5 15E
	Seen	1/9-5/10/17	Griend, NETHERLANDS 53 15N 5 15E
	Seen	21/3 & 28/4/18	Marshside, Merseyside
	Seen	29/04/2019	Southport, Merseyside
	Seen	24/05/2018	Reykjarfjörður, ICELAND 65.37.28N 23.28.13W
	Seen	16-17/10/18	Griend, NETHERLANDS 53 15N 5 15E
	Seen	20/03/2019	Southport, Merseyside
	Seen	07/04/2019	Ainsdale, Merseyside
	Photo	23/02/2020	Heysham old Heliport
	Seen	26/02/2020	Heysham old Heliport

SANDERLING

N3WYGY	Ad	07/04/2019	Bolama, GUINEA-BISSAU, 11°31'N 15°54'W
POL D59725	Seen	25/07/2019	Formby Point, Merseyside 4,802km NNE
Y/OYG	Ad	21/10/2018	O Grove, Pontevedra, SPAIN
	Seen	Nov 18 to Jan 19	O Grove, Pontevedra, SPAIN
	Seen	01/08/2019	Formby Point

Our first from Guinea-Bissau and one of four Spanish-ringed birds seen in our area, also two ringed on Sanday, Orkney.

DUNLIN

T74879	Adult	27/07/2017	Ynyslas,borth: c. 52°31'N 4°3'W (Ceredigion)
	Seen	31/05/2019	Knott End on Sea: 53°55'N 3°0'W (Lancashire) 170km NNE
	Seen	01/06/2019	Knott End on Sea
BT93178	First-year	08/10/2018	Ynyslas National Nature Reserve,Borth: 52°31'N 4°3'W (Ceredigion)
	Seen	24/07/2019	Ainsdale-on-Sea, Southport: 53°35'N 3°4'W (Merseyside) 136km NNE
BT88698	Adult	28/08/2018	Ynyslas National Nature Reserve,Borth: 52°31'N 4°3'W (Ceredigion)
	Seen	24/07/2019	Ainsdale-on-Sea, Southport: 53°35'N 3°4'W (Merseyside) 136km NNE
NR55964	First-year	14/09/2015	Ynyslas, Borth: c. 52°30'N 4°3'W (Ceredigion)
	Caught	22/03/2019	Altcar Rifle Range Foreshore, Hightown: 53°31'N 3°5'W 131km NNE
BTT88153	1st summer	02/06/2019	Ynyslas NNR Borth (Ceredigion)
	Seen	15/05/2019	Sunderland Point 181 km NNE
PLG	Adult	12/08/2016	Ujscie, Wisly: 54°21'N 18°55'E (Pomorskie) POLAND
JT61337	Seen	29/04/2019	Southport: 53°38'N 3°1'W (Merseyside) 1,432km W
PLG	Second-year	10/07/2019	Ujscie Wisly: 54°21'N 18°57'E (Pomorskie) POLAND
JT36130	Seen	17/12/2019	Southport: 53°36'N 3°1'W (Merseyside) 1,433km W
ESI T091196	1st Winter	13/08/2019	O Vao OGrove (Pontevedra) SPAIN 42 27N 08 52 W
	Seen	13/01/2020	O Vao OGrove (Pontevedra) SPAIN 42 27N 08 52 W
	Seen	13/05/2020	Sunderland Point 1358km SSW
Pol D59238	Adult	08/03/2019	Evoa Vila Franca de Xira, Santarém, PORTUGAL
	Caught (schinzii)	02/08/2019	Altcar Rifle Range, Hightown, Merseyside 1702km NNE

REDSHANK

| DD49337 | First-year | 26/09/2018 | Welwick Pond: 53°38'N 0°1'E (East Riding of Yorkshire) |
| | Seen | 17/03/2019 | Conder Green: 53°59'N 2°50'W (Lancashire) 191km WNW |

DE56499	Adult male	07/09/2017	Harty (Kent)
	Seen	16/4-29/4/2019	Eric Morecambe Complex
	Seen	04/03/2020	Eric Morecambe Complex 399km NW

Last year's Welwick pond-ringed bird returned to Leighton Moss in spring 2020.

BLACK-HEADED GULL

EY26801	Adult	26/02/2014	Pine Lake, near Warton: 54°8'N 2°44'W (Lancashire)
	Seen	21/04-26/5/14	Carrickfergus: 54°42'N 5°48'W (Antrim) 208km WNW
	Seen	22/06/2016	Carrickfergus
	Seen	25/12/2016	Pine Lake
	Seen	01/08/2017	RSPB Hodbarrow: 54°11'N 3°16'W (Cumbria) 35km WNW
	Seen	02/02/2018	Pine Lake
	Seen	26/03/2018	RSPB Hodbarrow
	Seen	13/03/2019	Pine Lake
	Seen	12/04/2019	Carrickfergus Leisure Centre
	Seen	24/11 & 30/12/19	Pine Lake
1A173680	Adult male	05/05/2018	Inseln Bohmke und Werder GERMANY 53 57N 14 1 E
	Seen	01/03/2020	Pine Lake 1096 km W
EY90323	Nestling	06/06/2014	Martin Mere, Burscough: 53°37'N 2°52'W (Lancashire)
	Hit by car	04/12/2019	Ploermel: 47°55'N 2°22'W (Morbihan) FRANCE 635km S
EY26820	Adult	04/01/2015	Preston Docks: 53°45'N 2°44'W (Lancashire)
	Seen	06/01/2015	Preston Docks
	Seen	14/10/2015	Preston Docks
	Seen	18/09/2016	Preston Docks
	Seen	27/07/2017	Preston Docks
	Seen	27/10/2018	Preston Docks
	Sick (disease)	26/06/2019	Porkhov: 57°45'N 29°33'E (Pskov Oblast) RUSSIAN FED. 2,048km ENE
TJEC	Ad F	05/06/2011	Przykona, Radyczyny, Przykona, Wielkopolskie, POLAND
	Seen	21/01/2019	Whinney Hill Tip, Altham
EZ82418	Nestling	02/07/2019	Elvanfoot (S Lanark)
	Seen	03/05/2020	Conder Green 169 km SSE
VH19	Nestling	05/06/2010	Hirsholm, Frederikshavn, DENMARK 57 29N 10 37E
	Seen	to 18/6/10	Hirsholm, Frederikshavn, DENMARK 57 29N 10 37E
	Seen	16/02/2011	Pennington Flash, Greater Man.
	Seen	25/01/2014	Kilbarrack, Dublin, Ireland
	Seen	06/03/2017	Kilbarrack, Dublin, Ireland
	Seen	01/03/2019	Seaforth Nature Reserve
	Seen	24/09/2019	North Bull Island, Dublin, Ireland
HA13053	Adult	29/03/2010	Sąvartynas, Klaipėdos, LITHUANIA
/ P353	Seen	01/05/2017	Kalvių karjerai, Klaipėdos, LITHUANIA
	Seen	25/09/2019	Cocker's Dyke, Fylde
EA40587	Nestling	12/06/2019	Martin Mere, Burscough: 53°37'N 2°52'W (Lancashire)
	Seen	12/09/2019	Gormanston Beach: 53°38'N 6°12'W (Meath) 220km W
A40584	Nestling	12/06/2019	Martin Mere, Burscough: 53°37'N 2°52'W (Lancashire)
	Seen	29/08/2019	Carr Vale near: 53°12'N 1°19'W (Derbyshire) 112km ESE
	Seen	15/10/2019	Shawell Lagoons: 52°24'N 1°13'W (Warwickshire) 174km S
ET49724	Nestling	01/07/1998	Wheldrake Ings Nature Reserve, York: 53°53'N 0°56'W (York)
	Seen	24/05/2019	WWT Martin Mere: 53°37'N 2°52'W (Lancashire) 131km WSW
EY90323	Nestling	06/06/2014	Martin Mere, Burscough: 53°37'N 2°52'W (Lancashire)
	Sick (hit by car)	04/12/2019	Ploermel: 47°55'N 2°22'W (Morbihan) FRANCE 635km S

Plenty of returning Danish and Norwegian birds eg one first ringed in Denmark in 2010 still wintering along the quayside at Lancaster.

MEDITERRANEAN GULL

PLG	Adult Female	16/05/2011	J.Rynskie, Rybical: 53°55'N 21°31'E (Warminsko-Mazurskie) POLAND
FN16096	Seen	24/09/2014	Skippool, Poulton le Fylde: 53°51'N 2°58'W (Lancashire) 1,597km W
	Seen	07/08/2016	Brockholes Quarry: 53°45'N 2°37'W (Lancashire) 1,576km W
	Seen	01/11/2018	Mill Quarter Bay, Strangford Narrows: 54°19'N 5°32'W (Down) 1,753km WNW
	Seen	03/09/2019	Skippool, Poulton le Fylde: 53°51'N 2°58'W (Lancashire) 1,597km
FS15738	Adult Female	17/05/2016	Mietkowskie Lake, Lower Silesia, POLAND
Red PUH9	Seen	05/06-26/06/16	Swidnica, Bioelektrownia, POLAND
	Seen	25/11/2016	San Lorenzo, SPAIN
	Seen	31/01-08/02/17	Marin Harbour, Pontevedra, SPAIN
	Seen	25/04/2018	Mietkowskie Lake, Lower Silesia, POLAND
	Seen	08/03/2018	A seca-poio, Pontevedra, SPAIN
	Seen	04/07-08/08/18	Seaforth NR
	Seen	27/11/2018	A seca-poio, Pontevedra, SPAIN
	In colony	10/05-12/06/19	Skoki Duze, POLAND
	Seen	21/07/2019	Seaforth, later Crosby beach

NLA	Nestling	22/06/2018	Wervershoof, de Kreupel: 52°46'N 5°13'E (Noord-Holland) NETHERLANDS
3746547	Seen	08/06/2019	Preston Docks: 53°43'N 2°40'W (Lancashire) 540km WNW
5357903	Nestling	18/06/2016	Zwillbrocker Venn, Flamingo-Insel, Borken GERMANY 52 44N 6 42E
ANNE	Seen	30/09/2016	Mutton Island, Galway, Ireland 1070km WNW
	Seen	07/04/2019	Les Mordeaux, Maine et Loire FRANCE 47 19N 0 6W
	Seen	15/04/2019	Les Bretonnieres, Montreul sur Loire FRANCE 47 35N 0 23W
	Seen	11/07/2020	Skippool Creek, Wyre Estuary
5409036	Ad F	16/06/2012	Steinkirchen, Stade, GERMANY
AKZH	Seen	20-21/7/2013	Heysham outfalls
	Seen	August 2014	Formby
	Seen	May-June 2016	Texel, NETHERLANDS
	Seen	01/05/2019	Steinkirchen, Stade, GERMANY
	Seen	25/07/2019	Formby Point
Yellow AZHT	Nestling	11/06/2019	Rehbach Gravel Pit, Leipzig, GERMANY 51 15N 12 17E
	Seen	14/07/2019	Skippool Creek, Wyre Estuary, Fylde 1071km WNW

This and the next are 2/166 chicks ringed at the site in June 2019.

Yellow AZTZ	Nestling	11/06/2019	Rehbach Gravel Pit, Leipzig, GERMANY 51 15N 12 17E
	Seen	13/09/2019	Heysham Power Station outfalls c1080km WNW

Returning Dutch LCG and German ANLT & ASRE seen Heysham outfalls late summer, ASRE subsequently at usual wintering site, Coruna SPAIN 29/11/19. The returning Czech veteran lost its main food source, anglers scraps, due to closure of most of Heysham north wall. It was photographed in October 2019, possibly seen in December 2019, but searched for and not found during the remainder of the winter to the normal departure in late Feb.

COMMON GULL

5407416	Ad	26/06/2012	Kiel, Schleswig-Holstein, GERMANY
/ AL16	Seen	09/05/2014	Kiel, Schleswig-Holstein, GERMANY
	Seen	28/04/2015	Kiel, Schleswig-Holstein, GERMANY
	Seen	20/04 & 22/06/16	Kiel, Schleswig-Holstein, GERMANY
	Seen	28/01/2019	Cocker's Dyke, Fylde
5164108	Nestling	13/07/2017	Lillesand, Aust Agder, NORWAY
	Seen	16/07/2019	Formby Point

GREAT BLACK-BACKED GULL

HT95158	Nestling	22/07/2013	Calf of Man: c. 54°3'N 4°47'W
	Seen	03/07-05/07/15	Hoylake: 53°23'N 3°11'W (Merseyside) 130km SE
	Seen	14/09/2019	Birkdale: 53°38'N 3°2'W (Merseyside) 124km ESE
	Seen	28/12/2019	Ainsdale Beach: 53°36'N 3°3'W (Merseyside) 124km ESE

HERRING GULL

GR71584	Adult Female	22/06/2013	Rosemount, Aberdeen: 57°8'N 2°6'W (Aberdeen)
	Seren	19/02/2019	Sclattie Quarry Industrial Estate, Bucksburn, Aberdeen 6km NW
	Seren	04/03/2019	Southport Marine Lake, Merseyside: 53°39'N 3°0'W (Merseyside) 392km
GR71990	Adult Male	01/05/2014	Rosemount, Aberdeen: 57°8'N 2°6'W (Aberdeen)
	Seen	28/11/2015	Marine Lake, Southport: 53°38'N 3°0'W (Merseyside) 393km S
	Seen	30/12/2017	Chanters Landfill, Greater Manchester: 53°31'N 2°27'W 402km S
	Seen	23/12/2018	Southport Marine Lake, Merseyside: 53°39'N 3°0'W (Merseyside) 392km S
	Seen	01/04/2019	West Achath, Aberdeenshire: 57°11'N 2°27'W (Aberdeenshire) 21km WN
GR57344	Adult Male	10/06/2013	University, Hillhead, Aberdeen: 57°9'N 2°5'W (Aberdeen)
	Seen	17 & 23/01/2019	Whinney Hill Tip, Altham: 53°46'N 2°21'W (Lancashire) 377km S
GV20584	Nestling	29/06/2018	Isle of May: 56°10'N 2°33'W (Fife)
	Seen	02/04/2019	Southport Beach: 53°38'N 3°1'W (Merseyside) 283km S
GV20587	Nestling	29/06/2018	Isle of May: 56°10'N 2°33'W (Fife)
	Seen	17/01/2019	Whinney Hill Tip, Altham: 53°46'N 2°21'W (Lancashire) 268km S
GR98388	Adult	19/05/2014	South End Haws, Walney Island, Cumbria
	Seen	23/04 & 29/05/15	South End Haws, Walney Island, Cumbria
	Seen	18/12/2015	Richmond Bank, Warrington 82 km, SSE
	Seen	09/03 & 17/05/17	South End Haws, Walney Island, Cumbria
	Seen	21/01/2019	Whinney Hill Tip, Altham, Lancashire 60 km, ESE,

Included for nostalgia - there was a time when virtually every large gull recovery was from the huge Walney colony; now badgers etc have reduced breeding success there to low single figures.

YC08	1st summer	31/05/2017	York
/GV54531	Seen	10/01/2018	Dungeness, Kent
	Seen	17/01/2019	Whinney Hill Tip, Altham
YC37	1st summer	31/05/2017	York
/GV54760	Seen	06/02/2018	Wimereux "beach" Pas-de-Calais,FRANCE
	Seen	08/01/2019	Whinney Hill Tip, Altham
7K6B	1st summer	21/08/2015	York
GV31610	Seen	01/01/2016	Minsmere,Suffolk,England

| | Seen | 28/12/2018 | Cotesbach Landfill site, Leicestershire , England |
| | Seen | 23/01/2019 | Whinney Hill Tip, Altham |

LESSER BLACK BACKED GULL

| GV58173 | Nestling | 07/07/2018 | Langden Head: 53°56'N 2°39'W (Lancashire) |
| | Seen | 17/11 & 24/11/19 | Richmond Park: 55°49'N 4°14'W (Glasgow) 233km NNW |

Odd location for a 2nd W bird

| GV42807 | Adult | 05/06/2016 | Langden Head: 53°56'N 2°39'W (Lancashire) |
| | Seen | 08/01-10/01/19 | Dakhla: 23°40'N 15°55'W (Western Sahara) WESTERN SAHARA 3,543km SSW |

Longest distance to the SW located for 2019

SANDWICH TERN

A by-product of the wader ring-reading by Peter Knight and Rose Maciewitz was a significant number of Sandwich Terns: 28 of these were from Cemlyn, 15 from Hodbarrow, 13 from Lady Island's Lake, 3 from Northumberland and two from the Ythan.

L-NIT	Nestling	19/06/2019	Slijkplaat, Haringvliet, Zuid-Holland NETHERLANDS
1585810	Seen	11/07/2014	De Putten, Camperdiun, NETHERLANDS
	Seen	19/07/2014	Slutter-zuid, Texel, NETHERLANDS
	Seen	14/07-19/07/17	Hable D'Ault, Cayeux-sur-Mer, Somme, FRANCE
	Seen	26/07/2018	Rhos Point, Clywd
	Seen	24/07/2019	Ainsdale
DK52586	Nestling	20/06/2015	Inner Farne, Northumberland
	Seen	03/07/2017	East Chevington, Northumberland
	Seen	03/08/2017	East Wemyss, Fife
	Seen	11/08 & 14/08/17	Coquet, Northumberland
	Seen	29/05/2018	Ham Wall, Somerset
	Seen	19/07 & 28/09/18	Kartong, GAMBIA
	Seen	16/07/2019	Formby Point
DK52806	Nestling	04/07/2014	Coquet, Northumberland
	Seen	09/12/2014	Joao Vieira Island, Bijagos, GUINEA-BISSAU
	Seen	27/08 & 01/09/16	Ainsdale
	Seen	17/04/2018	Coquet, Northumberland
	Seen	25/07/2019	Formby Point
	Seen	28/07/2019	Rhos Point, Clywd
DE02201	Nestling	23/06/2015	Inish, Lady Island's Lake, Wexford
	Seen	03/09/2017	Rhos Point, Clywd
	Seen	27/08/2018	Rhos Point, Clywd
	Seen	21/01/2019	Walvis Bay Oyster Beds NAMIBIA
	Seen	21/07 & 25/07/19	Formby Point
DE65708	Nestling	05/06/2013	Forvie, Ythan Estuary
	Seen	13/11/2017	Gansbii, Western Cape, SOUTH AFRICA 10379kmS
	Seen	21/05-21/05/18	Hodbarrow, Cumbria
	Seen	20/08/2018	Rhos Point, Clywd
	Seen	10/10/2018	Strand, Western Cape, SOUTH AFRICA 10319km
	Seen	16/03/2019	Mile 4 saltworks, NAMIBIA 8979km
	Seen	15/07/2019	Rhyl, Clywd
	Seen	21/07/2019	Formby Point
	Seen	28/07-25/08/19	Between Rhyl and Conwy. Clywd

Selection comprises the only Dutch bird and all those including African sightings.

COMMON TERN

BLB	Adult	07/04/2005	La Somone: 14°28'N 17°4'W SENEGAL
99Z21293	Seen	14/05/2017	Preston Dock: 53°45'N 2°44'W (Lancashire) 4,543km NNE
	Seen	30/06/2019	Preston Dock
FPP	Second-year	29/03/2011	Mile 4 Saltworks, Swakopmund: 22°34'S 14°31'E NAMIBIA
4H58786	Seen	28/06/2014	Preston Dock, Preston: 53°45'N 2°44'W (Lancashire) 8,649km N
	Seen	21/05/2015	Preston Dock
	Seen	22/05/2016	Preston Dock
	Seen	28/05/2017	Preston Dock
	Seen	17/06/2018	Preston Dock
	Seen	12/05/2019	Preston Dock
FPP	Full-grown	06/04/2018	La Somone: 14°28'N 17°4'W SENEGAL
4H78869	Seen	30/06/2019	Preston Dock: 53°45'N 2°44'W (Lancashire) 4,543km NNE
ST62068 / U21	Nestling	27/06/2017	Watermead County Park, Leicester, Leicestershire
	Seen	05/08/2017	Seaforth, Mersey Estuary, Merseyside
	Seen	02/08/2019	Preston Dock, Ribble Estuary, Fylde
SR23944	Nestling	10/07/2015	Seaforth, Liverpool, Merseyside
	Seen 5 times	12/05-23/05/19	The Skerries, Isle of Anglesey 105km W

| SR96341 | Nestling | 02/07/2010 | Dublin Port, Dublin, Ireland |
| | Adult | 05/08/2019 | Seaforth, Liverpool, Merseyside 211km E |

GUILLEMOT

Y25939	Nestling	04/07/2018	Puffin Island: c. 53°18'N 4°1'W (Isle of Anglesey)
	Freshly dead	18/06/2019	Potts' Corner, Middleton Sands: 54°0'N 2°53'W (Lancashire) 107km NE
Y29501	Nestling	22/06/2019	Puffin Island: c. 53°18'N 4°1'W (Isle of Anglesey)
	Freshly dead	06/10/2019	Formby: 53°33'N 3°6'W (Merseyside) 67km ENE

RAZORBILL

| K27427 | Nestling | 18/06/2011 | Puffin Island: c. 53°18'N 4°1'W (Isle of Anglesey) |
| | Dead | 21/06/2019 | North Shore, Blackpool 86km NE |

We post all tideline seabird recoveries but the place of origin is increasingly the same (see also Shag!)

BARN OWL

| GC91235 | Nestling | 15/06/2019 | Near St Helens, Merseyside |
| | Long dead in barn | 04/03/2020 | Near Longridge, Lancashire 32km N |

The longest movement reported.

MAGPIE

EZ69815	Juvenile	02/07/2017	Sutton Weaver, Runcorn: 53°18'N 2°41'W (Halton)
	Caught by ringer	04/07/2017	Sutton Weaver, Runcorn: 53°18'N 2°41'W (Halton) 0km
	Killed by raptor	30/03/2019	Great Altcar, near Formby: 53°32'N 3°1'W (Lancashire) 34km NW

WAXWING

| NW93611 | First-year Male | 24/11/2018 | Bridge of Don, near Aberdeen: 57°10'N 2°6'W (Aberdeen) |
| | Seen | 20/01/2019 | Banks: 53°39'N 2°55'W (Lancashire) 394km S |

SAND MARTIN

| S458282 | Adult | 14/08/2019 | Brockholes Quarry Lancs 53.46 N 2.37 W |
| | Caught by ringer | 31/08/2019 | Sandouville Seine Maritime France 49.28 N 0.19 E 518km 157deg SSE |

CETTIS WARBLER

| AKC5855 | Juvenile male | 22/09/2018 | Leighton Moss, near Silverdale, Lancashire |
| | Caught by ringer | 05/05 & 18/05/19 | Brook Vale, Liverpool, Merseyside 79km S |

Correction of sex from last year's report and an extra date

ATD4130	Juvenile Female	24/07/2019	Halton Moss: 53°20'N 2°40'W (Halton), Cheshire
	Caught by ringer	19/10/2019	Fleetwood: 53°54'N 3°1'W (Lancashire) 66km NNW
AKC5872	1st winter male	24/09/2018	Leighton Moss
	Breeding male	08/06/2020	Woolston Eyes Warrington 89 km S

Quite a few recoveries of birds moving north and north-west to winter in our area but no records as yet of where our locally-born birds disperse. In this respect the Leighton Moss capture dates are typical for autumn passage migrants and prospective wintering birds. The more clear-cut status at Middleton/Heysham suggests passage birds/prospective winterers arrived between late September and the end of October.

WILLOW WARBLER

| RV917 | Juvenile | 04/08/2019 | Brockholes Quarry: 53°46'N 2°37'W (Lancashire) |
| | Caught by ringer | 29/08/2019 | Bermeo: 43°25'N 2°43'W (Vizcaya) SPAIN 1,151km S |

CHIFFCHAFF

| LHH734 | Juvenile | 22/06/2019 | Leighton Moss, near Silverdale: 54°9'N 2°47'W (Lancashire) |
| | Caught by ringer | 03/10/2019 | Titchfield Haven National Nature Reserve: 50°48'N 1°14'W (Hants) 387km SSE |

SEDGE WARBLER

HF9975	First-year	02/08/2019	Leighton Moss, near Silverdale: 54°9'N 2°47'W (Lancashire)
	Caught by ringer	11/08/2019	Tour Aux Moutons, Donges: 47°19'N 2°4'W FRANCE 763km S
ADA2871	Juvenile	11/08/2018	Middleton Nature Reserve: c. 54°1'N 2°54'W (Lancashire)
	Caught by ringer	07/05/2019	Middleton Nature Reserve: c. 54°1'N 2°54'W (Lancashire) 0km 0y 8m 26d
	Caught by ringer	19/08/2019	Marais-Moisan-Ouest, Messanges: 43°48'N 1°22'W FRANCE 1,142km S

REED WARBLER

Z051393	First-year Female	08/08/2015	Llangorse Lake: c. 51°55'N 3°15'W (Powys)
	Caught by ringer	18/05/2018	Brockholes Quarry: 53°46'N 2°37'W (Lancashire) 210km N 2y 9m 10d
	Caught by ringer	19/05/2019	Brockholes Quarry: 53°46'N 2°37'W (Lancashire) 210km N 3y 9m 11d
	Caught by ringer	28/05/2019	Brockholes Quarry: 53°46'N 2°37'W (Lancashire) 210km N
POL	Full-grown	09/04/2017	Salreu: 40°43'N 8°34'W (Aveiro) PORTUGAL
A371238		21/04/2019	Martin Mere WWT: 53°37'N 2°51'W (Lancashire) 1,497km NNE
S728397	Juvenile	17/07/2019	Leighton Moss
	Caught by ringer	19/08/2019	Chenal (Charente Maritime} France 45 30N 0 49 W 974 km S

BLACKCAP

S458106	Juvenile	10/07/2019	Brockholes Quarry: 53°46'N 2°37'W (Lancashire)
	Caught by ringer	14/07/2019	Brockholes Quarry
	Caught by ringer	14/09/2019	Mansands Devon 384KM N
S405939	First-year Female	26/09/2018	Sandwich Bay Estate: 51°16'N 1°22'E (Kent)
	Caught by ringer	17/09/2019	Billinge Hill 373km NW
ACE2152	First-year Female	15/09/2018	Five Houses, Calbourne: 50°41'N 1°23'W (Isle of Wight)
	Caught by ringer	24/07/2019	Barnacre Res 372km NNW
AVE8996	1st W Female	05/10/2019	Middleton NR
	Caught by ringer	06/04/2020	Parnassiaweg (Noord-Holland) NETHERLANDS 527 kmESE
ADA1620	1st S Male	15/04/2018	Middleton NR
	Killed by cat	23/04/2020	Bogmarsh Holme Lacy (Herts) 227 km S

GARDEN WARBLER

S457525	Juvenile	02/07/2018	Brockholes Quarry: 53°46'N 2°37'W (Lancashire)
	Caught by ringer	11/07/2019	Stanford Reservoir: 52°24'N 1°7'W (Northamptonshire) 182km S

GOLDCREST

KRC754	First-year Male	20/10/2019	Wales Farm, Plumpton: 50°53'N 0°4'W (East Sussex)
	Caught by ringer	05/11/2019	Ince Blundell: 53°31'N 3°1'W (Merseyside) 353km NN
LHH927	Full-grown Male	14/10/2019	Middleton Nature Reserve: c. 54°1'N 2°54'W (Lancashire)
	Caught by ringer	19/11/2019	Woolston Eyes No 3 Bed: 53°23'N 2°31'W (Warrington) 75km SS

STARLING

SFH	Nestling	19/05/2005	Kaarina, Varsinais-Suomi: 60°25'N 22°22'E (Turku-Pori) Finland
A671969	Ring only	(12/05/2019)	Bilsborrow, Preston: 53°50'N 2°45'W (Lancashire) 1,670km WS

These 'metal detector recoveries' occasionally appear

NOS	Juv Female	21/08/2019	Jomfruland Lok 2 (Telemark) NORWAY 58 09 N 9 35E
7638542	Caught	17/12/2019	Challan Hall, Silverdale, North Lancs 922 km WSW

REDWING

RL20231	First-year	20/10/2019	Queen Adelaide Railway Scrub: 52°24'N 0°17'E (Cambridgeshire)
	Caught by ringer	09/11/2019	Underhand, Newton: 53°55'N 2°27'W (Lancashire) 249km NW
RY31120	First-year	19/11/2018	Billinge Hill, near Billinge: 53°30'N 2°43'W (Merseyside)
	Long dead on ship 17/11/2019		Oil Rig Snorre B, Tampen: 61°31'N 2°12'E NORTH SEA 938km NNE

ROBIN

Z302341	First-year	19/09/2015	Brook Vale, Liverpool: c. 53°27'N 2°59'W (Merseyside)
	Predated	19/02/2019	Norton Fitzwarren, Taunton: 51°1'N 3°9'W (Somerset) 272km S
Z619658	Adult	06/10/2018	Hilbre Island, Wirral, Merseyside
	Caught by ringer	22/10/2019	Thornton, Merseyside 20km NE

Quite likely to be passing through both sites on autumn migration

REDSTART

ADA1202	Nestling	28/05/2019	Colleyholme Wood Nr Slaidburn
	Taken by cat	22/04/2020	Windmill Hill Bristol (Bristol) 286 km S

PIED FLYCATCHER

AND4708	Nestling	11/06/2018	Stork House, Bransdale: 54°20'N 1°2'W (North Yorkshire)
	Caught in nestbox	12/05 & 15/05/19	Outhwaite Wood, Roeburndale, Wray 106km WSW
ANF6087	Nestling female	06/06/2019	Llethr Woods Llanwrthwl (Powys)
	Caught in nestbox	15/05/2020	Greenbank, upper Hindburndale 211 km NNE
ADH6770	Nestling female	09/06/2018	Low Crag Lartington (Durham)
	Caught in nestbox	21/05/2020	Haw Wood, Hindburndale, nr Wray 63 km SW
Z494767	Nestling female	11/06/2016	Cwn Clydack (Swansea)
	Caught in nestbox	16/05/2019	Botton Mill, upper Hindburndale 275 km NNE
	Caught in nestbox	13/05/2020	Botton Mill

The longest movements from data received during the period under review. Plenty of movements of 30km or less.

S373701	Nestling female	09/06/2017	Barbondale, south Cumbria
	Caught in nestbox	18/05/2019	Cragg Wood, Newton-in-Bowland 36 km S
	Caught in nestbox	17/05/2020	Winder Wood, upper Roeburndale 19 km S
ADA2242	Nestling female	03/06/2018	Winder Wood, upper Roeburndale
	Caught in nestbox	01/06/2019	Greenbank, upper Hindburndale 8 km E
	Caught in nestbox	16/05/2020	Chipping 22 km SSE

Two 'valley-hoppers'. In contrast, a Winder Wood female from 2014 has returned each year to breed in Roeburndale, including 2020.

GREY WAGTAIL

AKC5231	First-year	15/09/2018	Heysham NR, Lancs
	Seen	15/12/2019	Mancetter: 52°33′N 1°30′W (Warwickshire) 188km SSE
ARB6492	First-year	17/09/2019	Heysham NR, Lancs
	Seen	19/01/2020	Ninesprings (Yeovil Country Park), Somerset 345 km, S

Usually a clear majority of sightings are from autumn passage/winter localities. The Somerset bird is the third longest movement from the study (& Wiltshire and Hampshire). Also four birds wintering close to the ringing sites.

ADA0043	First-year	23/09/2017	Heysham NR, Lancs
	Breeding female	30/03/2020	River Cocker, Cockermouth, Cumbria 74 km, NNW
ARB6464	First-year	16/09/2019	Heysham NR, Lancs
	Breeding female	20/04/2020	Killington Lake, Cumbria 37 km NNE
AVE8856	First-year	14/09/2019	Middleton Nature Reserve, Lancashire
	Breeding male	20/03 & 25/03/20	Teviot Haughs, Scottish Borders 169 km N
ARB6429	First-year	02/09/2019	Heysham NR, Lancs
	Breeding male	26/03/2020	River Brock, Brock, Lancashire 13 km, SE
Z296608	First-year female	07/10/2014	Middleton Nature Reserve, Lancashire
	Seen	21/01 & 22/02/15	Warton Marsh, south Ribble estuary
	prob breeding F	04/04/2020	Blackpool North shore 23 km SSW

In addition, the Crawshawbooth, Rossendale breeding male of 2019 returned to the same area to breed in 2020. Note that the last three breeding season records, undoubtedly a product of local walking during C-19, were from the south of the ringing site. Z296608 could have spent its whole of its lengthy on-going life in the Fylde after departure from the ringing site.

CHAFFINCH

Y999462	First-year Female	15/10/2013	Hightown: c. 53°31′N 3°3′W (Merseyside)
	Freshly dead (cat)	17/05/2019	Hayhill, Ayr: 55°24′N 4°26′W (East Ayrshire) 229km NNW
Z749115	First-year Male	08/01/2017	Mere Sands Wood, Rufford: 53°37′N 2°50′W (Lancashire)
	Caught by ringer	28/02/2019	Dalston, Carlisle 135km N

Remaining at or near breeding area as an adult?

| Z707678 | First-year Male | 26/11/2016 | Petre Cresent, Rishton: 53°45′N 2°24′W (Lancashire) |
| | Caught by ringer | 04/04/2019 | Rodjedal, Barnarp: 57°43′N 14°13′E (Jönköping) SWEDEN 1,127km ENE |

GREENFINCH

| NY22596 | 1st W Female | 18/10/2017 | Heysham NR |
| | Dead | 12/05/2020 | Sedbergh 42 km NE |

A typical October passage bird originating/breeding to the NE

LINNET

| AJD6518 | First-year Male | 26/11/2018 | Pilling Marsh: 53°55′N 2°53′W (Lancashire) |
| | Caught | 07/05 & 28/06/19 | Holland, North Ronaldsay: 59°21′N 2°26′W (Orkney) 604km N |

Another excellent recovery on the same theme as those in the 2018 report.

LESSER REDPOLL

Y927677	First-year Male	02/11/2013	Pett Level, Sussex: 50°54′N 0°40′E (East Sussex)
	Caught by ringer	25/02/2019	Kemple End: 53°51′N 2°28′W (Lancashire) 392km NNW
S374327	Adult Female	02/04/2017	New Laithe Farm, Newton: c. 53°55′N 2°28′W (Lancashire)
	Caught by ringer	11/02/2019	Chilworth: 51°12′N 0°32′W (Surrey) 329km SSE

GOLDFINCH

S470789	Adult Female	26/10/2017	Eastcote: 51°34′N 0°23′W (Greater London)
	Caught by ringer	12/04/2019	New Laithe Farm, Newton: c. 53°55′N 2°28′W (Lancashire) 297km NNW
S374451	First-year Male	13/04/2017	New Laithe Farm, Newton: c. 53°55′N 2°28′W (Lancashire)
	Caught by ringer	28/12/2019	Rue Salinas, Wirwignes: 50°40′N 1°46′E (Pas-de-Calais) FRANCE 464km S
ACF5670	First-year Female	07/04/2019	Crawford, near Up Holland: 53°31′N 2°45′W (Lancashire)
	Caught by ringer	09/04/2019	Leswalt, Stranraer: 54°56′N 5°5′W (Dumfries and Galloway) 220km N
AJD6754	First-year Female	04/04/2019	Laidleys Walk, Fleetwood: c. 53°55′N 3°1′W (Lancashire)
	Caught by ringer	11/04/2019	Leswalt, Stranraer: 54°56′N 5°5′W (Dumfries and Galloway) 175km N

Two excellent examples of the timing of spring passage but did they involve a sea crossing of the outer Solway or the long way round 'along the A75'?

SISKIN

D448907	Adult Female	25/02/2019	Kemple End: 53°51′N 2°28′W (Lancashire)
	Hit by car	09/06/2019	Gruids, Lairg: 57°58′N 4°25′W (Highland) 474km N
S803373	First-year Female	15/04/2017	Inchberry, near Fochabers, Moray: 57°34′N 3°9′W (Moray)
	Caught by ringer	02/03/2019	Kemple End: 53°51′N 2°28′W (Lancashire) 416km

REED BUNTING

| AHF8133 | Adult Female | 26/11/2018 | near Suffolk Water Park, Bramford: c. 52°5′N 1°5′E (Suffolk) |
| | Dead | 23/11/2019 | Paythorne: 53°57′N 2°15′W (Lancashire) 305km N |

Obituaries

Andrew Cadman

Pete Marsh/John Wilson

Andrew, an active supporter of the Society for many years, passed away on 20 October 2019 at the age of 88. He was a schoolmaster at Rossall School from 1956 to 1990, a location that was an ideal place to observe migration at first-hand before the school day started; he was in the vanguard of vis-miggers contributing substantially to a national project to study bird migration. He taught for a period in Libya, watching birds there of course, and then retired to Over Kellet where he became more involved in an organisational capacity. He served on the committee of the Lancaster and District Bird Watching Society, becoming Honorary Secretary in the late 1990's and eventually Chairman in the early 2000's.

He was an enthusiastic bird ringer with the North Lancashire Ringing Group, both in his garden at Over Kellet and with many of the group's projects both at Heysham Nature Reserve and Leighton Moss RSPB Reserve. He helped with a study of Sand Martins on the river Lune and was really pleased when six of the ringed birds were found in their wintering quarters in Senegal, West Africa. Ringing of wintering Redwing was another project which he was particularly keen on, producing recoveries in Italy, Greece and, amazingly, in Azerbaijan. He regularly visited Canada on ringing expeditions, which serendipitously helped him to immediately identify Lancashire's only White-throated Sparrow (of the tan morph) when it turned up in a net at Heysham NR in 2008. He travelled widely in Africa and the Americas.

Andrew had many other interests and this proved extremely useful in the pub quiz league team where his ability to answer the more obscure 'cultural' questions provided the perfect balance to the rest of us populists and film director buffs. He was a kind and considerate person, ever ready to help and share his knowledge and enthusiasm. He will be sorely missed.

Malcolm E. Greenhalgh

Philip H. Smith

A great Lancastrian, Dr Malcolm E. Greenhalgh, passed away in Manchester Royal Infirmary on 25th October 2019 at the age of 73. Born in Bolton, he was raised in Kirkham and Preston, passing his 11+ and attending the Kirkham Grammar School, where he won the Zoological Society of London Prince Philip Award for his 1965 report entitled "Ruff migration on the Ribble Estuary." Malcolm gained a place at Lancaster University, obtaining an Honours Degree in Biological Sciences before going on to study for a Ph.D. (1975) on the breeding birds of the Ribble Estuary, supervised by Prof. W.G. Hale at Liverpool Polytechnic.

I first got to know Malcolm in the late 1960s as an enthusiastic bird-watcher and recorder. His initials (MG or MEG) were a familiar sight in Lancashire Bird Reports from 1962 to 1974, after which his allegiance switched to angling. His ebullient, fast-talking personality came to the fore during an epic birding trip with Andrew Lassey (of Flamborough fame) and me, in August 1969, to the Forth, Lindisfarne and Teesmouth, starting with several days' sea-watching at Fife Ness. Andrew's detailed report lists 134 birds recorded, highlights including four species of shearwater, Long-tailed Skua, Black-necked and Red-necked Grebes, Black Guillemot, Roseate Terns, Barred Warblers and over 350 Little Gulls (at Kilconquhar Loch). The same year, Malcolm also became one of the earliest contributors to the Birds of Estuaries Inquiry, later the Wetland Birds Survey, counting waterfowl on the Ribble's enormous Banks Marsh.

During his "birding period", Malcolm produced a remarkable number of well-written scientific papers and short notes, mainly on the Ribble Estuary and surrounding countryside, involving an impressive amount of field-work. In a 1975 article on the breeding birds of the Ribble marshes, he wrote eloquently about the various threats to this habitat, especially from reclamation, prophetically raising the "pressing need for a large saltmarsh reserve on the Ribble". Only three years later, this came about when the, then, Nature Conservancy Council purchased and designated the Ribble Estuary National Nature Reserve (4365 ha).

Just before his 40th birthday in 1986, Malcolm resigned from his teaching position and devoted the rest of his life to free-lance writing, public speaking and working as a fly-fishing consultant in the British Isles and elsewhere. He was also a Vice President and enthusiastic supporter of the Wild Trout Trust. Over the next 30 years Malcolm wrote about 25 books, mainly on fly-fishing, but also on history, natural history, gardening and cookery, reflecting an enormous breadth of interest and knowledge. Significantly, almost all his books were awarded a five-star rating on Amazon.

Malcolm searching for Marsh Gentians, Highfield Moss, August 2007 (Phil Smith)

Perhaps his last publication was a typically erudite and detailed treatise on freshwater fish for the Lancashire & Cheshire Fauna Society's Vertebrates of Lancashire (2017).

I saw less of Malcolm in his later years but I well remember being invited to a Ribble feast, in which the starter was Glasswort *Salicornia* from the saltmarsh, followed by Sea Trout from the river, while the sweet was a crumble of Bramble picked from the Ribble Valley. I also joined him in August 2007 on the superb raised bog of Highfield Moss near his Lowton home to count the relict population of Marsh Gentian *Gentiana pneumonanthe* at its last South Lancashire locality, now a Lancashire Wildlife Trust Nature Reserve.

A Selected Biliography for M.E. Greenhalgh

SCIENTIFIC PAPERS & NOTES

Greenhalgh, M.E. 1965a. Shelduck numbers on the Ribble Estuary. *Bird Study* 12: 255-256.
Greenhalgh, M.E. 1966. The oystercatcher population of the Ribble Valley. *Bird Study* 13:330-331.
Greenhalgh, M.E. 1967. The Ruff in Lancashire. *Naturalist* 903: 117-118.
Greenhalgh, M.E. 1968a. The autumn migration of waders through the Inner Ribble Marshes, Lancashire. *Naturalist* 906: 79-84.
Greenhalgh, M.E. 1969a. The populations of Redshank and Dunlin on the saltmarshes in northwest England. *Bird Study* 16: 63-64.
Greenhalgh, M.E. & Greenhalgh, P.A. 1970. Glaucous and Iceland Gulls in Lancashire. *Naturalist* 914: 93-94.
Greenhalgh, M.E. 1971a. The breeding bird communities of Lancashire salt-marshes. *Bird Study* 18: 199-212.
Greenhalgh, M.E. & Greenhalgh, P.A. 1971b. The Ruff as a winter visitor to Lancashire. *Nature in Lancashire* 2: 34-35.
Greenhalgh, M.E. 1974a. Population growth and breeding success of a saltmarsh Common Tern colony. *Naturalist* 931: 121-127.
Greenhalgh, M.E. 1974b. The Pennine gullery. *Bird Study* 21: 146-148.

Greenhalgh, M.E. 1975a. Aspects of the ecology of an increasing Black-headed Gull colony. *Naturalist* 933: 43-51.

Smith, P.H. & Greenhalgh, M.E. 1977. A four-year census of wading birds on the Ribble Estuary, Lancashire/ Merseyside. *Bird Study* 24: 243-258.

Greenhalgh, M.E. 2004b. The freshwater fishes of Lancashire, Merseyside and Cheshire. *Lancashire & Cheshire Fauna Society* general report no. 105: 23-33.

BOOKS

Greenhalgh, M.E. 1975. *Wildfowl of the Ribble Estuary*. WAGBI, Sevenoaks.

Greenhalgh, M.E. 2001. *The pocket guide to the freshwater fish of Britain & Europe*. Mitchell Beazley.

Greenhalgh, M.E. & Ovenden, D.W. 2006. *Collins pocket guide to the freshwater life of Britain and Northern Europe*. Harper Collins.

Greenhalgh, M.E. 2009b. Ribble: valley and river. *A local natural history*. Carnegie, Lancaster.

Greenhalgh, M.E. 2011a. *The pocket guide to freshwater fish of Britain and Europe*. Bounty Books.

Greenhalgh, M.E. 2017. Freshwater fish. In: White, S.J. (ed.) *The Vertebrates of Lancashire*. Lancashire & Cheshire Fauna Society publication no. 122, pp. 4-29.

Barry McCarthy
3 November 1948 – 6 January 2020

John Dempsey

About ten years ago we were shivering under mosquito nets in a couple of shacks in southern Mexico, not far from the Guatemalan border. A typically tough day in the field, we'd been out from 5am to 10pm searching for birds – the type of day Barry loved. It wasn't a bad shack and as usual I was sharing with Barry, as we both allegedly snored quite badly. We were never shown any proof of this of course (video and phone recordings can be faked), but it meant we inevitably ended up sharing rooms when Marshside's finest went birding around the world. Anyway, at about 2am that night, Barry, fast asleep and snoring like a chainsaw, sat bolt upright and uttered the immortal words: "Great days, great days, never to be forgotten". Then he fell back to slumbering. Even in the Land of Nod he couldn't contain his love of birding and travelling or his joy whenever exploring our spectacular global village.

There are so many people who will have travelled so many roads, across deserts and oceans, through forests and up the highest mountains on all continents to enjoy birding with Barry. His knowledge, preparation and ready wit made him the perfect travelling companion, although as a confirmed and expert map navigator, I suspect he viewed the arrival of SatNav technology as the fall of civilisation. But Barry was more than a confirmed globetrotter – this proudest of dads was as happy on his local patch at Marshside as he was in a rainforest or vast tropical delta. As "Mr Marshside", what he didn't know about the site wasn't worth knowing, and he was always happy to share his knowledge with inquiring open minds. His book "The Birds of Marshside" is still the go-to text for all serious visitors to the marsh. As a stalwart of the Lancashire Bird Report and recorder for many years, his analytical, dispassionate approach to data made him a formidable judge of records.

Those who believe there were shortcuts to gaining such knowledge occasionally got short shrift and simple, clear advice – "You buy a book, you read the book, you go birding, you learn". I may have edited that legendary response for the more sensitive amongst us. Away from birding, Barry was an affable man, who hid his intellect with a laconic modesty, but his love of cinema, history, music and literature meant he would readily astonish friends with his knowledge during even the most obscure of conversations. Who knew he was good friends with blues/rock guitar legend Rory Gallagher during his earlier life in Cork? Or that he was a folk singer of some renown in the days before "the snoring years"? He was tolerant, open-minded man until confronted with bigotry or authoritarianism, when his eloquence would rapidly deflate such foolish approaches to life. As a Doctor of Psychology at UCLAN, his lectures were posted onto YouTube by students, and became required viewing by many, whether they attended his popular courses or not!!! He loved capturing the most complex ideas and concepts in simple clear terms. This explains why his favourite moment in cinema was the terse, pivotal point in the "Wild Bunch", when the Tector character utters the line "why not?" summing up all the intense emotions the characters feel in just two words. I think it was also why he always chose the trickiest groups of birds to learn before he set off on an expedition with the crew.

Barry always chose the flycatchers, the drabber and more obscure the better – he relished the challenge and was equal to the task of putting a name to these difficult to identify birds. His herculean seawatches from Formby Point, often lasting for hours at a time, largely staring at empty waves, summed his determination up perfectly – he knew sometimes you have to put the effort in, and was rewarded with a string of rare seabirds over the years. How many times did we rise stiff-legged from the dunes to head home without seeing very much of anything, only to hear a smiling Barry explaining: "Some days you get the bear, other days the bear gets you". The Tobacco Dump will never be the same.

Paul Thomason, who has perhaps covered more miles than anyone with Barry in recent years (they completed five blockbusting weeks in Argentina just before Christmas 2019) sums it up perfectly when he says: "Bazzo was a great travelling companion, enjoying the highs, dealing positively with the lows. Also his fantastic memory helped with identifying new birds. He once said if there was a tiger on the right and a pipit on the left of the safari jeep, he knew which way he'd be looking." I doubt the big stripey cat would have got a look in. And Neill Hunt added: "Barry was an inspiration, the one you could always turn to talk about stuff, not just birding. He was our sensible, reliable friend."

Great days, great days, never to be forgotten.

Barry after a hard day's birding in Argentina in 2019 (Paul Thomason)

Steve White adds: Barry was a lynchpin in the work of the Lancashire & Cheshire Fauna Society for more than two decades. He was a member of the county records committee and wrote several sections of the annual bird reports – managing to find something to say about Feral Pigeons for 20 years! It was always a pleasure to receive his drafts as nothing ever needed to be changed – and we shared a love of the semi-colon!

He helped organise our two major atlas surveys in 1997-2000 and 2008-2011, taking on responsibility for chivvying Southport and West Lancashire birders into the field.

Alongside the 'Birds of Marshside' (2001), the publication of the county avifauna (The Birds of Lancashire & North Merseyside) in 2008, which he co-edited, will stand as a fitting memorial.

Ringing Bearded Tits at Leighton Moss 1992 - 2019

John Wilson

Bearded Tits first bred on the Leighton Moss reserve in 1973 (Wilson 1993). Between 1975 and 2019 we have ringed 2983 new birds, 663 of which as nestlings mainly in the nest boxes which were first installed in 1997. Ringing was first done as part of a study by Colin Bibby of the RSPB into the diet of Bearded Tits (Bibby1981) between 1975 and 1980 when 422 new birds were ringed. We had a target of collecting 120 faecal samples; when we caught a bird we held it for a short time in a clean bag in the hope that it would produce a collectable sample. Many more were caught than were needed to produce the samples, which was great because the controls they produced provided an interesting contrast with those from later ringing as shown in the section on Irruption and Movements below.

We then got permission to start again in 1992, ringing 233 new birds and handling 236 retraps in that first year. We developed a programme over the next few years aimed primarily at studying the breeding population and survival, developing a standard programme of using five ringing sites spread throughout the reedbed and, as much as weather and water levels would allow, these were worked in rotation. When spraying of the reed edge with dalapon was general practice, we noticed how young Bearded Tits congregated in these dead reed areas especially on mornings following rain or a heavy dew, so we used to spray small areas by the ringing rides to attract them. We also provided small grit trays along the rides in autumn. We started individual colour-ringing in 2000, installed the grit tray along the Causeway in 2004 and from then on the number of sightings exceeded retraps.

In 2004 five large areas of reed were destroyed by bed-lowering as part of a project to provide better conditions for Bitterns. The reed was killed and is only slowly returning, these areas had previously been some of the best areas for our nest box studies and one of our best ringing sites was also destroyed. We therefore moved this site to the nearest remaining reed area to continue using five sites. I feel that the bed lowering substantially reduced the area available to Bearded Tits and is one of the main reasons why the population has not returned to the pre-2001 levels.

Because Bearded Tits are not territorial and do not sing, they are extremely difficult to census. On one occasion while watching a nest with young, I could see four males, the only aggression was from the female if an intruder male approached the nest box. Studies of captive populations have shown that females often mate with several males.

Ringing to a standard plan gives a much better idea of populations than any other survey method. For example, the study produced statistics which highlighted the catastrophic decline over the 2000/01 winter. In 2000 we caught 75 adult males and 44 adult females and ringed 275 juveniles. The autumn and winter saw a period of prolonged exceedingly high water levels from October to December, followed by a cold spell in January. In 2001, despite the same level of ringing activity, we caught only seven adult males, five adult females and 18 juveniles (Wilson & Peach 2006). We were also able to record the recovery and fluctuations of the population over the following years.

Bearded Tit, Leighton Moss, 24 November 2019 (Paul Ellis)

We were extremely successful in catching a high percentage of the population. In the 17 years from 1993 to 2009 we ringed 1665 new birds, had 6819 retraps and 1345 sightings but we only caught 15 adults which had not been ringed – fewer than one per year. We did, however, catch 73 ringed adults which had not been caught in the intervening years, 38 of them males and 35 females – these need to be taken into account when estimating population size.

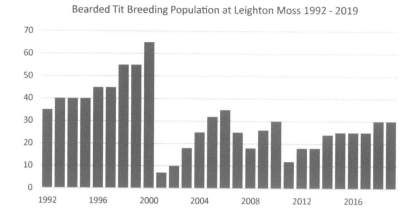

Bearded Tit Breeding Population at Leighton Moss 1992 - 2019

Nestlings

Between 1997 and 2018 we ringed 674 nestlings, mainly in our nest boxes. Of these 354 (53%) were retrapped as juveniles and 193 survived to their first breeding season. With colour-ringing we were able to identify adults at the nest boxes (Wilson 2015).

Survival

With 14733 records from 1992 to 2019, made up of 1880 new birds,674 nestlings, 7677 retraps and 4502 sightings, an analysis of survival needs full statistical treatment by an expert. Survival rates vary from year to year depending in part on the weather as the decline from 2000 to 2001 detailed above shows.

However, I have looked at the survival from breeding season to breeding season (see Table 1) which gives the numbers of birds which have survived for the number of breeding seasons. In this I have only included nestlings if they were caught as juveniles. The figure of 2223 is the total ringed for the first time in a given year as juveniles; of these 811 have survived giving a survival rate of 36.5%. However, there is considerable annual variation. The poorest survival was in 2000 when out of 270 only five survived to the next breeding season – a survival rate of 1.9%. This compares with 2005 when 30 out of 52 survived (57.1%).

Our oldest bird is a national record of seven years and three months and there are two others which survived for seven years.

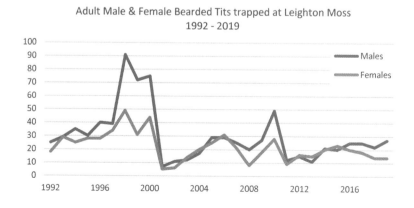

Adult Male & Female Bearded Tits trapped at Leighton Moss 1992 - 2019

The graph above shows the numbers of adults of each sex caught over the period 1992 to 2019. There appears to have been an excess of males over females from 1996 to 2000. I looked at survival of first-year juveniles between 1996-99: 110 of 203 males (52.2%) and 82 of 187 females (43.5%) survived to the next breeding season. So in this crude analysis, males appeared to survive better than females. However, a full statistical study is needed taking into account ringing and retrap dates and also retrap frequency as males are retrapped more often than females.

Numbers of Bearded Tits which have Survived to the next Season 1992-2016

Year	Total ringed	1 year	2 years	3 years	4 years	5 years	6 years	7 years
Number	2223	434	201	112	37	21	3	3

Irruptions and Movements

Irruptions have been a feature throughout, although they vary from year to year depending to some extent on the weather and size of the population. They usually occur from late September through October to early November. Weather certainly plays a part with most movements taking place during several days of good, preferably calm weather.

The movement starts with groups of birds calling excitedly and flying over the top of the reed. They then suddenly start to climb and move usually in a south-westerly direction ,climbing to 50 to100 metres. Very often they stop up for two or three minutes before dropping back into the reedbed but sometimes numbers or the whole group fly out of sight.

My most vivid memory was in October 2006. I was ringing with Andrew Cadman on the Griesdale ride, suddenly there was a loud bout of calling and c. 30 Beardies started flying towards the nets over the top of the reeds calling all the time, we thought we were in for a record catch! They dropped into the reeds just short of the net, then with a loud bout of calling took off over the nets and away to the west, gaining height all the time. We caught just three stragglers!

My impression is that irruptive behaviour, although still occurring each autumn, has been at a much lower level in recent years than previously. When it does occur, only small groups take part and, although there has been some high flying reported, they soon drop back into the reeds; no birds have been seen to leave with certainty in recent years.

However, birds certainly have left the reserve in times past as nine recoveries show. The interesting thing is that six of the recoveries came from the 422 ringed in the 1970s; four of these were caught together on 11 January 1980 at Blacktoft Sands RSPB reserve in Humberside. Three these were birds in their first year along with a four-year-old female. Two other birds were controlled that winter at Coventry and near Bolton.

Despite ringing a further 2561 birds from 1992 to date, we have had only three reports of identifiable birds away from the reserve. Two of these were local, Morecambe and Walney Island, the latter a colour-ringed bird returned to Leighton. The only one moving any distance was ringed as a nestling in 1994 and caught the following May at a new breeding site in Cleveland. There was also at least one report of ringed birds at Marton Mere Blackpool in winter, but this was before we did individual colour ringing.

References

Bibby,C J..1981 Food Supply and diet of bearded tit. *Bird Study* 28 201-210.

Wilson J 1993 Colonisation by Bearded Tits of Leighton Moss Lancashire. *British Birds* 86, 352-358.

Wilson,J & Hartley I.R. 2007 Changes in eye colour of juvenile Bearded Tits *Panurus biarmacus* and its use in determining breeding productivity *Ibis* 149 407-411

Wilson J. & Peach W. 2006 Impact of an exceptional winter flood on the population dynamics of Bearded tits *Panurus biarmacus Animal Conservation* 9: 463-473.

Wilson J (2014) The gritting behaviour of Bearded Tits *Panurus biarmicus Ringing & Migration* 29 37-40.

Wilson J (2015) A nest-box and colour-ringing study of Bearded Tits *Panurus biarmacus* at Leighton Moss Lancashire, *Ringing & Migration* Vol.30 75-80.

The Massive Redwing Roost at Longridge Fell

David Hindle

In the late afternoon of 4 November 2019 two local birders and work colleagues from Birdquest, Pete Morris and Kris McBride, were walking east along a forest track on Longridge Fell; the weather was windy with rain coming in from the west. As dusk approached they noticed hundreds of Redwings landing in Bracken and low vegetation at the side of the track.

They returned to the site the following evening, with more favourable weather conditions, and were surprised to observe a constant stream of thousands of Redwings flying into the coniferous woodland to roost within close proximity to the road at Kemple End. The news was put out to local birders and on 13 November, an estimated 22000 flew into the roost site. On subsequent evenings many birdwatchers and even a BBC Winterwatch cameraman gathered to watch this spectacle.

I visited the site on 18 November, arriving at 15.30 hours and on this occasion numbers peaked after sunset between 15.45 and 16.15 hours. The flocks seemed to adopt regular flight-lines from primarily a south to south-easterly direction over the Ribble valley and were going through at a rate of approximately 600 to 1000 per minute at the peak time.

Numbers probably peaked on 13 December, 2019, when 35,500 were documented by one observer and on the following evening, when 37,500 were claimed. It's worth noting that all observations were made from an area at the top of Kemple End and so it is possible that there were arrivals from other directions and hence an under-estimate of the numbers present!

By the end of February 2020, numbers had fallen considerably – at 18.00 hours on 28 February only fifteen were counted by one observer at the Kemple End watchpoint.

An additional bonus to birders was up to twenty to thirty Woodcocks leaving the forest at dusk. Certain species roost communally to offset predation but each evening Peregrine Falcons and Sparrowhawks were seen to take Redwings.

This event raised a number of questions. Firstly, where did the extraordinary numbers originate – in Lancashire or further afield in northern England? What flight-lines were followed – apart from the Ribble valley did they perhaps utilise the Whalley Gap and follow the course of the River Calder?

Without doubt Kemple End, at the eastern end of the ridge of Longridge Fell, features prominently in the landscape and is heavily afforested. Forests are on record as roost sites for Redwings but for how many years have they been roosting communally in coniferous woodland on Longridge Fell? There

Redwings at Kemple End, January 2020 (Mark Breaks)

were plentiful berries that winter which may have some relevance in explaining the large numbers emanating in the Ribble Valley.

Large Redwing roosts are not without precedent but not in such numbers. Certainly the numbers at this site were unprecedented in Lancashire if not further afield – the Birds of Lancashire and North Merseyside (2010) documented the following roosts with far fewer numbers: "Winter roosts often form in Rhododendron or conifer plantations; they may build up substantially, increased by cold weather influxes as in January 1984, 1000 were in a plantation at Billington near Blackburn and 1500 at Formby Hall, and in late January and February 1986, when 1,000 roosted at Lancaster University."

Thanks are due to Tony Cooper of the East Lancashire Ornithologists Club for allowing access to documented records.

Dragonflies in Lancashire 2019 (VC59 & 60)

Steve White

After unconfirmed but probable ('what-else-could-they-have-been') sightings of Vagrant Emperors at three sites on 23-27 February our second confirmed record, after one in Manchester in 2017, came on 27 June when three males and a female were found on Ainsdale NNR on the Sefton Coast.

Male Small Red-eyed Damselfly,
International Garden Festival site, Liverpool,
12 August (Phil Smith)

After decades of restriction to a single site in Lancashire, Banded Demoiselles are now breeding in numbers everywhere, while the Beautiful Demoiselle remains a rarity. Prior to 2018 there were just three records, all of wandering insects, anywhere in the three 'counties', when a male was found in suitable habitat in the West Pennine Moors. Then in May 2019 another male was discovered close to the Cumbrian border; breeding has yet to be confirmed at either site.

There are no doubts about our later colonist, though. The region's first Small Red-eyed Damselflies were discovered on 9 August at Towneley School, Burnley and 50 miles away at Liverpool's Garden Festival site. Numbers increased to six during the month to six in Burnley and 22 in Liverpool, and mating and ovipositing was observed at both sites. Greater Manchester's first records appeared soon after on the Leeds-Liverpool Canal in Leigh on the 23rd and Marriot Golf course in Worsley on the 26th.

In contrast, Large Red-eyed Damselflies showed no sign of expanding their range to the north of the Leeds-Liverpool Canal in Aintree and Wigan, although two new sites were discovered in Liverpool.

Keeled Skimmer remains firmly established at one Lancashire site but made its first appearance in Greater Manchester on Smithills Moor on 23 August.

Male Ruddy Darter,
International Garden Festival site, Liverpool,
12 August (Phil Smith)

Migrant Red-veined Darters were much in evidence from the third week of June, predominantly on the Sefton and north Lancashire coasts, where records included 20+ at Ainsdale and four flying in off the sea with 120 Painted Ladies at Heysham on 27 June.

The Ruddy Darter continues to be a very scarce and probably threatened species, with its only stronghold on the Sefton Coast, but a few also turned up at a handful of other sites this year, including the Small Redeye sites in Liverpool and Burnley.

Description Species

British Birds Rarities

Descriptions of nationally rare species (for the list, see British Birds Rarities Reports or their website) should be submitted to the British Birds Rarities Committee via the County Recorder at the address below. Since 2007 the BBRC has no longer been accepting paper records. Paper submissions, including sketches, should therefore be electronically scanned and sent by email to the County Recorder as low resolution jpegs or pdfs. Photographs should also be sent as jpegs. Digital copies of the BBRC submission form are available from the County Recorder. If descriptions are submitted directly via the BBRC website could copies of these also be sent to the County Recorder to be added to the Lancashire archive. We are aware, however, that a diminishing number of birders do not have access to the necessary equipment; if this is the case please continue to send paper records to the County Recorder who will process them before sending them to the BBRC.

The following records have been accepted by the BBRC since the publication of our last report:

- Stilt Sandpiper, Lunt Meadows, 17 to 21 May 2019
- Iberian Chiffchaff, Pilling Lane Ends, 3 May to 23 June 2019
- Long-billed Dowitcher, MMWWT, 20 to 25 August 2019
- Red-breasted Goose, Marshside, 8 September 2019
- North American Canada Goose, south Ribble marshes, 30 January to 31 March 2019
- North American Canada Goose (same as 2019), south Ribble marshes, 3 January to 18 February 2020
- Long-billed Dowitcher, Marshside & Crossens, 10 January to 5 February 2020

The following records are under consideration by the BBRC:

- Barolo Shearwater, Heysham & Rossall Pont, 20 September 2018
- Eastern Black-eared Wheatear, Fluke Hall, 1 to 16 September 2019

The following record was found to be not proven by the BBRC:

- Gyr Falcon, Slipper Hill Reservoir, 18 February 2019

County Description Species

Descriptions of species considered to be county rarities (listed below and marked with an asterisk in the text) should be sent to the County Recorder, preferably as soon after the sighting as possible. Most descriptions now come in by the preferred email route, many with digital images attached, but paper records are perfectly acceptable. The increase in digital submissions has meant that the county records committee has been able to circulate records and make decisions promptly. Current members of the committee are Steve White (non-voting Chair), Chris Batty, Mark Breaks, Stuart Darbyshire, Chris Kehoe, Gavin Thomas and John Wright.

The job of the committee is to assess every record of a species that requires a description and they have an obligation to apply the rules even-handedly. On odd occasions this means that a perfectly good record will fail to be accepted (normally through lack of detail). It is very rare that a record is thought to be incorrect, just that it is not 100% proven or there is some doubt.

Many county rarities get to be seen by many observers and an increasing proportion are now photographed, and the committee generally accepts such records on the nod – but it is still important that someone writes the record up so that all records can be reviewed by future generations.

All records of scarce migrants and rare breeding birds are submitted each year for publication in British Birds. This makes it vital that we are confident about the accuracy of all records. Descriptions need to be as full as possible - if anyone needs any guidance, please contact the county recorder:

Steve White, 102 Minster Court, Crown Street, Liverpool L7 3QD.

E-mail: stevewhite102@btinternet.com

Please note that both Lesser Spotted Woodpecker and Turtle Dove are now so rare in the county that they are 'description species', and that records of both Willow and Marsh Tit outside of their known ranges also need to be supported by descriptions.

Lesser Scaup, Kentish Plover and all taxa of both Subalpine Warbler and Arctic Redpoll are now treated as national rarities and assessed by the BBRC.

Species and Subspecies Requiring Full Descriptions

These are all marked with an asterisk in the systematic list

Taiga Bean Goose
Black Brant
American Wigeon
Ring-necked Duck
Surf Scoter
Black Grouse
White-billed Diver
Cory's Shearwater
Great Shearwater
Sooty Shearwater
Balearic Shearwater
Wilson's Petrel
Night Heron
Purple Heron
Glossy Ibis
Red-necked Grebe
Honey Buzzard
Black Kite
White-tailed Eagle
Montagu's Harrier
Rough-legged Buzzard
Golden Eagle
Spotted Crake
Corncrake
Common Crane
Stone Curlew
Black-winged Stilt
American Golden Plover
Temminck's Stint
White-rumped Sandpiper

Buff-breasted Sandpiper
Pectoral Sandpiper
Red-necked Phalarope
Lesser Yellowlegs
Long-tailed Skua
Little Auk
White-winged Black Tern
Roseate Tern
Sabine's Gull
Ring-billed Gull
Caspian Gull
Turtle Dove
Nightjar
Alpine Swift
Hoopoe
Bee-eater
Wryneck
Lesser Spotted Woodpecker
Red-footed Falcon
Golden Oriole
Red-backed Shrike
Woodchat Shrike
Chough
Woodlark
Shore Lark
Short-toed Lark
Red-rumped Swallow
Penduline Tit
Marsh and Willow Tit
    (out of normal range)

Greenish Warbler
Arctic Warbler
Pallas's Warbler
Radde's Warbler
Dusky Warbler
Siberian Chiffchaff
Barred Warbler
Dartford Warbler
Icterine Warbler
Melodious Warbler
Blyth's Reed Warbler
Marsh Warbler
Red-flanked Bluetail
Rose-coloured Starling
Nightingale
Bluethroat
Red-breasted Flycatcher
Citrine Wagtail
Grey-headed Wagtail
Richard's Pipit
Olive-backed Pipit
Common Rosefinch
Common (Mealy) Redpoll
Serin
Lapland Bunting
Cirl Bunting
Ortolan Bunting
Little Bunting

Migrant Dates 2019

The table of first and last dates is a regular feature of the bird report giving an at a glance view of actual and expected first arrival and last departure dates. The table summarises the following information:

- The earliest spring arrival and latest autumn records in 2019.
- The earliest recorded spring and latest recorded autumn records.
- The average (mean) first arrival and last departure dates 1990-2019.
- The trends for earlier or later arrival or departure where these are statistically significant between 1990 and 2019.

Records of overwintering and sickly birds have been omitted.

	Spring				Autumn			
	2019	Earliest	Mean	Trend	2019	Latest	Mean	Trend
Garganey	21/3	24/2/95	29/3		21/11			
Osprey	19/3	4/3/05	22/3	Earlier	24/9	15/11/14	10/10	
LRP	22/3	8/3/10	19/3		25/9	19/10/76	16/9	
Dotterel	28/4	29/3/89	21/4					
Whimbrel	24/3	11/3/78	7/4		12/10	6/11/88	2/10	
Wood Sandpiper	24/4	14/4/83	2/5		26/9	5/12/12	18/9	
Sandwich Tern	30/3	13/3/90	26/3		22/10	2/12/94	15/10	
Little Tern	20/4	12/4/13	23/4		9/8	23/10/03	12/9	
Common Tern	15/4	30/3/07	12/4		15/10	17/11/77	13/10	Earlier
Arctic Tern	15/4	1/4/94	16/4		9/10	18/11/11	10/10	
Black Tern	25/4	11/4/80	29/4		31/8	23/11/14	10/10	
Cuckoo	14/4	23/3/00	16/4	Earlier	3/9	9/10/07	30/8	
Swift	25/4	1/4/04	16/4		29/9	4/12/63	5/10	
Sand Martin	25/2	24/2/90	10/3		29/9	13/10/72	5/10	
Swallow	22/3	5/3/14	21/3		4/12	31/12/86	22/11	
House Martin	28/3	17/3/63	31/3	Earlier	12/10	31/12/81	26/10	
Willow Warbler	29/3	23/3/15	29/3		2/10	18/11/89	10/10	
Wood Warbler	23/4	14/4/79	24/4			26/9/67		
Sedge Warbler	8/4	27/3/03	11/4		25/9	14/11/96	29/9	
Reed Warbler	6/4	5/4/11	13/4	Earlier	18/9	14/11/93	13/10	
Grasshopper Warbler	5/4	3/4/14	15/4	Earlier	7/9	4/10/12 & 13	20/9	
Garden Warbler	13/4	6/4/11	18/4	Earlier	25/10	13/11/95	12/10	Earlier
Lesser Whitethroat	16/4	3/4/14	18/4	Earlier	7/10	23/11/99	3/10	
Whitethroat	15/4	2/4/14	15/4	Earlier	26/9	23/10/90	1/10	
Ring Ouzel	28/3	7/3/16	21/3		15/10	11/12/00	4/11	
Spotted Flycatcher	4/5	14/4/15	30/4		21/9	15/11/79	2/10	
Pied Flycatcher	18/4	7/4/11	15/4			3/11/01	20/9	Earlier
Redstart	11/4	28/3/68 & 12	9/4	Earlier	16/9	10/11/82	2/10	
Whinchat	21/4	20/3/76	20/4		17/10	12/11/79	11/10	
Wheatear	26/2	26/2/03 & 19	10/3		16/10	27/11/11	31/10	
Yellow Wagtail	12/4	24/3/96	10/4		13/10	11/11/95	10/10	
Tree Pipit	6/4	17/3/57	4/4		21/9	1/12/12	4/10	